The Albanians

THE ALBANIANS

Europe's Forgotten Survivors

Anton Logoreci

Westview Press
Boulder, Colorado

Copyright © 1977 by Anton Logoreci

London, England

Published in 1978 in the United States of America by

Westview Press, Inc.

5500 Central Avenue

Boulder, Colorado 80301

Frederick A. Praeger, Publisher and Editorial Director

Library of Congress Cataloging in Publication Data

Logoreci, Anton.
  The Albanians.

  Bibliography: p.
  Includes index.
    1. Albania—History. 2. Albanians.

1 Title.
DR941.L63   1978   949.65   77-14985

ISBN 0-89158-827-2

Printed and bound in Great Britain

For Doreen and Philip with love

CONTENTS

ILLUSTRATIONS

Following page 104

ACKNOWLEDGEMENTS

In writing the main section of this book, which covers the period of communist rule from the end of 1944 to the present day, I have relied on the Albanian press and other official publications, despite their shortcomings. I am also indebted to three works published in the United States which deal with different phases of communist rule: Professor S. Skendi's *Albania* (1957); Professor N. Pano's *The People's Republic of Albania* (1968) and E. Keefe's *Area Handbook for Albania* (1971). Like most writers on the affairs of eastern Europe, I have found the BBC Summaries of World Broadcasts and the research papers of Radio Free Europe (Munich) very valuable.

My sources for the earlier periods of Albanian history are listed in the bibliography at the end of the book. But if I had to single out one work which has been particularly illuminating and helpful this would be Professor S. Skendi's seminal *The Albanian National Awakening: 1878–1912* (1967). I am also grateful to him for giving me valuable advice on books and other sources pertaining to the communist period.

I am also deeply indebted to my wife Doreen who, apart from typing the manuscript, has made innumerable improvements to it; and to my friend Harry Hodgkinson who drew the map.

A.L.

NOTE

With regard to Albanian place-names, I have kept the in-definite forms used in the country itself, e.g. Durrës, Shkodër, Vlorë etc. An exception has been made in the case of the capital : the more familiar form Tirana (instead of Tiranë) is used throughout.

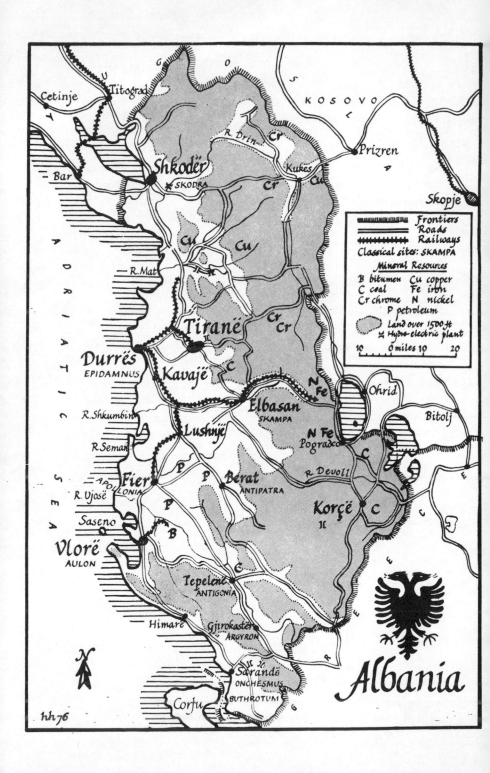

Cetinje

Titograd

G O S

O

KOSOVO

S

L

Prizren

Bar

R. Drin.

Cr

Skopje

Shkodër

SKODRA

Kukes

Cr

Cu

Cu

Cu

Cr

Cr

Cu

R. Mat

Tiranë

Cr Cr

Durrës

EPIDAMNUS

Kavajë

C

N

Fe

Ohrid

Elbasan

SKAMPA

Bitolj

R. Shkumbin

Lushnjë

N Fe

Pogradec

R. Seman

P

C

Fier

P

P

Berat

R. Devoll

APOLLONIA

ANTIPATRA

R. Ujosë

P

Korçë

C

Saseno

B

C

Vlorë

AULON

Tepelenë

ANTIGONIA

R E

E

C

E

Himarë

Gjirokastër

ARGYRON

N

hh 76

Sarandë

ONCHESMUS

Corfu

BUTHROTUM

G

Albania

ADRIATIC SEA

Introduction

FROM ANCIENT ILLYRIANS TO MODERN ALBANIANS

E DWARD GIBBON DESCRIBED Albania as a country "within the sight of Italy which is less known than the interior of America". More than a century later, in the 1910 edition of the *Encyclopaedia Britannica*, James Bourchier, who had served as correspondent of *The Times* in the Balkans, reported that little progress had been made towards "a scientific knowledge of this interesting land and its inhabitants". He ascribed the lack of progress in understanding Albania to the inaccessible character of the country; the lawless disposition of its people; the difficulties presented by their language and complex social institutions; the inability of the Turkish government, which ruled the country until 1912, to secure the safety of prospective travellers there.

Similar complaints have often been voiced since Bourchier published his essay more than 60 years ago. These have been particularly frequent since the second world war when a régime was established in Albania which adopted, for a variety of reasons, a policy of rigid political, economic and cultural isolation from the rest of Europe. Yet it would be wrong to attribute the country's present state of isolation wholly to contemporary political or ideological factors. The interaction of the stark facts of geography and history had played a crucial rôle in the process of erecting the walls that separated Albanians from one another as well as from other Europeans. Some 70 per cent of the country's area is mountainous and barren; only the soil of the remaining coastal plain, which was marshy until shortly after the second world war, is comparatively fertile. Less than 10 per cent of the total area was under cultivation as recently as the early 1940s. The forbidding mountainous landscape had proved an obstacle to intercourse both between the various regions of Albania and between the country itself and the outside world.

In addition to these crippling natural disadvantages the

country had suffered, in the course of two millennia, a staggering succession of foreign invasions and occupations which had allowed its people little breathing space or energy to spare for enterprises unconnected with their actual physical survival or the preservation of their national identity and language. The long period of Ottoman rule spanning nearly five centuries had inevitably had the most lasting political, cultural and social consequences, leaving in its wake a legacy of backwardness with which modern Albanians have had to wrestle as best they could in the twentieth century.

Although scholars are still debating the origins of present-day Albanians, there is general agreement that they are probably the descendants of the Illyrian tribes who constituted the southern kingdom of Illyria in the third century BC around Scutari (Shkodër) and the bay of Kotor. The various Illyrian tribes, however, occupied a much larger area stretching to the Danube in the north and covering the greater part of the Balkan peninsula. After a century of constant warfare between Illyrians and Romans along the Adriatic coast, the Roman empire annexed Illyria and made it one of its provinces. Illyria and the rest of the Balkans enjoyed a good deal of economic prosperity and cultural advancement under Rome for some two centuries. The bitter squabbles between the local tribes subsided with the establishment of the Roman system of government. The Romans also built aqueducts and roads, the most famous of these being the Via Egnatia. This military highway linked Durazzo (Durrës) on the Albanian coast with Constantinople, passing through Albania and Macedonia.

After Rome's imperial enterprise, the next momentous event not only for Albania but for the Balkan peninsula as a whole was the irruption of the Slavs into the area between AD 600 and AD 800. They crossed the Danube in waves, spreading desolation throughout Illyria, forcing large numbers of its inhabitants to retreat into the highlands, where they exchanged the life of farmers for that of shepherds. The Byzantine and Roman cultural centres of the greater part of the Balkans, including Albania, were destroyed in the course of these invasions.

The latter part of the fourteenth century saw the irruption of yet another formidable power in southern Europe—the Ottomans—one that was destined to have a profound effect on the subsequent historical development of all the Balkan peoples, and of the Albanians in particular. Marching along the Via Egnatia towards the west, the Ottoman armies first reached the Albanian coast in 1385. Within a few years the local petty chiefs had been either won over or subdued. The Ottomans then superimposed their own system of military fiefs—or *timars*—on the old feudal structure of the Albanian clans. As the *timar*-holders of the middle ages were the ancestors of the influential Albanian landowners of the twentieth century, some grasp of the Ottoman feudal system is crucial to the understanding of the political and social development of modern Albania. The conversion of the majority of Albanians to Islam is one of the permanent legacies of the long period of Ottoman rule. How this came about, when the rest of the inhabitants of the Balkan peninsula, apart from the Bosnians, remained attached to Christianity, is another topic that requires investigation.

Albania's dark age of Ottoman rule was relieved by one single flash of lightning produced by the extraordinary career of George Kastrioti, or Scanderbeg (1405–1468). After serving as a young man in the Ottoman army he deserted it and returned to his native land where he led a successful revolt against his former masters for some 25 years. His revolt, aided to some extent by Naples and the Papacy, was partly religious and partly nationalistic in character. Although after his death the country reverted to complete Ottoman subjugation, Scanderbeg's daring exploits had nevertheless played a major rôle in inspiring his countrymen's subsequent struggles against foreign rule and in shaping their national consciousness. Were it not for Scanderbeg's example, kept alive by a strong oral tradition, the numerous acts of resistance, followed by savage reprisals, with which the period of Turkish rule is pock-marked, would probably have been inconceivable.

But continuous opposition to foreign domination, which caused widespread devastation and anarchy, bore little fruit in terms of real political autonomy or independence. Despite their great sacrifices and heavy losses the Albanians lagged far behind, for instance, the Greeks and the Serbs, who managed to free themselves from Turkish rule in the 1830s. One of the reasons for this unsatisfactory state of affairs was the lack of effective political leadership at a time when the European nationalist movement of the nineteenth century was at its height. After the conversion of the majority of the people to Islam, many of the

country's most gifted and ambitious men emigrated to Turkey in
search of careers in the Ottoman military and civil administration. Some of them achieved positions of power and influence in
different parts of the empire. Their departure thus created a
serious political and cultural vacuum in the country itself. The
spread of the Moslem religion had another serious consequence.
Under the Ottoman system of government, the subjects of the
empire were divided into national groups, or *millets*, not according to their ethnic origin or language but according to their
religious beliefs. Because of their Moslem religion, most Albanians
were therefore classified as Turks. This meant that the only
schools they could attend were Turkish or Greek schools. Education and the publication of books or newspapers in Albanian were
forbidden.

The Ottoman refusal to recognize that Albanians were not
Turks but a people with a distinct identity of their own proved a
formidable barrier to their cultural and political advancement.
They were consequently almost totally unprepared for the complex power game, the new acquisitive propensities and the fierce
national rivalries that accompanied the decay and final dissolution of the Ottoman empire between 1880 and 1914. Modern
Albanian nationalism was to some extent an offspring of the fear
that, far from gaining its freedom, the country would be partitioned between Turkey's successor states in the Balkans. The
threat of dismemberment was responsible for bringing into being
the Albanian League, a nationalist organization set up in 1878
for the purpose of opposing the ruling of the Congress of Berlin
to cede districts inhabited by Albanians to Montenegro and
Serbia. Although the League may have achieved limited practical
results, its influence on the political thinking and the national
consciousness of subsequent generations has been both powerful
and pervasive. What had helped to keep its spirit alive to the
present was the fact that the threat of dismemberment had
continued to haunt Albanian political leaders of every persuasion
ever since.

Although the country managed to throw off the trammels of
Ottoman rule in 1912, its independence proved illusory : shortly
after the outbreak of the first world war its territory was overrun by the armies of most of the belligerents. If all foreign troops
were unwelcome so soon after independence, none were more so
than those of Italy, Serbia, Greece and Montenegro, countries

which cherished designs of permanent occupation. Serbia and Greece had already acquired substantial Albanian minorities when Albania's frontiers were decided by the great powers in 1913. However, at the end of the war it was Italy, one of the victorious states, which was in a far stronger position than the Balkan countries to retain its troops in Albania for the purpose of staking a political claim on its future. The issue was temporarily settled by the Albanians themselves when they rose against the Italian armed forces in 1920. But within a few years Italy was able to achieve part of its ambitions by imposing on the country a virtual protectorate.

1920 was a turning-point in the modern history of Albania. It marked the beginning of true independent statehood as opposed to the declaration of nominal independence from Turkish rule 8 years earlier. Given the political anarchy of the immediate post-war period, the absence of a coherent administration, the uncertainty about the international status of the fledgeling state, the achievements of those feverish 12 months were remarkable. A national congress was convened to deal with the situation. Working under strong external and domestic pressures, it proved highly effective both as a policy-making body and as a focus of national unity. Its principal achievement in foreign policy was to make it plain to Albania's neighbours and to the peace conference at Versailles that the majority of its people was determined to defend their national rights and lay the foundations of the new state. The congress was also responsible for setting up the basic structure of a central and local administration.

Some of the political leaders and administrators who were active during the early stages of this national revival had held important positions in the Ottoman government. With all their qualities and shortcomings, they continued to exercise a good deal of influence in Albania's affairs right up to the second world war. A young politician who distinguished himself from the beginning and who became the dominating figure in the country's public life during the next twenty years was Ahmet Zogu (1895–1961). As minister of the interior in the first Albanian government he was in a better position than most other politicians to stamp his personality on the political scene and gradually establish a system of personal rule. Zogu's real power lay in the clans of northern Albania to which his family belonged. After a stormy early career he became president of the republic in 1925; within 3 years he had transformed himself into Zog 1, king of the Albanians. The book discusses his attempts to cope with the country's many daunting problems during his 14 years as president and king. One of Zog's biggest headaches was his alliance with Mussolini's Italy on which he was wholly dependent for economic aid as well as military and political support. A sharp conflict soon arose between fascist Italy's policy of economic and political penetration and the Albanian government's desire to retain a measure of control over its affairs. In the end Mussolini had his way in this unequal contest, with the result that many of the country's acute internal problems were unresolved by the time Italy decided to destroy Albania's independence by invading it in April 1939. Thus barely two decades of precarious independent existence were over; the old cycle of direct foreign rule and oppression was once again in full swing. "No one has come to this land except as an enemy, a conqueror, or a visitor devoid of understanding", Carlo Levi wrote in *Christ Stopped at Eboli* about the wretched conditions of the inhabitants of southern Italy on the eve of the second world war. This also described fairly accurately what many Albanians, living on the opposite shore of the Adriatic, felt about their own plight.

The second world war was a period of great confusion and disorder in Albania. The Italian occupation was superseded in 1943 by German nazi rule. At about the same time a bitter civil war broke out between the communist partisan forces on the one hand and the nationalist and royalist resistance units on the other. The main part of the book is devoted to the history of the communist régime which emerged victorious at the end of 1944 under the leadership of Enver Hoxha (b. 1908), who had commanded the partisan forces during the war. The régime's agricultural, industrial, educational and social policies are discussed, as are the dramatic shifts in its post-war alliances: first from Yugoslavia to the Soviet Union, then from the Soviet Union to China. In the course of its troubled existence the Albanian régime had scored some notable successes in several fields. But it had also managed to erect a totalitarian system of rule, unparalleled in communist Europe, upon foundations of diverse layers. One of these consisted of the Ottoman legacy of social and cultural backwardness, coupled with political and administrative anarchy. Another was the layer of fear and suspicion of the outside world created by Albania's desperate struggle for survival throughout the greater part of its history. Upon these old flinty layers Hoxha's régime had superimposed two brand new ones of its own making. The first is its utopian claim (inspired by a potent amalgam of Mao Tse-tung's revolutionary doctrines and Stalinism) to exercise absolute control over the minds and lives of its people. The other is the neurotic fear that other countries might challenge its right to such a claim and perhaps attempt to remove the leadership that enforced it. One of the major consequences of these forces working together was the almost complete insulation of Albania from Europe and the rest of the world. The country's post-war generation, the best educated in all its history, was consequently prevented from having any direct contact with the political, cultural, scientific and technological developments of a rapidly changing world. In addition to assessing these trends, the book attempts to ascertain the influence that China has had on Albania's domestic affairs since the two countries forged their strange alliance in 1961.

Chapter 1

LONG NIGHT OF OTTOMAN RULE

THE SLAV INVASIONS of the Balkans between AD 600 and AD 800, besides destroying some of the Roman and Byzantine cultural centres of the region, caused great havoc among its ancient inhabitants such as the Thracians and Illyrians. They were massacred in large numbers, deported or forced to retreat into the mountains. The invasions also dealt a severe blow to the military strength and political cohesion of the Byzantine empire itself. The province of Illyria had for centuries provided some of the ablest recruits for the armies of the empire. This valuable source of manpower was cut off by the widespread devastation that the long series of Slav invasions left in their wake. The foundations of Byzantium were further eroded in the succeeding centuries by a number of less formidable but nevertheless ambitious local kingdoms and principalities. In the tenth century, for instance, the Bulgarians founded a kingdom of their own which comprised parts of Serbia, Albania, Macedonia and Greece. In the following century the Normans launched two naval attacks on the eastern empire, establishing bridgeheads on the Albanian coast. The Normans were followed by the Angevins, who occupied the ancient city of Durazzo on the same coast and proclaimed Charles d'Anjou king of Albania.

But the most powerful challenge to the weakened Byzantine empire came from the Serbian monarch Stefan Dušan (1331–1355). Although he failed in his supreme ambition to replace the Byzantine emperor at Constantinople, Dušan did manage to carve out for himself the largest kingdom of the age in the Balkan peninsula. This embraced most of Albania, parts of Macedonia and Greece as well as Serbia. But after the death of the Serbian monarch in 1355 his kingdom split up into small territorial units ruled by various noble families.

However, it was the Ottoman Turks who, after setting foot near Gallipoli in 1355, gave the final blow to the Byzantine

empire and established their own rule in the Balkans by the end
of the fourteenth century. This expansion and conquest were
assisted by certain local political, economic and social factors.
The general decline of the central authority of Byzantium and
of its successor principalities was accompanied by the emergence
of a new feudalism throughout the region. Ambitious, self-seeking
local leaders as well as religious foundations started laying hands
on land which had previously belonged to the state. The new
landowners were thus in a position to collect directly from the
peasants such taxes and feudal dues as they saw fit. The domains
of the Balkan leaders were also in a constant state of expansion
and contraction. Their ever-changing alliances were often accompanied by bitter quarrels; occasionally a prince would ask for the
protection of the Ottoman army, thereby coming under its over-
lordship. But the Ottomans would not have been able to benefit
from any of these weaknesses and divisions had they not brought
to their imperial endeavour certain distinctive qualities and
assets. They had a clear-cut policy which was carried out by a
centralized administration buttressed by great military strength.
When it formed the Janissary corps (or new soldiers) after the
capture of Adrianople (Edirne) in 1361, the Ottoman state set
up the first standing army in Europe. The unruly mercenary
forces of the small Balkan principalities were hardly a match for
the new army, which possessed an additional advantage in its
burning conviction that it waged holy war in the name of Islam.

. After occupying Adrianople, the Ottoman armies advanced to
the west along three main routes. The first of these followed the
direction of the Via Egnatia, the Roman highway linking
Constantinople with the ancient port of Durazzo (Durrës) on the
Albanian coast. The new conquerors from the east reached this
coast in 1385, after an appeal from an Albanian chieftain for
military aid against a rival. Another line of advance was against
Thessaly and the port of Salonica which was captured in 1387.
The third line of advance followed the highway leading from
Constantinople to Belgrade. These rapid successes so alarmed
the peoples of the Balkans that many of their feudal leaders
decided to forget their past quarrels for the time being and form
a coalition against the common enemy. Serbian, Bulgarian,
Bosnian, Romanian and Albanian forces under the command of
the Serbian prince Lazar engaged the Ottoman armies in the
plain of Kosovo in 1389. This improvised Balkan coalition,

which received no help from the Christian nations of western
Europe, suffered a great defeat at the hands of the more dis-
ciplined and better trained Janissaries. After the battle of Kosovo
the Christian inhabitants of the Balkans lost their precarious
freedom, and the Turks established an empire of vassal principalities in Europe and Anatolia. But defeat did not allay the
restlessness or the spirit of rebellion of the Balkan vassals. They
staged one revolt after another against the new imperial power,
offering the latter the opportunity of removing troublesome
dynasties and bringing vassals under direct control.

Continuing their westward drive, the Ottoman armies proceeded to consolidate their occupation of Albania by superior
military power coupled with a policy of making the best possible
use of local divisions. In 1393 they took over Scutari (Shkodër)
and large areas of northern Albania. A Turkish presence so close
to the Adriatic coast alarmed the Venetians who in the early
middle ages had maintained a string of trading posts on Albanian
soil. In a desperate effort to protect their maritime and commercial interests, they occupied Durazzo in 1392; 4 years later they
managed to wrest Scutari from the Turks. These losses did not,
however, prevent the Ottomans from conquering the rest of the
country by 1417.

In the meantime, the Ottoman empire met its first great
defeat, not in Europe, but in the heart of Anatolia. The
Mongolian cavalry commanded by Timur (or Tamerlane)
destroyed the proud Ottoman army at the battle of Ankara in
1402. Sultan Bayazid was taken prisoner and died in captivity
shortly afterwards. The leadership of the empire was in a hopeless
disarray for some 10 years following this disaster, with the sultan's
sons fighting one another for the succession. Although Constantinople was reprieved for another 40 years, the nations of Europe
allowed this precious breathing-space to slip by. In the end, it was
left to the Hungarians and the Albanians to resist with their own
meagre resources the enormous power of the revived Ottoman
state.

The establishment of Ottoman rule in the Balkans passed
through two main stages. During the initial stage the various
dynasties and feudal families were gradually brought under the
jurisdiction of the central government. But apart from this, their
status remained more or less unaltered. This was followed by the
introduction of a new system of military government and land

tenure. The transition between the two stages was effected by a new land and population survey which was instrumental in causing a radical change in the whole system of land tenure. When the survey was carried out, all agricultural land became the property of the Ottoman state. The bulk of this was then re-distributed as military fiefs, or *timars*, among local *sipahis* (horsemen) in return for military service. As the main purpose of this arrangement was to ensure the empire an abundant supply of hardened warriors for its campaigns of conquest, the land granted to the *sipahis* was not hereditary as was the case with the feudal system of western Europe. It could be withdrawn whenever the fief-holder failed to fulfil his military obligations. Part of the income of the horsemen derived from tithes and other taxes levied on the peasants. These dues were regulated by legislation, the total income of each *sipahi* depending on his personal status in the feudal hierarchy. However, the main source of wealth of the new ruling caste and, indeed, the very success of the *timar* system itself depended to a large extent on the spoils of war. When the wars of conquest became less frequent, the *sipahis* sought ways and means of enriching themselves at home.

The *timar* system together with the Ottoman administrative structure were introduced in Albania following a land and population survey carried out in 1431–32. Of the first 335 *timars* that were set up about half were granted to Albanian converts to Islam, 16 per cent to Christians and the rest to Turkish settlers from Anatolia. The fact that Christians were allowed to hold any military fiefs at all is an indication that no attempt was made at the beginning to force people to embrace the Moslem faith. Personal allegiance to the empire was all that was required. Resort to forceful conversions came later. So in those areas in which the new system of land tenure was introduced there were two main social groups: feudal lords who had contracted to render military service to the government, and peasants (or *rayas*) who, in addition to cultivating the land, served as armed retainers of their immediate masters in time of war. The position of the peasants, who made up the vast majority of the population, was no worse than it had been under pre-Ottoman régimes; perhaps in some ways it was distinctly better. The new centralized administration, with its elaborate tax laws and regulations, ensured the peasantry the kind of protection it had hardly enjoyed when it was at the mercy of the personal whims of

independent feudal bosses. Once the latter became Ottoman
fief-holders they were subject to certain restraints and inhibitions
by virtue of their being local representatives of the imperial
government.

In addition to units of armed peasants led by *sipahis*, the
Turks maintained in towns confingents of the formidable Janissaries which were under the direct authority of the sultan.
Having been formed with prisoner-of-war recruits, the standing
army was later replenished with Christian children levied in
many countries of the Balkans, including Albania. After their
conversion to Islam these young recruits were subjected to inten-
sive military training and indoctrination. They were also permanently cut off from both their families and their native lands. A
third military establishment was an auxiliary armed force made
up of native peasants outside the *timar* framework who were
exempted from taxation in return for performing certain military
duties.

The Ottoman land and population survey was not, however, a
smooth or straightforward operation. In fact it encountered such
opposition in Albania that 1431–32 marked the beginning of the
country's long and often ruinous resistance to Turkish domination. Fearing that registration would open the way to government
control and taxation, many villagers of the mountain regions
clashed with Ottoman officials and with prospective military
fief-holders. A number of powerful vassals in other parts of the
country also took up arms when asked to contribute part of their
estates to the new land tenure arrangements. Encouraged by
Venice, the kingdoms of Náples and Hungary, the Albanian
revolt spread and proved successful for a short while. But by
1434 the Turks had subdued the rebellious vassals and had
forced them to join the ranks of *timar*-holders. Yet they failed
to subdue the clans of the northern highlands and of one or two
districts of southern Albania. Because of the inaccessible and
difficult terrain of these areas and the warlike propensities of their
inhabitants, the clans remained outside the control of the Turkish
feudal and military structure. In the end the Ottoman authorities saw no other alternative but to recognize the clans' right to
self-government in accordance with their ancient customary
laws. Their only obligation to the state was the payment of an
annual tribute, which they frequently failed to meet.

The highlanders, who were to prove a more or less continuous source of trouble to the Turks throughout their rule, displayed their passion for freedom and their military qualities under the command of George Kastrioti (1405–1468) or Scanderbeg, as he is better known, the Albanian feudal chieftain who fought against Turkey with remarkable, and sometimes spectacular, success for a quarter of a century (1443–1468). Although his early life remains shrouded in obscurity, it seems fairly certain that his father, John Kastrioti, on becoming an Ottoman vassal, sent young George to the sultan's court as hostage. After renouncing his Christian faith, at least nominally, he joined the army in which he appears to have quickly made his mark. He took part in several Ottoman campaigns both in Asia Minor and in Europe, reaching the rank of general. Although everything seemed to point to a distinguished career in the military hierarchy of a rising empire, he nevertheless decided to throw up everything for the highly dangerous life of a hunted rebel. The motives behind his decision are not very clear. Having perhaps remained a staunch Christian at heart, Scanderbeg may have been disgusted with the very idea of continuing to take part in wars fought for the expansion of an Islamic state. One or two historians have suggested that the plight of his fellow countrymen in the 1430s, when they were conquered and then punished by the Turks for having dared to rebel, may have preyed on his mind. After all, his own father, who had attempted to secure for himself, with Venetian help, a measure of autonomy as a feudal chieftain in northern Albania, was reduced to submission a few years before his death. But whatever his real motives, Scanderbeg decided to abandon the Ottoman cause at the battle of Niš in Serbia in 1443 when the Turkish army in which he served was defeated by Christian forces commanded by the Hungarian John Hunyadi (c. 1387–1456). He captured Krujë, his father's seat in northern Albania, and recovered the greater part of his family's possessions. After proclaiming himself a Christian he asked the local inhabitants, both Turkish and Albanian, to choose between Christianity and death. Many of them were massacred for refusing to renounce Islam. Although this ruthless policy suggests that Scanderbeg saw himself engaged in a religious war against his former masters, religion was not the sole motive of his rebellion. He was also, perhaps primarily, concerned with becoming an independent feudal lord, as opposed to a mere Ottoman vassal. Pitted against the might of the Ottoman empire at its zenith,

such ambition would have been quixotic and futile had Scanderbeg not possessed military genius and a political vision unrivalled
among his Albanian feudal contemporaries. Realizing that the
complete lack of unity or agreement among the latter had greatly
helped Ottoman expansion, he achieved an extraordinary
political feat shortly after his return home. This was the creation
of an alliance among some of the most powerful feudal chieftains.
They agreed to pool their military and financial resources in a
joint struggle against Turkey under Scanderbeg's command.
During the next 25 years he fought, with forces rarely exceeding
ten thousand, several battles against Ottoman punitive expedi-
tions. On three occasions these were led by two sultans in person :
Murad II (1421–1451), and Mehmed II (1451–1480), the conqueror of Constantinople. Although Scanderbeg lost one or two
battles during his career of rebellion and the people of his
domain suffered enormous losses and untold misery, he was never
actually subdued. His military successes were due to the
flexibilty of his skilful guerilla tactics. One example of these
tactics was when he lured large units of Turkish cavalry
into a narrow mountain valley, where they were surprised
and cut to pieces by Albanian guerilla forces hiding in the
dense forests of the surrounding hills. Yet another type of
tactics was employed in the sieges of Krujë, the focus of his
power. While the town itself was defended by a small Albanian
force, the far larger besieging Ottoman armies were constantly attacked and their communications disrupted by
Scanderbeg himself who remained outside Krujë at the head of
other Albanian units. In his unequal struggle against the Turks
he had one great advantage over his European contemporaries;
this was his intimate and thorough knowledge of Ottoman
military theory and practice.

The situation which the Turks faced in fifteenth-century
Albania was in many ways strikingly similar to that of the
Scottish Highlands described by Samuel Johnson in *A Journey to
the Western Islands of Scotland* (1775). Mountainous countries,
Johnson writes,

are not easily conquered, because they must be entered by
narrow ways, exposed to every power of mischief from those
that occupy the heights; and every new ridge is a new fortress,
where the defendants have again the same advantages. If the

assailants either force the strait, or storm the summit, they gain only so much ground; their enemies are fled to take possession of the next rock, and the pursuers stand at gaze, knowing neither where the ways of escape wind among the steeps, nor where the bog has firmness to sustain them.

Scanderbeg's military successes evoked a good deal of interest and admiration at the Papal state, Venice and Naples, themselves threatened by the growing Ottoman power across the Adriatic. The Albanian warrior played his hand with a good deal of political and diplomatic skill in his dealings with the three Italian states. Hoping to strengthen and expand the last Christian bridgehead in the Balkans, they provided Scanderbeg with money, supplies and occasionally with troops. One of his most powerful and consistent supporters was Alfonso the Magnanimous (1416–1458), the Aragonese king of Naples, whose dream was to build a Catalan empire stretching from Barcelona to Constantinople. As the eastern frontier of his Italian kingdom was only 50 miles from the Albanian coast, Alfonso decided to take Scanderbeg under his protection as vassal in 1451, shortly after the latter had scored his second victory against Murad II. In addition to financial assistance, the king of Naples undertook to supply the Albanian leader with troops, military equipment as well as with sanctuary for himself and his family should the need arise. As an active defender of the Christian cause in the Balkans, Scanderbeg was also closely involved with the policies of four Popes, one of them being Pius II (1458–1464) or Aeneas Sylvius Piccolomini, the Renaissance humanist, writer and diplomat. Profoundly shaken by the fall of Constantinople in 1453, Pius II tried to organize a new crusade against the Turks; consequently he did his best to come to Scanderbeg's aid, as two of his predecessors, Nicholas V and Calixtus III, had done before him. This policy was continued by his successor, Paul II (1464–1473).

Scanderbeg's relations with Venice, on the other hand, were far more complex and uneasy. As the main concern of the Venetians was to protect their possessions in Albania, they were prepared to subsidize him so long as he fought against the Turks without becoming, at the same time, too powerful and hence a real menace to the security of Venice's outposts. Given this unstable relationship, whenever the Albanian leader was successful Venice tried to undermine his position by intriguing with his rivals or by negotiating with the Turks behind his back. On one occasion (in 1448) fighting did actually break out between Venetians and Albanians. Although the Venetians were beaten, Scanderbeg was obliged to patch up a compromise peace with them because he could ill afford a war on two fronts. His death from natural causes in 1468 opened the way not only to the conquest of the greater part of Albania by the Turks but also to the disappearance of most of Venice's possessions in the country during the next three decades. "Like Sophocles' Ajax," the nineteenth-century German historian Fallmerayer writes, "Scanderbeg withdrew from the scene before the end of the great Albanian tragedy."

Albania certainly paid a very high price for its long and bitter struggle against the Ottomans under Scanderbeg's leadership. The many battles fought on its soil and the savage Turkish reprisals caused immense human and material devastation. Several of its flourishing cities were either completely destroyed or else reduced to wretched villages. Large numbers of their inhabitants abandoned them and sought refuge in safer outlying areas. Trade was brought to a standstill and many ancient crafts declined or perished altogether. The conquest also caused great havoc to the country's churches, monasteries, houses of the nobility, as well as to its cultural and civic centres. Another dramatic outcome of full Ottoman occupation was to set in motion waves of Albanian migrations to Italy, involving many thousands. This exodus began towards the end of the fourteenth century when the Turks first set foot in Albania. It swelled immediately after Scanderbeg's death, reaching a climax between 1480 and the early 1500s, although the waves of migrations on a smaller scale continued for some time to come. The greater part of these Albanian refugees settled in Calabria and Sicily in small compact communities where their descendants still live today. But in this extraordinary movement of people the country lost à substantial part of its political, economic and cultural élite. The resulting national impoverishment was a serious one.

Although Scanderbeg's epic struggle ended in disaster and may have helped to strengthen the determination of the Ottomans to ensure that their vulnerable western province should never again fall into unfriendly hands, it did nevertheless serve one important historical purpose. It demonstrated that the Albanians were prepared to face the most overwhelming odds to preserve their racial identity, their language and their way of life. Scanderbeg's example thus played a crucial rôle in inspiring subsequent acts of resistance to foreign domination. It also gave the Albanians the necessary self-confidence and the will ultimately to achieve national independence. His extraordinary career became in time both the living symbol and the fountainhead of Albanian nationalism.

Scanderbeg's posthumous renown was by no means confined to his own country. Voltaire thought the Byzantine empire would have survived had it possessed a leader of his quality. A number of poets and composers have also drawn inspiration from his military career. The French sixteenth-century poet Ronsard wrote a poem about it, and so did the nineteenth-century American poet Longfellow. Antonio Vivaldi's list of rarely performed compositions includes an opera entitled *Scanderbeg*.

When the Turks occupied Albania, the northern half of the country was Catholic and the southern half Orthodox. At the beginning they pursued a fairly consistent policy of religious tolerance. After the fall of Constantinople in 1453, the sultan granted the Patriarch of the Greek Orthodox church the right to exercise supreme authority over all Orthodox Christians of the empire. The Albanian Orthodox, who came under his jurisdiction, were allowed to practise their religion provided they paid the capitation tax levied on non-Moslem subjects. But this policy of tolerance was not extended to the Catholics, whose church was persecuted because of its links with Naples, Venice and the Papacy. Records show that after the first 35 years of Ottoman rule less than 3 per cent of the population had become Moslem. The early conversions were voluntary and were brought about by the desire to avoid paying taxes or to secure employment in the Ottoman administration. But the attitude of the Turks towards the Catholics hardened as a result of Scanderbeg's opposition to their rule in alliance with the Italian states. The situation was further aggravated by the Turkish naval defeat at Lepanto in 1571 by the Holy League between Spain, Venice and the Papacy. While the defeat encouraged the Albanian Catholics to defend their church as best they could under very difficult circumstances, it made the Ottomans even more suspicious of their Albanian subjects who maintained ties with the Catholic countries of Europe.

The spread of Mohammedanism in Albania and other parts of

the Balkans was given a special impetus by the Bektashis, an
heretical Moslem sect whose doctrine and outlook were generally
more acceptable to Christian communities than those of the
official Sunni Mohammedanism of the Turkish state. The
Bektashi sect was pantheistic; it attached greater importance to
the spiritual side of religion than to its external manifestations; it
did not demand observance of the Islamic rites of prayer and
fasting; it allowed women to appear unveiled in public and to
mix socially with men. The tolerance of the Bektashis towards
other religions was an additional advantage they had over other
Mohammedans. They put all these assets to good use when they
became the official religious order of the Jannisary corps towards
the end of the sixteenth century.

A systematic campaign of conversions began at about the same
time and lasted throughout most of the next century. Apart from
the social discrimination suffered by Christians, the Turks applied
coercion by more stringent fiscal measures. The poll tax paid by
Christians was gradually increased to break down their resistance.
This resistance was already weakened by the general decline of
Christian churches, particularly of the Catholic church, because
of earlier persecutions. Ecclesiastic organization, the clergy's
theological training and discipline were badly undermined. As a
result of these combined pressures, about two-thirds of the population had joined the Mohammedan fold by the end of the
seventeenth century. This breakdown in the Turkish policy of
religious tolerance appears to have been caused by a desire to
create in the Albanian province a compact mass of Moslems so
firmly anchored—ideologically, politically and socially—to the
basic interests and philosophy of the Ottoman state that the
province would be immune to western political and religious
blandishments.

Following these changes, Albanian Moslems were unevenly
distributed throughout the country. Most of them were to be
found in Kosovo, now part of Yugoslavia, and in the central
areas. Catholics were confined to the northern town of Shkodër
(Scutari) and its neighbouring highlands, whilst the majority of
Orthodox Christians lived in the southern districts of Korçë and
Gjirokastër. Of the small Christian communities that were left,
the Catholics had the hardest time of all. Being under constant
suspicion as potential opponents of Ottoman rule and as reluctant tax-payers, they were harassed and subjected to every kind

of government pressure. Members of the Orthodox church, on the other hand, fared somewhat better because they enjoyed the protection of the Greek Patriarch of Constantinople. But for this comparative freedom from persecution they paid the penalty of being taken for Greek nationals, an anomaly that was later to cause political complications and to have serious consequences for Albania's emergence as an independent nation-state. In the face of pressure to turn them into Moslems, some Christians resorted to the curious stratagem known as crypto-Christianity. This meant that they professed Islam in public and bore Mohammedan names while continuing to practise Christianity in the privacy of their homes. They were thus in a position to deal with government authorities on a more or less equal footing and thereby avoid some of the penalties imposed on overt Christians.

After Scanderbeg's death the *timar* system of land tenure was extended to all parts of the country so that by 1520 there were three times as many *timar*-holders as had existed before he had appeared on the scene. The horsemen, who did not own land but were allowed to derive revenue from it, lived in villages where they held themselves in readiness for military service. But their normal income from the *timars* was, as we have seen, modest; the only way they could amass wealth was through the spoils of the wars of conquest. The structure of the *timar* system was gradually undermined when such wars began petering out after the middle of the sixteenth century. The system was further eroded by the general decline of the empire and the devaluation of its currency. Seizing the opportunity offered by these upheavals, the Albanian *sipahis* transformed themselves, in the course of time, from military servants of the empire into hereditary landowners. They acquired new estates for themselves and their families through buying land from weaker *timar*-holders and impoverished peasants or by encroaching on common land. Divested of any military obligations, some of them transferred their residences to the towns, thus becoming absentee landlords. The peasants were the ones who suffered most of all from this orgy of acquisition. They became a classic example of the proverbial policy of grinding the faces of the poor and the weak. From the chief beneficiaries of this radical change in land tenure there arose the big landowners, or *beys*, who were to become some of the country's most influential leaders during the nineteenth and twentieth centuries.

The weakening of the central government and of the *timar* system led to a state of general anarchy and lawlessness in which many Albanian feudal lords were engaged in a bitter struggle for economic and political supremacy. The field was dominated by two families which managed to wield considerable local authority in defiance of the government at Istanbul. The Bushati family in the north and Ali Pasha Tepelena in the south set up two virtually independent principalities during the latter part of the eighteenth century. Ali Pasha, in particular, proved remarkably successful. Aided by his sons, he brought under his rule southern Albania, parts of Greece and Macedonia. Because of the strategic importance of his territory during the Napoleonic wars he was courted by Britain and France and was deeply involved in Byzantine diplomatic intrigues with both powers. Ali was one of those monstrous tyrants whose career might easily have caught the imagination of Shakespeare had he lived in an earlier age, as his English biographer William Plomer suggests. He did in fact catch the imagination of Lord Byron who visited him at Tepelenë in 1809 and recorded his impressions of the man and of his bizarre court in *Childe Harold's Pilgrimage* and in letters to members of his family and friends.

At first Turkey did not challenge the growing power of Ali Pasha and the Bushati family as they counter-balanced one another and also helped to keep in check ambitious local officials. But drastic measures were taken when the Ottoman government considered that things had gone too far. A military expedition was sent against Ali who was killed in 1822, thus bringing to an end a blood-stained career of defiance which had lasted for more than three decades. The power of the last of the Bushatis was destroyed some ten years later.

At about the same time the Turkish government had to contend with another more formidable rebel of Albanian origin, the governor of Egypt, Mehmed Ali. After having seized power and become virtually independent from the Sublime Porte, he modernized the country's armed forces with French technical aid. Ottoman attempts to remove him proved unsuccessful and Mehmed Ali not only helped to lay the foundations of modern Egyptian nationalism but created a royal dynasty which lasted until 1952.

This record of almost continuous Albanian opposition to Ottoman rule had, however, a somewhat paradoxical counter-

part in the large number of Albanians who distinguished themselves as loyal servants of the empire. At least thirty grand viziers
(prime ministers) were of Albanian descent. So was the Köprülü
family which provided Turkey with no less than four grand
viziers during the second half of the seventeenth century and
the early 1700s.

After the disappearance of the powerful Albanian pashas
some of the country's smaller rulers began to assert their authority
and unwillingness to submit to direct control from Istanbul.
They too, like their more ambitious predecessors, came into
conflict with the centralizing policy of the Ottoman government.
The latter decided to deal with the problem by the expediency
of stark atrocity. The Turkish authorities invited 1,000 Albanian
leaders to attend a meeting at Monastir (Bitola) in Macedonia
on 26 August 1830. Five hundred of them were massacred on
the spot by Turkish troops. However, neither this nor subsequent
repressive measures succeeded in curbing Albanian opposition
and restlessness. In fact, these increased after the introduction
in 1839 of a number of political and administrative reforms
(*Tanzimat*). A regular army, based on conscription, was set up to
replace the Janissaries who had been disbanded some years
earlier. Greater central control was restored, coupled with the
promise of eliminating corruption and arbitrary behaviour on the
part of local officials. The reforms also guaranteed equal rights
to all Ottoman subjects, regardless of race or creed. These
changes were put into effect rather haphazardly because of the
different types of opposition they encountered. The northern
highlanders were wholeheartedly against the reforms as they
marked the end of the autonomy they had enjoyed for so long.
The introduction of 5 years' conscription service in the new
regular army was resented by most Albanians, but especially by
the peasants for whom it meant neglecting their land and their
families. Another source of irritation was higher taxes. The
accumulation of all these grievances led to a new series of
uprisings. These may have caused Turkey a good deal of trouble
but proved not only very costly but politically barren as far as
the Albanians were concerned.

The question that inevitably presents itself is why it was that
this relentless if confused struggle for freedom, with its awful
treadmill of violence and counter-violence, did not manage to
coalesce into a constructive nationalist movement sooner than it

did? One simple answer is that the most successful Albanian rulers of the age who might have provided the necessary political leadership of such a movement were totally unfit to do so. Albania's misfortune was that men like Ali Pasha Tepelena and members of the Bushati family proved to be narrow-minded, self-seeking, ignorant autocrats who remained unmoved by the plight of their fellow countrymen and untouched by the revolutionary fervour of modern nationalism. Many of the lesser rulers who succeeded them suffered from the same disabilities.

Yet the tribulations and sacrifices of the great majority of the people throughout the Ottoman period, in particular during the eighteenth and nineteenth centuries, may not have been altogether wasted. Some Albanian communities abroad, hence open to the heady ideas of nineteenth-century nationalism, were so moved by the seemingly endless sufferings of their countrymen at home that they felt the urge to come to their aid as best they could by means of political thought as well as action.

Chapter 2

DELAYED INDEPENDENCE

THE OTTOMAN POLITICAL and administrative reforms (*Tanzimat*) of 1839 were reaffirmed and amplified by a new decree issued in 1856. Apart from introducing compulsory military service and increasing central government control, the reforms promised equal educational opportunities to all subjects of the empire who were organized into separate communities known as *millets*. The criterion on which these communities were founded was neither ethnic origin nor language, but religious affiliation. In the case of the Albanians this meant that in the eyes of Ottoman law they were split into three separate *millets*: Moslems, who made up the majority of the population; Orthodox Christians; Roman Catholics. Members of the larger group were classified as Turks, even though they were of a different ethnic origin; members of the Orthodox church were considered to be Greeks because of their religion, whilst the small Roman Catholic minority formed a somewhat ambiguous *millet* of its own. This fragmentation along religious lines entailed serious cultural and political fragmentation as well.

In the 1840s a large number of Turkish primary schools were opened in many parts of the country. Their main purpose was to propagate the Islamic faith and inculcate political and ideological allegiance to the Ottoman state. At about the same time, Greek language schools, which had existed in southern Albania for many years, increased in number and went on doing so during the greater part of the nineteenth century. These schools were sponsored and financed by the Greek Orthodox church. As a result, Albanian Moslems and Orthodox Christians who desired to acquire education had two choices open to them: to attend foreign schools, in which their native tongue was not taught, or go without any education at all. The second choice was to be the lot of the great majority. Turkish and Greek educational policies, although very different in scope and purpose in all other respects, were in agreement on one issue. This was that Albanians were to be denied the right to maintain schools of any sort in their own language so that Moslems and Orthodox Christians could be more readily assimilated into the Turkish and Greek cultural communities respectively. The Turks had largely achieved their purpose through the conversion of most Albanians to Islam. Greece did its best to emulate this success by forcing Orthodox Christians into its particular cultural sphere. The instrument of this policy was the Greek Orthodox church. The Patriarch of Constantinople and the senior members of the Orthodox hierarchy, who were usually Greeks, tended to identify the welfare of the church as a whole with purely Greek national interests. This tendency became more pronounced after Greece had achieved independence in 1821. One of the consequences of the continuous pressure to hellenize the Orthodox faith during the Ottoman period was to induce the Serbs, Bulgarians and Romanians to establish national churches quite independent of the Patriarch. The Albanians, on the other hand, were in no position to take such a step before the early part of the twentieth century.

The Roman Catholic church, though weak and under constant Ottoman pressure, somehow managed to retain a certain freedom of action so that it eventually became the custodian of the Albanian language and cultural heritage. A number of bishops and priests of the Catholic church were the first Albanian writers. The earliest book in the language is a *Liturgy* by Father Gjon Buzuku published in 1555. Other religious works appeared during the seventeenth century. The first Latin-Albanian dictionary (1635) was the work of Father Frano Bardhi who was attached to the bishopric of Shkodër (Scutari). The main aim of these clerical writers was no doubt to serve the Roman Catholic church and to propagate its teaching as best they could. But they also appear to have been very much aware of the need to cultivate their native language and make it as efficient a vehicle of their faith as possible.

In 1616 Albanian Roman Catholics were placed under the protection of Austria which undertook to build churches, religious institutions and schools. In terms of secular education, this protection became a practical proposition only in 1855 when an Albanian primary school, financed by the Austrian government, was opened in Shkodër. Later on a number of Austrian-sponsored religious schools were started in the same city. Spurred by the desire to counter Austrian influence in Albania, Italy decided towards the end of the nineteenth century to set up its own schools in Catholic areas, in which both Italian and Albanian were taught.

But these Austrian and Italian efforts, though useful and destined to play a significant rôle later on, made very little impact on the general cultural scene of the nineteenth century. The deep religious divisions of the country and the almost total absence of Albanian secular schools set a number of educated Albanians living in Italy, Turkey and Romania thinking about what should be done to channel the continuous acts of resistance to Ottoman rule along more constructive nationalist lines. Naum Veqilharxhi, one of the early pioneers of the nationalist movement who had emigrated to Romania, summed up the problem facing his countrymen when he wrote in the early 1800s that "a nation deprived of knowledge is a slave, and knowledge can only be acquired in one's native tongue". After stressing the danger to national emancipation stemming from schooling in foreign languages, he appealed to all educated Albanians to do everything in their power to spread the teaching of Albanian among the people. The urgent need to open clandestine Albanian schools became the cardinal objective of a number of small but influential patriotic societies and groups which cropped up in Romania, Turkey and Italy.

The descendants of the Albanians who had emigrated to Calabria and Sicily after Scanderbeg's death were to play a major part in this movement of cultural and political revival. Under the influence of the romantic and nationalist ideas of the early nineteenth century, a number of Italo-Albanian scholars, writers and publicists began studying the history, dialects and folklore of their own communities as well as of their country of origin. The most outstanding of these was the poet Girolamo de Rada (1814–1903) who was born in a small village in Calabria where he spent most of his life. He published a good deal of romantic poetry in the local Albanian dialect, largely inspired by ancient legends and folklore. But the mainspring of his whole life and career was the cultural and political liberation of the land of his forebears across the Adriatic. Norman Douglas writes in his *Old Calabria* that de Rada—"an Albanian seer" as he calls him—lived in his native village "brooding on Albanian wrongs,

devising remedies, corresponding with foreigners, and writing—
ever writing; consuming his patrimony in the cause of Albania".
One of the great achievements of this passionately romantic
nationalist was to inspire a flourishing literary movement among
the Albanian-speaking communities of both Calabria and Sicily.
As many Sicilian Italo-Albanians were deeply involved in the
struggle for the unification of Italy of the 1860s, some of the
liberal and nationalist ideas of that struggle spilled over into the
campaign for freeing Albania from Ottoman domination. Useful
patriotic, political and cultural links were also forged between the
old Albanian settlers in Italy and groups of more recent Albanian
exiles in Turkey, Greece, Romania and Bulgaria. The benefits of
this cross-fertilization were to become apparent during the last
two decades of the nineteenth century.

The first real test of this infant nationalist movement came
with Turkey's defeat by Russia in the war of 1877–78. In its
desire to strengthen its allies in the Balkans and thereby curb
Austro-Hungarian influence in the region, Russia imposed the
harsh treaty of San Stefano on Turkey. Albania was one of the
principal victims of the peace terms which ceded to Bulgaria,
Serbia and Montenegro substantial territories inhabited by
Albanians. This turn of events faced Albanian nationalists, at
home and abroad, with a formidable problem : how to bring
about the country's liberation from Ottoman rule without causing
at the same time its partition among several states? Fearing that
Russia would dominate the enlarged state of Bulgaria, Austria
and Britain pressed Moscow to submit the peace settlement to
the Congress of Berlin which met in June 1878 and was attended
by Russia, Turkey, Austria-Hungary, Britain, France, Italy and
Germany. At the same time a meeting of Albanian nationalist
leaders was held in the town of Prizren, in Kosovo, for the
purpose of organizing political and military opposition to the
treaty of San Stefano. One of the first acts of the Albanian
League, which was set up at the Prizren meeting, was to address
a memorandum to the Berlin Congress. This stated *inter alia* :
"Just as we are not and don't want to be Turks, so we shall
oppose with all our might anyone who would like to turn us
into Slavs or Austrians or Greeks. We want to be Albanians."
Although as a result of the deliberations of the European powers
in Berlin Albanian territorial losses were somewhat reduced in
size, the Albanian League nevertheless decided to oppose them.

Albanian nationalist committees were formed in many parts of the country for the purpose of organizing meetings and drawing up protests against the Berlin decisions. Fighting also broke out between Albanians and Montenegrins. The attitude of the Turkish government to the activities of the League was highly equivocal. At the beginning it supported the League in the desperate hope that Albanian opposition to the expansionist tendencies of the Slav states would help to prop up the weakened Ottoman rule in the Balkans. However, when the Albanians began substituting political protests with armed force, the Turks discovered that the Albanian movement had undergone a sea-change within a short time : it now demanded nothing less than complete autonomy within the empire. The more sophisticated leaders of the League came to realize that the very precarious territorial unity of their country would crumble together with the rotten structure of the Ottoman empire itself unless some sort of autonomy and political cohesion were achieved before it was too late. But as these aspirations clashed with the centralist ambitions of Istanbul, Turkey decided to suppress the Albanian nationalist organization by armed force. All its leaders were arrested in March 1881 and exiled to remote parts of Turkey. Turkish troops also occupied the north-eastern districts which had come under the political and military sway of the League.

Although the League was not able to prevent the loss of some Albanian territory to neighbouring countries or to gain any administrative autonomy for itself, it was by no means a complete failure. One of its main achievements was to speak for the first time with a single voice on behalf of the great majority of Albanians who for centuries had been involved in numerous uncoordinated uprisings which had borne little or no fruit in terms of political freedom or independence. When the problem of Albania was briefly raised at the Congress of Berlin, Bismarck had curtly dismissed it with the remark : "There is no Albanian nationality". Yet after the united action of the Albanian nationalists between 1878 and 1881 the European powers could not dismiss the Albanian question altogether or sweep it under the carpet for very long. It had by then become an international problem that was to come up, on and off, during the next four decades or so. The harsh experience of the League also served to make some of the more clear-sighted nationalist leaders aware of the wide gap that existed between their immediate political aspirations and the deep-seated social, economic and cultural backwardness of the overwhelming majority of the people whose rights they defended. This increased their eagerness to overcome by every available means the pernicious effects of Ottoman opposition to Albanian schools and to the publication of newspapers and books in Albanian. In the absence of a common religious heritage, the cultivation of the Albanian language was seen as the most effective method of forging links between the various religious and regional communities.

No one has made a greater contribution to the political and cultural awakening of the Albanians in the nineteenth century than the three remarkable Frasheri brothers—Abdyl, Naim and Sami—who managed to serve the Ottoman government in various capacities while at the same time doing their best to undermine its rule in Albania. They were a gifted and cultivated trio who put their diverse and complementary talents at the service of the nationalist cause. Abdyl Frasheri (1839–1894), the eldest brother, was the true leader of the Albanian League. It was his skills in political organization, in diplomacy and in propaganda which helped to make the League an effective nationalist movement. Without his leadership the League would certainly have been far less successful than it turned out to be, and might probably have failed to come into being at all. Naim Frasheri (1846–1900), besides being one of the best lyric and romantic poets of the language, became the widely acknowledged poet of the nationalist movement. He wrote a number of works on Scanderbeg and other historical and patriotic subjects which became very popular and thus helped to fortify and keep alive the hopes of national emancipation. He was also active in the fields of education and nationalist propaganda. He wrote several school books on a wide variety of subjects; made translations from Persian and French, and published numerous articles on political and cultural themes. Sami Frasheri (1850–1903) was a scholar and political thinker who wrote both in Turkish and Albanian. His main Turkish work is a six-volume encyclopedia entitled *Universal Dictionary of History and Geography* (1894). Like his brother Naim, he was a skilful and prolific propagandist of the nationalist cause. His most valuable contribution to this was the pamphlet "Albania's Past, Present and Future" (1899) in which he discussed some of the problems facing the country after the Congress of Berlin and outlined various measures that should be taken to bring about its independence from Turkish rule and to secure its stability once independence had been achieved. Sami Frasheri criticized the Ottoman policy of equating Albanian Moslems with Turks and Albanian Orthodox Christians with Greeks. He condemned Greek efforts to hellenize Albanian Orthodox Christians in the hope of eventually detaching them politically from the rest of their countrymen. He pointed out that Albanians would not be able to preserve their nationality or language so long as Turkey continued to oppose the opening of Albanian schools, while allowing other Balkan nationalities to do as they pleased at the Albanians' expense. Sami Frasheri therefore believed that the prolongation of Ottoman rule could only lead to partition between Slavs and Greeks. Although the Albanians by themselves were in no position to drive the Turks out of Europe, he urged them to prepare themselves politically and culturally for the day when that happened. He advocated that they should campaign for the recognition of their national rights by Turkey, and that they should set up a republic with a parliamentary form of government after its rule had disappeared.

The Frasheri brothers were able to play a unique and many-sided rôle in the nineteenth-century nationalist movement because, apart from their outstanding abilities, they had certain distinct advantages over many of their contemporaries. They were highly educated and spoke, apart from Albanian, Turkish, Arabic and several European languages. They thus had not only an inside knowledge of the Ottoman political system but also a wide acquaintance with contemporary European political and cultural trends. All three were deeply influenced by the ideas of the French revolution as well as of the European nationalist movements of their time. Their religious affiliation also set them apart. Although Moslems by birth, they did not belong to the large Sunni sect, which embraced the rulers of the Ottoman state and the majority of their subjects. They were members of the heretical Bektashi sect. This placed them at an oblique angle to the whole ethos of the Ottoman empire. In his essay "The European Witch-craze of the 16th and 17th Centuries", Professor H. R. Trevor-Roper writes that "heretical ideas, intellectual in origin, are often assumed by societies determined to assert their independence". In the previous chapter we saw how the Bektashis, with their unorthodox outlook and their liberal attitude towards other religions, were instrumental in propagating the Islamic faith in the Balkans after they had become the official religious order of the Janissaries at the end of the sixteenth century. As their somewhat mysterious power and influence grew throughout the empire, their loyalty to the state and their heretical ideas became more and more suspect. But the Bektashis suffered a serious setback when their powerful protectors, the Janissaries, were disbanded in 1826. It was at about this time that the heretical sect began gaining ground among Albanians, both at home and abroad. They transmuted its doctrines into a useful vehicle for their national aspirations and endeavours. The Frasheri brothers bestowed intellectual and political respectability on the conversion of the majority of the inhabitants of southern Albania to Bektashism. They did this largely by their selfless dedication to the cause of political and cultural emancipation. Their example was greatly enhanced by the poetic and humanitarian vision of Naim Frasheri who succeeded in investing the teachings of the heretical sect with a highly personal mixture of the ideals of brotherly love, of ethical conduct and of national freedom. Having propagated these views among his countrymen throughout most of his life, he summed them up in his pamphlet "Notebook of the Bektashis" published in 1896, which is a sort of religious-cum-nationalist tract. Devoid of any religious dogma, the pamphlet lays stress on fundamental values of perennial philosophy such as wisdom, love, human brotherhood and tolerance. "The true Bektashis respect a man of whatever religion he may be; they hold him their brother and their beloved; they never look on him as a stranger." Its political message is couched in somewhat more practical and down-to-earth terms: "Let them [the Bektashis] strive night and day for the nation . . . for the salvation of Albania and the Albanians, for the education and civilization of their nation and their country, for their language . . . for all progress and improvement". While it would be untrue to say that Naim Frasheri's lofty and unworldly sentiments animated the majority of those Albanians who, for one reason or another, joined the ranks of the Moslem heretics, his political and religious ideas did help to shape the profound influence which the Bektashis had exerted on the evolution of Albanian nationalism in the nineteenth century and the early part of the twentieth. The pervasive religious tolerance of the Bektashis may have also been partly responsible for the absence of any serious religious strife in modern Albania.

Albania's turbulent emergence on the nineteenth-century European political scene succeeded in arousing the interest of a number of German and Austrian scholars in the origin of its people and the relationship of their language to other European languages. According to an earlier rather nebulous theory, the Albanians were held to be the descendants of the Pelasgians who were supposed to have inhabited the whole of the Balkan peninsula and the Mediterranean basin in prehistoric times. Such Indo-European languages as Greek, Latin and Illyrian (hence modern Albanian) were thought to have sprung from the language spoken by this somewhat mythical people. However, later researches in comparative philology gradually undermined the Pelasgian theory and finally demolished it. The German linguist Franz Bopp was the first to provide real evidence in 1854 that Albanian occupied a quite separate position in the family of Indo-European languages. His line of enquiry was pursued by other European scholars. Towards the end of the nineteenth century Gustav Meyer, an Austrian philologist, propounded the theory that Albanian was a dialect of ancient Illyrian. In one of his works he analysed a few hundred basic Albanian words, tracing their Indo-European origin. Meyer's findings were endorsed by subsequent scholars who elaborated and refined them without, however, introducing much that was strikingly new. The results of these linguistic studies were taken up by a number of Italo-Albanian writers who made use of them in the propaganda of the nationalist movement in which they were actively engaged. Scholarly evidence that Albanians were neither Turks, Greeks nor Slavs but members of a distinct ethnic group with a language of its own helped to strengthen their case for granting Albanians the same national rights as other ethnic groups had either won for themselves or were in the process of doing so.

The dissolution of the Albanian League in 1881 was followed by a brief period of relative peace before a series of local revolts and uprisings started all over again. As so often in the past, one of the causes of strife was the attempt of the Turkish authorities to collect old taxes or impose new ones. Another was their policy of disarming the rebellious inhabitants of the northern highlands. A third source of resentment was the decision to send into exile Albanian leaders accused of persistently inciting popular disaffection or rebellion against the Ottoman administration. But on the whole these operations were of a local character and were mostly confined to the north. The absence of any real military and political co-ordination also rendered them somewhat ineffective. Nevertheless, from time to time the rebels did voice some of the nationalist demands inspired by the Albanian League, such as the right to open Albanian schools, the request to withdraw arrogant and corrupt Turkish officials from the country and to grant it administrative autonomy. The fears of the Albanian nationalists about what might happen to their country when Turkey withdrew from the Balkans altogether became apparent when they were willing to co-operate with Turkish forces on occasions when these were involved in hostilities with either Slavs or Greeks.

After the Congress of Berlin, the rivalry between Austria-Hungary and Italy for political influence in Albania became greater than ever. The Habsburgs were in a stronger position by virtue of the right they had possessed since the seventeenth century to exercise protection over the Roman Catholic community. But with the progress of the nationalist movement, they gradually modified this policy by extending protection to the rest of the population. Vienna supported the Albanian demand for autonomy because it believed this might act as a bulwark against the expansion of Slav influence in the Balkans. Italy's policy in Albania was largely a response to Austro-Hungarian policy and was designed to check Habsburg influence there. Both sides competed in the field of education, each one subsidizing religious schools of its own. In some of these a feeble attempt was made to introduce the teaching of the Albanian language. Albanian nationalist support veered between Austria-Hungary and Italy according to the bewildering changes that occurred in a highly unstable political situation. In time, however, many nationalist leaders tended to favour Austria-Hungary. They believed that Vienna had no intention of annexing the country and that its policy was relatively disinterested. Italian support, on the other hand, was suspected more and more of being motivated by ambitions of territorial acquisition.

After the abortive attempts at political reform between 1861 and 1876, Turkey fell for a generation under the harsh despotism of Sultan Abdul Hamid II, known as Abdul the Damned. The movement of the Young Turks tried to remedy this state of affairs by reviving the liberal constitution of 1876 which the sultan had discarded. Albanian nationalists were closely allied to the Young Turks whom they helped to depose Abdul Hamid in 1909 and bring their reforming administration to power. In the early stages of the revolution, the Albanians were enthusiastic about the radical reforms promised by the Young Turks. They seized the opportunity which the revolution offered them to open Albanian nationalist clubs and schools in many parts of the country and press their demands for full autonomy. New political leaders emerged, some of whom were members of the Young Turk movement, while others were prepared to support its more progressive policies. The most outstanding of these was Ismail Kemal (1844–1919) who had held several high government positions in many parts of the Ottoman empire and had been an exponent of radical constitutional and political reforms. However, he and many other Albanian nationalists were deeply dismayed when the Young Turks decided to block any measure which led to decentralization or autonomy, thus proving to be no less determined to oppress subject nationalities than their predecessors. The melancholy outcome of this revelation was more widespread Albanian revolts followed by more Turkish reprisals.

One of the major consequences of the chauvinistic policy of the Young Turks was the Balkan War of 1912. The policy was responsible for uniting Greeks, Serbs, Montenegrins and Bulgarians into a common front. In October 1912, they all declared war on Turkey. The war placed the Albanians in the awful predicament they had dreaded for so long. Their territory was invaded by all the Balkan allies who claimed to come as liberators but were in fact determined to partition the country between themselves. Faced with this situation, some Albanians fought on the side of Turkey, believing that by doing so they would best safeguard their country's territorial integrity. Turkey's quick defeat in the Balkans spurred Albanian nationalists to go into action under the able leadership of Ismail Kemal, who succeeded in enlisting the political and diplomatic support of Austria-Hungary. At a meeting of representatives from all parts of the country held at Vlorë (Valona) on 28 November 1912, Ismail Kemal formally proclaimed Albania's independence. The meeting entrusted him with the formation of the first provisional government. Shortly after, a conference of ambassadors of the great European powers was convened in London to discuss the problems raised by the Balkan War. On the demand of Austria-

Hungary, to which Russia agreed, the conference recognized the independence of the new Albanian state. In 1913 its new frontiers were decided by the great powers. In this settlement Albania lost the province of Kosovo to Serbia. But the dream of national freedom for which the Albanians had fought for so long amidst the most appalling difficulties had hardly come true before it was dissolved into the nightmare of the first world war and its aftermath.

Chapter 3

AHMET ZOGU'S AUTHORITARIAN RÉGIME

THE FUTURE OF the new state was placed in the hands of the conference of ambassadors of the great powers which met in London throughout 1913. One of its decisions was to proclaim Albania an independent principality ruled by a prince to be chosen by the European powers. The choice fell on Wilhelm zu Wied, an obscure, well-meaning German aristocrat who was ill-equipped to cope with the intractable problems of his new domain. He arrived in Albania in March 1914 and made the port of Durrës (Durazzo) his capital.

Prince Wied exercised power with the aid of two agencies: an Albanian government of landowners and former Ottoman officials, and an international control commission. The most powerful member of the government was Esad Toptani, a feudal lord with large estates in central Albania, who was both minister of the interior and of defence. Although he was supposed to act as the ruler's principal adviser on political and military affairs, Esad Toptani tried his best to make life as difficult as possible for the German prince so that he could himself become undisputed ruler of the new state. A master of the crafts of political intrigue and manipulation, Toptani used his influence to stir up local opposition to the government of which he was a member, thus aggravating the chaotic situation that already existed in the country. In the end, the great powers asked Prince Wied to give up his hopeless job. He left Albania in September 1914, thus bringing to an end 6 months of inglorious rule.

The outbreak of the first world war was to sweep away not only the intrigues of ambitious men like Esad Toptani but also Albania's fragile independence. In October 1914 Greece announced the occupation of the southern provinces, where its troops had been active for some time. A couple of months later, Italy, though still a neutral state, occupied the port of Vlorë

(Valona). During the summer of 1915 northern and central Albania were overrun by Serbian and Montenegrin troops. Their hold on the country was, however, short-lived. After badly defeating Serbia and Montenegro in the autumn of the same year, the armies of Austria-Hungary occupied some two-thirds of the country which remained under their control to the end of the war.

The entry of Austro-Hungarian troops was welcomed by many Albanians for a number of reasons. In the first place, they had driven out the Serbs and Montenegrins who had long-standing designs on Albanian territory. Secondly, the Habsburgs were seen as the only protectors of Albanian independence. Indeed, by its propaganda the Austrian military administration went all out to remind Albanians that Vienna had been chiefly responsible for setting up the new state at the London conference of 1912–13, and to persuade them that its policy of friendship and support would continue in the future. This astute propaganda was reinforced by action in several fields. A limited autonomy was granted to the occupied zone, in which a civilian administration, largely staffed by Albanian officials, was set up. A number of useful roads and bridges were built. The occupying power maintained Albanian schools and financed the publication of books and newspapers. Albanian students were sent to Austrian schools and universities on Austrian government grants. The fact that such encouragement came from an imperial power which denied freedom to several other national communities under its control did not appear as paradoxical to many Albanians. In their utter helplessness, the luxury of being able to choose one's protectors was not for them; they would have gone to the devil himself for political, diplomatic or any other succour. From the other belligerent camp, the French army, which had taken over the southern town of Korçë (Korcha) and its surrounding area towards the end of 1916, gave similar encouragement to political and cultural development in its zone of occupation.

By becoming a battlefield so soon after attaining nominal independence, Albania was not only denied the vital breathing space it needed to build an administrative structure from scratch, but also suffered great human losses as well as widespread devastation. With the defeat of Austria-Hungary in the war the Albanians lost the only European power which had shown any willingness to come to their defence. When peace came their

territory was at the mercy of Italy, Greece, Serbia and Montenegro. Then at the end of 1917 the Bolsheviks made public a
document which dealt yet another blow to their hopes for the
future. This was the secret Treaty of London, concluded in April
1915, by which Britain, France and Russia had bribed Italy to
enter the war on their side. In addition to Trentino, southern
Tirol and Trieste, Italy was promised full sovereignty over the
Albanian port of Vlorë as well as a protectorate over the greater
part of Albania. The country's northern and southern provinces
were to go to Serbia and Greece respectively. Albanian fears and
suspicions were further increased when the two main beneficiaries
of the secret treaty—Italy and Greece—agreed in July 1919 to
support one another when the Albanian issue was raised at the
peace conference.

These developments led Albanian nationalists to surmise that
their country was doomed if the peace settlement were to be
based on the old imperialistic policies of the great powers of
Europe. They were consequently immensely relieved when
president Woodrow Wilson enunciated his Fourteen Points as a
basis for a settlement. These laid down the principle of self-
determination and of "open covenants of peace openly arrived
at" which meant the disavowal of secret treaties in which peoples
and provinces were made objects of barter.

The dangers implicit in the secret Treaty of London, coupled
with President Wilson's new doctrine, galvanized the Albanians
into action. A special congress was held at the beginning of 1920
at Lushnjë, in central Albania, in which fifty delegates representing all regions of the country took part. It produced a
number of rapid decisions regarding foreign policy and domestic
affairs. After rejecting the partition plans embodied in the 1915
Treaty of London and similar other schemes, the congress
declared that Albania was an independent state, hence its people
were not prepared to accept a foreign protectorate in any shape
or form. The peace conference at Versailles was informed that
Albanians would take up arms in defence of their country's
territorial integrity and independence.

The measures which the Lushnjë congress introduced to deal
with the confused internal situation were equally important. As
Wilhelm zu Wied had not abdicated when he left in haste in
1914, constitutionally the country was still a principality. So a

regency council of four was set up to act on his behalf. A non-
elected senate was entrusted with parliamentary functions until
such time as a general election could be held. The political
structure of the new state was completed with the formation of
a government headed by Sulejman Delvina. The minister of the
interior of the new administration was Ahmet Zogu. When
the congress chose Tirana as the country's capital, he was given
the task of restoring some law and order to enable the legislative
and executive branches of government to function.

The problems facing the first post-war government were
daunting indeed. One of these was the great shortage of trained
people in every field of public affairs. Another was the state of
general anarchy caused by the fighting that had taken place in
Albania during the war years. At the beginning, the authority
of the government was confined to central Albania. But gradually
its power grew as it brought under control towns and provinces
evacuated by foreign troops. Perhaps the most formidable challenge was posed by Italy's refusal to withdraw its 20,000 troops
from southern Albania.

Italy's behaviour and the government's inability to cope with
the tricky situation engendered an atmosphere of bitter anti-
Italian feeling in the country. This in turn gave rise to a spon-
taneous popular movement in favour of direct military action.
A secret committee of national defence was set up in Vlorë in
May 1920. This sent an ultimatum to the commander of the
Italian forces, demanding that the towns of Vlorë, Tepelenë and
Himarë be handed over to the Albanian government. The ultimatum stated that Albanians "were not prepared to be sold like
cattle in the markets of Europe". The Italian navy replied by
opening fire on the Albanian irregular forces massed along the
outer defences of the port of Vlorë. The Albanians then stormed
the Italian outposts, capturing several of them and taking some
prisoners. They also made a desperate attempt to capture the
town itself but were driven back with heavy losses. In the meantime, volunteers rushed to Vlorë from many parts of the country.
As fighting continued for several weeks, secret talks were held
between Rome and Tirana to end the conflict. The determination
of the Albanians to rid their country of foreign troops received an
unexpected boost from the domestic convulsions of post-war
Italy. Italian socialists, in particular, were opposed to foreign
adventures like the protracted occupation of Albania. When

fighting broke out at Vlorë, violent demonstrations were staged in a number of Italian cities against the despatch of reinforcements to Albania. The transport of troops across the Adriatic was in fact seriously hampered by strikes organized by the seamen's and railway workers' unions. With an explosive situation at home and an uprising against its army abroad on its hands, the Italian government decided to cut its losses by agreeing, in August 1920, to withdraw its troops from Albania and recognize its independence and territorial integrity. The Italians managed, however, to retain the tiny island of Sazan (Saseno) which lies opposite Vlorë.

Although neither the Lushnjë congress nor the government in Tirana was directly responsible for the popular uprising which brought about the withdrawal of the Italian army, the new atmosphere of national unity did provide the necessary impulse for the uprising as well as for some of the other political successes scored in 1920. These in turn strengthened the country's self-confidence and will to action. The Albanians felt, perhaps for the first time in their history, that their own collective endeavours had helped in some measure to determine their own future by demonstrating that they were no longer prepared to be mere pawns in the political and diplomatic games of more powerful nations. When Italy gave up its policy of dominating Albania, Yugoslavia and Greece had little or no hope of pressing their own claims. Nevertheless, both countries did all they could to take advantage of Albania's weak position by stirring up trouble along its borders. However, after Albania's admission to the League of Nations in December 1920, this unsettled state of affairs eventually came to an end. One year later the country's 1913 borders were internationally reaffirmed, with certain minor concessions in Yugoslavia's favour.

The next few years were taken up with attempts to operate some sort of parliamentary government under very unpropitious circumstances. Three main social groups were involved in a confused struggle for power. The most important of these consisted of landowners, or *beys*, who were the direct descendants of the *sipahis* of the Ottoman empire, and of former officials of the Ottoman administration. They were all determined to retain some of the economic and political privileges they had enjoyed during centuries of foreign rule. The second group was made up of leaders of the northern clans who feared that by submitting to central government control they would forfeit the somewhat anarchic autonomy they had wrested from the old Ottoman régime. The third group included educated members of a tiny urban middle class who had played some part in the nationalist movement both at home and abroad. Representatives of these groups became members of parliament in the country's first real elections held in April 1921. In the absence of political parties in the true meaning of the term, there arose a number of unstable parliamentary factions representing largely irreconcilable interests and points of view. The landowners and the former Turkish officials were prepared to take part in the parliamentary charade in so far as this helped to enhance their power. Only a handful of well-educated politicians was willing or able to make a real success of parliamentary government. But they were in a minority; moreover, they had little or no influence among the mass of poor, illiterate peasants who were under the sway of powerful conservative politicians. Eventually the new parliament split into two broad factions: the conservative landowners and tribal chiefs led by Ahmet Zogu, the future king, and the liberal reformers headed by Fan Noli, a bishop of the Orthodox church.

The two political leaders could hardly have been more different in personality, background or outlook. Zogu, the clan chieftain and landowner, had distinguished himself as an energetic minister of the interior and leader of irregular forces in the early postwar years. He was an able administrator and a skilled politician. Noli, on the other hand, had spent most of his life in the United States, where he was educated, and had little or no real knowledge of the grave political, economic and social problems facing his countrymen. He was a poet, a historian and a musician of distinction. As Albania's first delegate to the League of Nations, Noli had defended its case with remarkable diplomatic skill. Yet when it came to domestic affairs he was no match for consummate politicians like Zogu or some of the former bureaucrats of the Ottoman empire.

Zogu became prime minister in the summer of 1922, retaining at the same time the portfolio of home affairs. His rapid rise to power and the ruthless efficiency he displayed in achieving it roused the suspicions not only of the more liberal parliamentarians but also of some of his fellow conservatives. As opposition to his rule gathered momentum in parliament, he managed to secure the support of the northern clan leaders, of army officers and of several landowners of central and southern Albania. His position, however, improved when his government secured a working majority in a general election held in December 1923. Yet within six months Zogu was swept from power in a fit of uncharacteristic political absent-mindedness and military ineptitude. He was dislodged by a feeble military coup staged by two army regiments, forcing him and several hundred of his political supporters to take refuge in Yugoslavia. His government was replaced by a moderately liberal and reformist administration under bishop Fan Noli.

The new prime minister's great reputation led many people to believe that a turning point had been reached in the country's political evolution. But such hopes were soon disappointed by some of the domestic and external policies of the government. Bishop Noli, himself an ardent supporter of parliamentary government, dealt a serious blow to the country's first experiment in liberal democracy when he failed to hold a general election. Although Albania's numerous domestic problems were neither of its making nor were they open to any easy solutions, Noli's administration made no real attempt to grapple with any of them. He attended the assembly of the League of Nations at Geneva and pleaded for an international loan under its auspices. At the same time, he did his best to nullify his plea by addressing the League in a somewhat patronizing and undiplomatic manner. He accused it, among other things, of having become an instrument of the great powers, a platform for grandiose rhetoric but little action. Such sweeping criticism would have caused resentment had it come from the representative of a major power; coming from the prime minister of Albania who had himself been at the birth of the League, it brought nothing but discredit to his government and to the country he represented. But the one act that perhaps sealed the fate of Fan Noli's government was its decision to recognize Soviet Russia, at a time when the nationalistic and right-wing governments of Greece, Yugoslavia and of the other Balkan countries regarded the communist régime in Moscow with the utmost suspicion. The big European powers also feared that Albania might become a hotbed of communist intrigue and subversion.

The overthrow of Fan Noli's government turned out to be just as easy as the removal of Zogu had been 6 months earlier. During his exile in Yugoslavia Zogu organized and trained a group of Albanian mercenaries with Yugoslav military and financial assistance. He also enlisted several seasoned veterans of General Wrangel's White Russian army who had sought refuge in Yugoslavia after the Bolshevik revolution. Aided and abetted by the Yugoslav government, these motley forces entered Albania in December 1924 and took over the country within a few weeks. Fan Noli and his ministers fled to Italy, from where they moved on to Paris, Vienna and other European capitals. Some years later Fan Noli himself passed this verdict on his 6 months' administration : "By insisting on the agrarian reforms I aroused the wrath of the landed aristocracy : by failing to carry them out I lost the support of the peasant masses". This is a rather glib and one-sided explanation of his failure, which was mainly due to a serious lack of hard commonsense and political realism in coping with the many domestic and external problems of a poor and weak country.

After having regained power, Ahmet Zogu quickly snuffed Albania's brief experiment in parliamentary government and proceeded to establish a personal authoritarian régime. At the beginning he ruled through four military governors directly responsible to him. Their absolute power was superimposed on the existing civilian administration. Stern measures were taken by the governors to disarm the population as well as deal with political opponents.

Some of Zogu's natural allies had always been the conservative landowners, or *beys*, of central and southern Albania, many of them men of wide administrative and diplomatic experience gained in the service of the Ottoman state. But the economic power and the political influence they wielded in their own districts made them uneasy and difficult partners for a man determined to set up a strong central government with himself as its linchpin. His problem was how best to deprive these men of the power they had exercised for many generations whilst making use of their administrative expertise. A sort of compromise was finally reached by allowing the *beys* to retain their estates in return for giving up their political ambitions. Zogu's vague promise to introduce agrarian reforms was to hang like a permanent threat over the landowners, thus ensuring their loyalty and good political behaviour. Many of them served as cabinet ministers or held well-paid positions as government officials, diplomats and courtiers during the 1920s and 1930s. In these posts they had a

good deal of influence, ample opportunities of enriching themselves, but little real power. Zogu's instinct was to place the
ultimate security of his administration in the hands of the tough
highlanders of north and north-eastern Albania, particularly of
the provinces of Mat and Diber, who had helped him to return
to power. Having started his career as a young tribal leader under
the Turks and other foreign rulers, he was reluctant to depend
entirely on the army or the police even when these had become
fairly efficient instruments of executive power. Consequently,
many of the clan chieftains were appointed reserve army officers,
armed and paid by the government, who held themselves ready
to answer their master's call in time of crisis. They were, in effect,
mercenaries pledged to defend the régime against domestic or
external threats.

In foreign affairs, Zogu made an unexpected change of policy
towards Yugoslavia which had been instrumental in getting him
back to power. He rejected the idea of close ties with that country
and opted for an alliance with Italy. There were several reasons
for this sudden shift. In common with other nationalists, Zogu
had resented Yugoslavia's persistent interference in Albania's
affairs in the immediate post-war period. Italy was in a far better
position than Yugoslavia to provide him with the economic, technical and military aid that his country needed. The Albanian
leader may have also believed that because Yugoslavia, unlike
Italy, had a land frontier with Albania, it presented a greater
potential menace to his own security. But the fact is that in matters of foreign policy and foreign economic aid Zogu hardly had
any choice; at best only a choice of evils. Britain and France
had not only shown no real desire to help his country but had
done all they could to push it into Italy's political sphere of
influence. The first economic and financial agreement between
president Zogu and Mussolini's government, concluded in May
1925, provided for the setting up of an Albanian national bank
and the granting of credits for Albania's economic development.
The true nature of the agreement was apparent in the choice of
Rome as the seat of the bank, and in the stipulation that the
Italian government would contribute 51 per cent of its capital.
In November 1926 the two countries signed a friendship and
security pact. This laid down that any disturbance of Albania's
political, juridical or territorial *status quo* threatened the vital

interests of both parties. They undertook to safeguard these interests by mutual co-operation. What this meant, in effect, was that Italy could intervene with its military forces in Albania whenever it saw fit. Finally, Albania's dependence on Italy was sealed by a 20-year defence treaty concluded one year later. This explicitly authorized Italy to go to its junior partner's defence should the latter be attacked.

These agreements enabled Italy to finance and equip the Albanian army to which a large number of Italian officers were attached in the capacities of organizers and instructors. Italian firms were granted monopolistic concessions for exploiting the country's oil and coal resources. The economic development funds were to be equally shared between schemes to modernize agriculture and plans for building new roads, bridges, schools and hospitals. But in practice very little was done to bring about any real improvement in farming, Albania's principal source of national income. Italy's main concern was to concentrate on building new roads and bridges, or improving existing ones, and modernizing the port of Durrës. These and similar other capital investments seemed designed to serve Mussolini's strategic purposes rather than Albania's economic development. Zogu soon became aware of the true nature of these policies and did all he could to counteract them. With the army under effective Italian control, he made sure that the police, the gendarmerie (a kind of constabulary) and the civil service remained under Albanian control. He arranged that the gendarmerie, entrusted with the task of maintaining law and order in the countryside, should be trained and supervised by retired British army officers, paid by the Albanian government, acting as inspectors. The British team was headed by an inspector-general directly responsible to the head of state. The post was held by two distinguished retired British officers: Colonel W. F. Stirling, who had been military adviser to Lawrence of Arabia, and General Sir Jocelyn Percy. Their presence in his administration was seen by Zogu as a token counterweight to excessive Italian influence.

In 1928 the president took a constitutional step that was to increase his dependence on fascist Italy as well as to widen the gap between him and his people. This was the transformation of the republic into a monarchy, a unique event in the modern history of Europe. After an officially inspired and orchestrated series of popular demands from many parts of the country, parliament voted, in September, to proclaim the president King of the Albanians, with Zog I as his official designation. The founding of the new dynasty and the spurious device that was used to bring it about caused misgivings at home and abroad. Some of the new king's countrymen thought the drastic constitutional change indicated that he was less concerned with Albania's political, economic and cultural advancement than with perpetuating his own rule. There were also legitimate fears that the country could ill afford the high cost of maintaining the monarchy. The most severe foreign criticism of the president's elevation to the throne came some years later from Kemal Atatürk, the president of Turkey. At a public reception in Ankara he complained to the Albanian minister about the strange political metamorphosis, which he likened to the staging of a small-time operetta, that had taken place in his country. Atatürk made it plain that he considered Albania's transition from republic to monarchy anachronistic.

The new king's family consisted of his mother, five sisters, several nephews and a large number of other relatives. Their incomes and the expenses of their separate establishments were derived from an ever-expanding civil list. In the context of Albania's great poverty, the monarchy soon became a pitiful incongruity. It also made the country, in the eyes of many people, synonymous with Ruritania. Its sorely tried people, the majority desperately poor peasants, became the laughing-stock of Europe, when what they needed was its compassionate understanding, not its derisive amusement. In short, Albania's upstart dynasty, with its gaudy trappings, succeeded in throwing a veil of insipid farce over an essentially tragic situation.

In domestic affairs Zog pursued a fairly consistent authoritarian policy punctuated by acts of great severity. In March 1925 government troops killed in northern Albania Bajram Curri, leader of a guerilla band opposed to the régime. At about the same time, Luigj Gurakuqi, a Catholic liberal politician and one of Fan Noli's closest associates, was murdered in Italy by an agent of the Albanian government. Some 6 years later a number of Albanian political exiles in Austria tried to assassinate Zog himself while on a private visit to Vienna. Although he had a narrow escape, one of his aides was killed and another wounded. The event marked the beginning of a series of revolts against the régime which were suppressed with a good deal of harshness.

One of these took place at Vlorë in 1932; its organizers were captured and given long prison sentences. A far more serious uprising occurred 3 years later at Fier, in central Albania, involving communists, landowners and members of the local gendarmerie force. Although quickly squashed, the Fier revolt caused a stir in Albania and abroad. Eleven gendarmes who had taken up arms against the government were executed without trial; some fifty other defendants were sentenced to death by a special tribunal, although their sentences were commuted.

This poorly organized, though genuine, opposition stemmed from two main sources. One was the feeling that Zog and his associates were gradually allowing fascist Italy to turn Albania into an outright protectorate. The other was the resentment caused by some of the policies and methods of the régime. After relying mainly on the power of the northern highlanders and of the big landlords, Zog's administration tried to expand its political network by attempting to enlist the support of other sections of the population. By the mid-1930s the country was roughly divided into those who had proved their loyalty to the king (they were known as "loyalists") and the rest of the population who made up the vast majority. Personal allegiance to the head of state, rather than professional qualifications, often determined one's employment in the civil service, the armed forces, the police, or one's chances of becoming a member of parliament. Many beneficiaries of this system of political patronage became arrogant and used their positions for the purpose of enriching themselves, their families and their friends. Those who were outside the magic circle felt left out in the cold. Members of a small professional class, and educated young people in particular, were dismayed by the selfish preoccupations of the régime and by its lack of any coherent social, political or economic objectives.

Two leading figures of the king's inner circle who best reflected its general philosophy and also did great harm to his reputation were Abdurrahman Krosi, one of Zog's closest friends, and Musa Juka, his minister of the interior for many years. Krosi, an illiterate peasant from the king's native province, had been a retainer of Zog's feudal family from the beginning of this century. When his master became president of the republic, he moved to Tirana and was elected (or rather appointed) member of parliament. Krosi never held any other official position. Yet his close proximity to the king, coupled with a mixture of native shrewdness, cunning and inordinate greed for power and wealth, enabled him to create, within a few years, a complex network of favouritism, bribery, financial corruption and general skulduggery. A great variety of individuals were caught in Krosi's insidious web at one time or another: cabinet ministers and civil servants; businessmen and shopkeepers; landowners and clan chieftains; peasants and town dwellers; rich and poor. Musa Juka, on the other hand, was the régime's police chief as well as the custodian of the absolute allegiance it demanded from its supporters and beneficiaries. A former Ottoman official, he retained many of the characteristics of the *ancien régime* bureaucrat: deviousness, procrastination, nepotism, venality, sycophancy. Besides controlling the police, he maintained a large number of informers and spies throughout the country. The highly centralized local government administration, divided into units known as prefectures and sub-prefectures, came under the jurisdiction of his department. Juka himself appointed the main executive officers of local government with whom he dealt directly. He once told a British journalist in the 1930s: "Many people would hang Krosi were it not for the king's protection." The same thing could have been said about Musa Juka himself.

Apart from his domestic problems, the king faced a good deal of pressure from Mussolini's government. In an effort to curtail excessive Italian influence, the Albanian government decided in 1933 to close all schools financed by Italy. This was done by the rather clumsy policy of placing the whole educational system under state control. Consequently, Albanian Catholic schools as well as those belonging to the Greek minority in southern Albania were shut down. Greece complained to the League of Nations and the case was referred to the International Court in the Hague. Albania was found guilty and eventually had to re-open the Greek schools. The Italian government reacted to the closure of its own schools by stopping the supply of credits. In reprisal, Zog took the bold step of expelling most of the Italian instructors attached to the armed forces. Relations between the two countries were seriously affected by these sharp exchanges. Mussolini's decision to suspend financial aid increased Albania's already grave economic difficulties. Nevertheless Zog stood firm. Although he possessed hardly any cards, he managed to play those he did have with skill and determination. His firmness was as widely appreciated by his own people as Mussolini's policy of blackmail was resented. The real test of the king's nerve, however, came when a large number of Italian warships appeared at the port of Durrës in June 1934 without prior warning. Zog decided to ignore the provocation, so Mussolini withdrew his fleet without having attained his immediate objective. But the Albanian leader could not afford to keep up this cat-and-mouse game for long without causing national bankruptcy or damaging his own position beyond repair. So within about a year a kind of uneasy truce was restored between Rome and Tirana and Italian financial aid was resumed.

Some progress was made between 1920 and 1939 in the neglected field of education. Elementary schooling was compulsory from the age of five to thirteen in towns, from the age of seven in the countryside. However, the acute shortage of teachers and the lack of school buildings, particularly in the villages, rendered this statutory obligation largely theoretical. Hence the problem of reducing illiteracy on a massive scale remained unresolved. By 1938 there were some 650 primary schools in the whole country. The development of secondary education was equally inadequate. By the beginning of the second world war no more than 20 secondary schools of various types, with an enrolment of 5,700 pupils, had been set up. Given this state of affairs, only 36 per cent of children of school age received education of any kind. Despite occasional political interference from the government, a network of private schools made a useful contribution to progress in education. The Jesuits and Franciscans had maintained Catholic primary and secondary schools in Shkodër for several generations. Two of the country's best secondary schools were financed by American foundations. As Albania had no universities of its own, young people wishing to acquire education had to do so abroad. The state granted some university scholarships, but their number was far too small to meet Albania's enormous needs for trained people. In 1936–37, for instance, there were some 400 students attending foreign universities; the number of university graduates in 1938 was only 90.

Yet despite these great deficiencies in education, and despite the country's general cultural backwardness, intellectual life during the 1930s was surprisingly lively in the capital and in one or two other centres. Newspapers and magazines of every type flourished, though some of them were short-lived. These provided a platform for intelligent debates on the country's political, economic, social and cultural problems. Some of these debates, however, were often conducted on a rather abstract level as they tended to ignore the crucial problem of the peasantry. Partly through lack of communications and partly through sheer apathy, most town dwellers were abysmally ignorant of the wretched conditions of the countryside. The peasants thus led a sequestered existence which had few links, other than those of taxation and military service, with the narrow society of officialdom and of the small urban population. The Italo-Ethiopian war (1935–36) and the Spanish civil war (1936–39) caused a good deal of interest and discussion, especially among young people. Most Albanians were, broadly speaking, opposed to Italy's and General Franco's sides in the two conflicts mainly for nationalistic reasons. It was the only way in which they could express their feelings with regard to fascist Italy's behaviour towards their own country. The interplay between Albania's acute internal problems, on the one hand, and the political and ideological issues raised by the fighting in Ethiopia and Spain, on the other, led to the formation of small groups of radical and left-wing elements. Stimulated to some extent by anti-Zogists living abroad, these groups were able to engage in widespread propaganda against the régime. A few left-wing army officers fled to Spain where they fought in the republican ranks. One of these was Mehmet Shehu, who became communist prime minister after the second world war. Some of the radical factions of the 1930s were to form the nucleus of the communist party that was set up in 1941.

Literature, particularly poetry, also flourished during the period between the two wars. The scene was dominated by three fairly representative writers. The most outstanding of these was Father Gjergj Fishta (1871–1940), Albania's greatest poet. He was in many ways a paradoxical figure. Although a Catholic and a member of the Franciscan order, Fishta was widely regarded in his lifetime as the national poet of a predominantly Moslem country. Yet the northern Albanian dialect in which he wrote, known as Geg, coupled with the intrinsic complexity of his vision, rendered some of his work largely incomprehensible to many of his readers. His most popular work, *The Lute of the Highlands*, is an epic poem of 30 cantos centred on Albania's long struggle for survival during the nineteenth and twentieth centuries. The villanies of its numerous enemies are flayed, the heroic feats of its people in meeting history's many challenges extolled. The poem's appeal rests on a simple message which embodies both black despair and shining faith : the despair engendered by Europe's political iniquities is counterbalanced by the poet's unshaken belief in his countrymen's readiness to overcome such iniquities and survive. But Fishta the national poet is also a satirical writer of savage power. In several comic narrative poems of Byronic bite he flays a number of foreign and local targets : European imperialism, the venality of politicians, religious hypocrisy, middle-class selfishness, peasant backwardness, civil service corruption and so forth. Ernest Koliqi (1903–1975) was a leader of the modern movement in prose and poetry and one of the country's outstanding intellectuals. He is a lyric poet with a genuine romantic vein as well as a fine short story writer. Although Koliqi began his literary career writing in the northern dialect, he did try, unlike Fishta, to bridge the gap between Geg and Tosk (the southern dialect) by helping to foster the development of a common literary language. A conservative and traditionalist by conviction, he felt that his cultural and political ambitions were thwarted under the monarchy. These found an unexpected outlet during Italy's occupation of Albania in the 1940s when Koliqi served as minister of education. The third leading literary figure of the pre-war period, Lasgush Poradeci (b. 1899), is the country's greatest lyric poet. An unworldly, non-political, mystical and difficult poet, he has a good deal of affinity with the Parnassian and symbolist poets of France. But Poradeci's voice, the musicality of his language, the fine craftsmanship of his verse are his own.

Hitler's occupation of Austria and Czechoslovakia between March 1938 and March 1939 greatly alarmed Mussolini about his ally's ultimate aims in Europe. Fascist Italy had to react quickly if it was not to be left far behind nazi Germany in the ruthless drive for territorial conquest. The only area in which Italy could expand with any degree of equanimity was the Balkans. The ground was carefully prepared by consolidating the friendly ties that had already been forged between Rome and Yugoslavia's right-wing government. After presenting king Zog with a series of unacceptable demands, Mussolini launched an unprovoked attack on its Albanian ally on Good Friday, 7 April 1939. After encountering a brief but fierce resistance, the Italian forces occupied most of the country within a few days. Zog and his family, together with some of his ministers, went into exile.

The deep sense of dereliction which most Albanians experienced in the spring of that year is best summed up by Carlo Levi's words quoted earlier, even though these were written in a quite different context : "No one has come to this land except as an enemy, a conqueror, or a visitor devoid of understanding."

Although it can fairly be said that Zog was a reformer of sorts, he was by no means a reformer like, say, Kemal Atatürk. His passion for social, political and cultural changes was feebler and more intermittent than that of the Turkish leader. Perhaps the greatest shortcoming of his régime was its failure to cope with the problem of the peasants. Little or nothing was done to improve their miserable living and working conditions, in spite of the fact that they were, in the true sense, the backbone of the country. The oxen-driven wooden plough continued to be the symbol of the archaic state of Albanian farming. With hardly any investments in agriculture and no proper credit facilities, Albania's peasants were gradually bled white by tax collector, landlord and moneylender. By the end of the 1930s many of them were reduced to penury.

Apart from some fairly significant improvements in education and in the other fields already discussed, Zog's principal achievement perhaps was to preside over the difficult task of laying the foundations of the Albanian nation-state. The various autonomous bailiwicks of obdurate tribal leaders and of self-seeking landowners were welded into a single national community. This in turn was provided with a somewhat ramshackle political, administrative and legal structure. Under the king's rule the ancient scourge of blood feuds was mitigated; a modicum of law and a good deal of public order were established throughout the country.

Chapter 4

FOREIGN OCCUPATION AND CIVIL WAR

ITALY'S INVASION OF Albania in April 1939 caused hardly a ripple on the waters of appeasement which had engulfed the democratic countries of Europe for some time past. Apart from the general policy of appeasement, Great Britain and France had over the years tacitly recognized Italy's right to do whatever it wished in Albania. Zog had tried to perform a balancing act in a highly ambiguous situation and failed. Mussolini was now free to transform the country into an outright Italian colony. R. A. Butler (Lord Butler), then a junior minister at the Foreign Office, went to see Neville Chamberlain at Downing Street on the Good Friday that Italy attacked Albania. He found the prime minister in his study, overlooking the garden, feeding the birds. Surprised by the minister's evident worry, Chamberlain said : "I feel sure Mussolini has not decided to go against us." When Butler spoke about the general threat to the Balkans, the prime minister told him : "Don't be silly. Go home to bed", and went on with the serious business of feeding the birds.[1]

Shortly after their entry in Tirana, the Italians set up a provisional government under Xhafer Ypi, a former senior official of Zog's régime. It was given the task of introducing a series of measures to bring about a union between the two countries. A so-called national assembly composed of landowners, clan chieftains and sundry pro-Italian politicians abolished the 1928 monarchical constitution and offered the Albanian crown to the king of Italy, Victor Emmanuel III. The Italian ambassador in Albania, Francesco Jacomoni, was appointed viceroy, or the country's effective ruler.

At the beginning Italian policy was based on the general assumption that Albania had not yet become a nation-state and

[1] Lord Butler, *The Art of the Possible*, Hamish Hamilton, London, 1971, p. 79.

that its society was still a mixture of Ottoman feudalism and ancient tribalism. This assumption disregarded the nationalist and political advances of two decades of independence. In pursuit of this policy, the provisional government which introduced the constitutional changes was soon replaced by another headed by Shefqet Verlaci, the country's largest landowner and a feudal lord in the classic mould. Ernest Koliqi, one of Albania's foremost writers and intellectuals, became minister of education. But his power and influence extended far beyond his own department. Koliqi was in many ways Italy's *éminence grise* in the country. As we saw earlier, he had made a name for himself as a poet and short story writer in the 1930s. However, he had gradually become embittered not only by the corruption and the malpractices of Zog's administration but also by his own inability to forge the kind of career to which he thought he was entitled. In view of his great reputation, Koliqi's decision to collaborate with the occupying power caused a good deal of consternation, particularly among young people who were incensed by the Italian invasion. Another pro-fascist politician who enjoyed the confidence of the Italians was Mustafa Kruja. A highly ambitious but frustrated politician, he had spent a large part of his life abroad as a protégé of Italy in opposition to Zog's régime. Kruja's political career was based on the simple notion that his country could not survive outside Rome's sphere of influence. Many Albanians were also dismayed by the alacrity with which several exiled politicians returned home in the wake of the invasion. This seemed to reveal the political bankruptcy of their long opposition to the previous régime.

Among the first measures designed to end Albania's status as an independent country was the abolition of the ministry of foreign affairs, accompanied by the withdrawal of Albanian dipplomatic missions abroad and the removal of their counterparts in Tirana. The country's army also became part of Italy's armed forces. The Italian fascists soon discovered that some of their political assumptions about their new colony were ill-founded. Merely securing the co-operation of a group of landowners, businessmen and pro-fascist elements, far from winning popular support, tended to strengthen the spirit of resistance in the country as a whole. The setting up of an Albanian fascist party and an Albanian militia did not meet with the enthusiasm which the colonial power had hoped for. The Italians began to realize that opposition to their occupation, though leaderless and not yet properly organized, was fairly widespread and was particularly strong among young people. This became evident during the celebrations that took place on 28 November 1939, the country's first independence day under foreign rule. Demonstrations of an anti-fascist character were organized in Tirana, Korçë, Vlorë and several other centres. Many of the ringleaders, among them several schoolteachers, were rounded up by the police and sent to special internment camps in Italy.

About a year later Mussolini was planning to embark on another military adventure, this time using Albania as his base of operations. The Italian dictator had nothing to show against Germany's successes in Europe during the summer of 1940. Hitler's occupation of Romania in October was the last straw: something had to be done quickly to prove that Italian fascism too was capable of similar feats. So an attack was launched against Greece at the end of October. By early December the Italian armies were hurled back into Albania and the Greek forces took over about half the area of the country. Mussolini had assumed that the war against Greece would be a military walkover. But he had failed to reckon either with the Greeks' heroic determination to defend their country, or with the singular unpreparedness of his troops to operate in the difficult terrain of Albania and Greece. Mussolini's armies were rescued from disaster when the nazi forces overran both Greece and Yugoslavia in April 1941.

One unexpected outcome of the Italo-Greek war was to embitter relations between Greeks and Albanians. When his country was attacked the Greek prime minister Metaxas stated that the Greeks were fighting not only to defend their country but to liberate Albania as well. However, in their moment of triumph the Greek forces acted more like conquerors who had come to secure the return of large Albanian provinces to Greece than liberators. A purely Greek administration was set up in Korçë, Gjirokastër and other occupied centres. These developments were resented by many Albanians, some of whom had carried out sabotage and harassing operations against the Italian armies. What the Greek government was in fact doing was to revive its old claim on southern Albania, one which had been rejected by the peace settlement of 1919. The claim was part of the expansionist doctrine known as the Great Idea by which Greece aspired to bring under its jurisdiction various parts of south-east Europe populated by Orthodox Christians. Although this doctrine had suffered a fatal blow in 1922, when Greece was defeated by Turkey in the war of Asia Minor, it was subsequently exhumed and was kept alive at the expense of a weak and vulnerable Albania. The issue was to poison relations between the two countries for many years to come.

The dismemberment of the Yugoslav state by Germany in the spring of 1941 raised another important issue affecting Albania. As a sop to Mussolini, Hitler allowed Italy's new possession in the Balkans to annex the Yugoslav province of Kosovo. This has a large Albanian population which had settled there during the mass migrations that occurred in the Balkans in the seventeenth and eighteenth centuries. Albanian tenant farmers began settling in Kosovo after the exodus of its Serbian inhabitants to Hungary in 1690. Albanian expansion into Macedonia continued during the following century. When Albania's present frontiers were settled in 1913, Kosovo and the other Albanian-speaking areas were assigned to Yugoslavia. After the first world war the Yugoslav government had adhered to the League of Nations' treaties for the protection of minorities. But as the Belgrade government was then dominated by Serbian nationalism, this adherence remained a dead letter as far as the Albanian minority was concerned. No Albanian schools of any kind were permitted in Kosovo; there was also grave political and economic discrimination against members of the minority. In 1930 the Albanian government complained to the League of Nations about this violation of elementary minority rights but got no satisfaction. By that time the whole international procedure for the protection of national minorities in Europe had proved cumbersome and largely ineffective. And Albania itself was in no position to put pressure on the Yugoslav government to change its policy in Kosovo.

The union of Kosovo with Albania under Italo-German auspices was well received by most Albanians at the beginning. Those who were committed to the fascist régime made the most of the new acquisition for propaganda purposes. But after a while the initial enthusiasm waned among the more sophisticated sections of the population, especially those engaged in underground activity. Although not averse to the idea that Kosovo should become part of Albania, they wished it could have been

brought about by some international agreement rathe<u>r</u> than by
the arbitrary decision of two rapacious powers bent on carving
up Europe between themselves. In the meantime, fascist Italy
did its best, while it could, to please nationalist and irredentist
opinion in Kosovo and Albania itself by opening a large number
of Albanian primary and secondary schools in the former Yugoslav province. These were the first such schools for more than
40 years. But the question of Kosovo continued to plague Yugoslav-Albanian relations during the latter part of the war as well
as in the post-war years.

A resistance movement against the occupying power began to
emerge in the early 1940s. The first guerilla band to operate
against the Italians was led by Abas Kupi, a former officer of
the gendarmerie under king Zog. After taking part in the defence
of the port of Durrës during the Italian invasion in 1939, Kupi
joined the king in exile. He returned to Albania two years later
and remained there throughout the war. As a highly experienced
guerilla fighter and a loyal supporter of Zog, his position and line
of action were fairly clear right from the beginning. But the same
cannot be said of the nationalist and communist resistance groups
which had to undergo several painful convulsions and complex
manoeuvres before they became at all effective. The rise of a
resistance movement was helped to some extent by a change of
government in Tirana. The Italians appeared to be dissatisfied
with the performance of Shefqet Verlaci and his government of
landlords and reactionary politicians. He was replaced in December 1941 by Mustafa Kruja, the faithful supporter of Italian
policy in Albania, who was allowed a little more freedom of
action than his predecessor. He was authorized to raise an independent Albanian army which was to operate alongside Italy's
armed forces. Kruja's administration was also permitted to set
free a large number of anti-fascists who had been interned earlier
on. However, both these measures had a boomerang effect : many
Albanian army recruits and released internees joined the resistance
movement. Far from improving, as the occupation authorities
had hoped, the internal situation deteriorated rapidly under
Kruja's leadership. As people became more and more restless and
defiant, the ranks of the guerilla forces swelled. The gradual
emergence of a communist resistance movement was particularly
worrying for the new administration.

The history of the Albanian communist movement is almost

as chequered and tortuous as the history of the Albanian nation-state itself. Its roots went back to the late 1920s when Fan Noli and his associates formed a national revolutionary committee in Vienna in opposition to Zog's régime. The committee established close links with the Communist International (Comintern) in Moscow which provided it with financial and political support. Although bishop Noli himself was not a communist but a radical in general sympathy with some of the policies of the Soviet government, several of his younger followers became communists after attending special political indoctrination courses in Moscow. The most successful of these was Ali Kelmendi, who was sent to Albania in 1930 for the purpose of organizing communist groups there. He was responsible for setting up communist cells in Korçë, Tirana and a few other centres, though he was not able to weld these into a proper party organization. The factions continued their quarrelsome, hence politically ineffective, existence until nazi Germany attacked Russia on 22 June 1941. Shortly after, the Yugoslav communist resistance movement led by Josip Broz Tito despatched to Albania two special envoys—Dušan Mugoša and Miladin Popovic—for the purpose of getting its strife-ridden communist groups to unite. Through a combination of persuasion and pressure, the two Yugoslavs did succeed in bringing the Albanian communist party into being on 8 November 1941. They remained in the country throughout the war, wielding great influence on communist political and military affairs.

Enver Hoxha, a member of the Korçë faction, was elected secretary-general of the party. He had first come into contact with communist doctrine as a university student in France in the 1930s. After attending the university at Montpellier for a brief period, Hoxha moved to Paris in 1931. There he came under the spell not only of the French communist party but also of a number of Soviet-trained Albanian propagandists then active in the student community. He returned home some 5 years later and pursued a career in teaching until the outbreak of the second world war. Between 1939 and 1941 Hoxha was involved in sporadic anti-Italian activities, though most of his time and energy were taken up by the political intrigues of the communist factions then in existence. His emergence as party leader after so much bitter controversy and strife was evidence of uncommon political agility as well as great personal ambition. The Albanian official record of the founding of the communist party and of Hoxha's election as leader in 1941 was completely rewritten, under his supervision, after Yugoslavia's break with Russia in 1948. The crucial rôle played by the Yugoslavs in this and subsequent events has disappeared altogether. Whenever Yugoslav political figures or Yugoslav policies are mentioned in Albanian publications they are made to serve as butts for censure and vituperation.

After its establishment and the election of its central committee, the communist party proceeded to set up a partisan movement capable of fighting the Italians. It convened a meeting of guerilla leaders and other anti-fascists at the village of Pezë, near Tirana, on 16 September 1942. The only non-communist of any significance who took part was Abas Kupi, the royalist guerilla leader. But despite the failure to obtain wider support, the meeting did create a united front organization called the National Liberation Movement. Its policy was to wage war against fascist Italy and its collaborators, to unite all Albanians, irrespective of their political views or religious beliefs, into a single anti-fascist organization. It was clear from the beginning that this body would be dominated by the communist party. Its desire to gain control of the whole resistance movement spurred a number of nationalists and other opponents of Italian rule to take stock of the situation. About a month later they formed a rival organization of their own known as *Balli Kombëtar* (National Front). This was a broad coalition of old conservative politicians, moderate liberals and agrarian radicals, held together by a passionate desire to free the country from foreign domination. Its leader, Midhat Frasheri, was a distinguished writer, scholar and former diplomat. He and his associates were republicans (hence opponents of Zog's return) who supported a programme of social, political and agrarian reforms. One of their peace aims was to secure the establishment of what they called an ethnic Albania; this meant, in effect, retaining the province of Kosovo. This policy coupled with the knowledge that the communist resistance movement was subject to powerful Yugoslav influence, became the cause of bitter rivalry, and eventually open hostility, between the nationalists and the communists.

At first the main zone of operations of the two guerilla organizations was southern Albania, with the communists concentrating in urban centres, whilst their rivals operated in the countryside.

Because of the underlying tension between them, each side took great pains to stick to its own area. The communist partisan units were highly mobile. They were given the task of sabotaging enemy military establishments and attacking Italian army and police officers in the cities. These actions were carried out with little or no thought of the reprisals against the civilian population that almost invariably ensued. In fact, the dislocation and the bitterness caused by Italian reprisals became valuable sources of new recruits for the partisans. The *Balli Kombëtar* guerilla units, somewhat larger than the communist ones, were organized on the traditional pattern of peasant insurrectionary movements. They benefited, to some extent, from the nationalist legacy of the 1920 revolt against the Italian army at Vlorë, still alive in some parts of southern Albania. As their support came from peasant volunteers, the leaders of *Balli Kombëtar* were more inclined than the communists to weigh the usefulness of a particular military operation against the harm that enemy reprisals might do to the families and villages of their followers. These differences in political outlook and methods of organization became steadily more pronounced. The communists never lost sight of their basic policy that the resistance movement was as much an engine of social and political revolution as of national independence. The *Balli Kombëtar* nationalists, on the other hand, were more concerned with the task of getting rid of foreign rule than with promoting their political and social ideals.

The underground activity of the communists in towns and cities soon produced results that were to prove very useful to their cause. They recruited a large number of students and young intellectuals by a judicious mixture of propaganda, coercion and cajolement. Itinerant propagandists had ready-made and seemingly watertight answers to many political, social and economic questions. Their task was made easier by the general political unsophistication and the prevailing intellectual and moral confusion. The communists were also, somewhat unexpectedly, successful with two other groups. They won the support of many clergymen of the Orthodox church and of several monks of the Bektashi sect. The adherence of the latter to the partisan cause was particularly significant because the Bektashis, as we saw earlier, had played an important part in the Albanian nationalist movement of the nineteenth century and the early part of the twentieth.

4—TA • •

The western allies and Russia gave their public blessing to Albanian resistance in December 1942. The American secretary of state, Cordell Hull, issued a statement which said that the United States government was not "unmindful of the continued resistance of the Albanian people to the Italian forces of occupation". With regard to post-war policy, Hull pointed out that this would be based on the Atlantic Charter (1941) which recognized the rights of all people to restore their national sovereignty and choose their own government. The British foreign secretary, Anthony Eden, made a similar declaration, with one important difference : he added the reservation that the country's post-war frontiers would be considered at the peace settlement. The Soviet official statement, like that of the United States, stuck to broad principles. But it was Britain's reservation on the frontier issue, introduced as a concession to the Greek government in exile, that caused serious misgivings among many Albanians. It certainly did nothing to enhance, and indeed may have harmed, the cause of the western allies in Albania during the war.

In the meantime, the internal situation appeared to be deteriorating fast. In addition to the problems of security stemming from the activities of the guerillas, the country's economic situation was showing signs of crisis. The cost of living had risen sharply since 1939 as a result of low productivity and a vast increase in the supply of paper money. In an attempt to cope with the mounting problems, the Italian authorities made two government changes in two months early in 1943. Mustafa Kruja, Italy's staunch ally, was succeeded by two political nonentities of the monarchist régime. Kruja's removal from office was a sign of some political confusion and loss of nerve in high quarters.

The communist party continued to strengthen its position in the country. It held its first national conference in March 1943 at which several important decisions regarding organization and future action were taken. The various partisan units were amalgamated into a national liberation army. A nation-wide campaign was launched to enlist the adherence of large sections of the population to the partisan cause. Particular stress was laid on the need to win over the peasants, who were to be the backbone of the liberation army. One of the conference resolutions urged the communist party to persuade workers and poor peasants that they were its natural allies. A common struggle would free them from hunger, misery and repression and so secure them a happier future. It was also decided to devote special attention to the recruitment of young men and women to the party's ranks. Enver Hoxha was re-elected secretary-general of the party. The conference, which embodied many of the political and military lessons learnt by the Yugoslav partisans in their own successful struggle, was a landmark in the campaign of the Albanian party to gain power and influence in the country.

Shortly after the conference, two British liaison officers, Colonel Neil McLean and Major David Smiley, entered southern Albania from Greece where they had been attached to guerilla units operating against the Germans. After establishing contact with the Albanian resistance movement they discovered that, like such movements in Greece and Yugoslavia, it was sharply split into communist and nationalist camps. The British officers' first efforts to bring the two sides together were helped by certain important developments in Italy. On 10 July allied troops landed in Sicily; some two weeks later Mussolini's régime collapsed in Rome. It was under the pressures of these events that the communist National Liberation Movement and the nationalist *Balli Kombëtar* agreed to discuss their differences at a secret meeting held at Mukaj, a village near the Albanian capital, on 3 August 1943. The two delegations decided to set up a joint committee which would direct the war effort and administer the liberated areas. The controversial issue of Kosovo was also discussed at some length. The meeting finally agreed that the issue should be settled by a plebiscite after the war. The nationalists held that Kosovo should remain within Albania's borders. Not to be outdone in the bid for popular support, the communists may have concluded that they, too, should take a similar stand on the matter. But the August 1943 agreement proved short-lived. The communist party repudiated it a few days later, maintaining that its representatives had undertaken commitments far beyond their official brief. Incensed by the decision that Kosovo's future should be settled by a post-war plebiscite, the Yugoslav communist party sent Svetozar Vukmanović-Tempo to Albania for the purpose of getting the communists there to go back on this decision as well as on their agreement to co-operate with the nationalists. This was promptly done. A fierce propaganda campaign was launched against the leadership of *Balli Kombëtar*. By making scapegoats of the communist delegates who had come to an understanding with the nationalists, Enver Hoxha's position as party leader was saved, in spite of the fact that he had originally supported the plan for a plebiscite in Kosovo. This wartime episode has been seriously obscured in subsequent Albanian official publications, although these do claim that Vukmanović-Tempo had tried to impose his will on the Albanian communist party, without, however, specifying in what way he had done so.

The fall of Mussolini brought in its wake the collapse of the Italian military and political establishment in Albania. The vacuum was quickly filled by the German forces which entered the country at the end of August. They occupied the main towns and drove the guerillas into the countryside and the hills. The Germans also took measures to defend the Albanian coast from a possible allied invasion across the Adriatic. These actions were accompanied by a reign of terror in those districts where the guerilla forces had been active. This was followed by a policy of studied moderation designed to ensure some sort of popular acceptance of the nazi occupation. Hermann Neubacher, Hitler's special roving envoy in the Balkans, was sent to Tirana in September to put the German scheme into action. An Austrian by birth, he did his best to persuade Albanian politicians that nazi policy was a natural sequel of the friendly policy which the Habsburg empire had pursued towards their country during the first world war. A group of politicians who had opposed Italian rule accepted Neubacher's offer to set up a new government under nazi protection. A national assembly was hurriedly convened in October. This brought to an end the country's union with the crown of Italy, abolished all fascist legislation passed since April 1939, and declared Albania's neutrality. A regency council of four members was also installed in Tirana. This was headed by Mehdi Frasheri, a former prime minister and one of the country's most respected politicians. But having come on the scene at a time when Albania was in a state of utmost chaos, Frasheri and his team faced problems which proved insurmountable.

After the downfall of the Italian fascist régime, the Albanian guerilla forces went on the offensive. In the north, the royalist units of Abas Kupi and other nationalist groups occupied several towns and scored other quick successes. In the south, communist gains were even more spectacular. Not only did the partisans manage to consolidate their hold on large areas of southern Albania but they also occupied the towns of Korçë, Gjirokastër and Elbasan. The activities of nationalist forces of *Balli Kombëtar* were mainly confined to the countryside around the southern port of Vlorë. However, many of these guerilla successes were wiped out a few weeks later when the Germans marched in. Amidst this turmoil, the Italian occupation forces went out of action. Some of their units placed themselves under the German command; others disintegrated. The communist partisans had a useful windfall when several hundred Italian soldiers decided to join them, together with a large amount of arms and military equipment.

In the absence of an allied landing from Italy, the British officers then in Albania tried to cope with the chaotic state of affairs as best they could. Their instructions were to forge some kind of unity between the various guerilla organizations, thus enabling them to concentrate on fighting the Germans. But the British military mission was under a serious handicap. Neither Britain nor the United States had worked out any clear policy on the future of Albania. Although king Zog spent the war years in London, he was unable to form a government in exile like other European leaders had done. Albania's and its king's misfortune was that the Italian invasion took place more than a year before fascist Italy entered the war. The recognition of Mussolini's acquisition in the Balkans by the western powers thus became part of their general policy of appeasement. Their subsequent statements on the country's post-war independence appeared too vague and unreassuring to many Albanians in 1943–44. Moreover, many non-communists thought that the simple British exhortation of killing as many Germans as possible, and damning the consequences, failed to take into account the immediate political dangers facing the country. One of these was the apparent determination of the communists to establish, with Yugoslav help, their own dictatorship after the Germans had left. Another was the spectre of partition between Greece and Yugoslavia that haunted the minds of many people.

But while the nationalists felt friendless and despondent about the future, the communist partisans were in a more hopeful frame of mind. They were better organized than most other resistance groups; they were confident that they could fight against the Germans as well as deal with their political opponents at home. This self-confidence was greatly enhanced by the knowledge that they enjoyed the powerful backing of Yugoslavia and the Soviet Union. Thus secure in the belief that their movement was the wave of the future, the communists decided to liquidate their main political opponents, the nationalist guerillas of *Balli Kombëtar*. This marked the beginning of a civil war which was largely fought in southern Albania and lasted about a year. It was accompanied by hideous massacres and atrocities (particularly on the part of the communists who were in a stronger position to inflict them) all too reminiscent of some of the fierce encounters with the Turks in the nineteenth century.

The *Balli Kombëtar* soon found itself in dire trouble. Lacking the single-mindedness, the aggressiveness and the draconian discipline of the communist partisans, its military structure began to disintegrate and the discipline of its units to break down. Under the pressure of hostilities, some of these units went over to the Germans, thus enabling the communists to lump the *Balli Kombëtar* leaders together with the members of the government in Tirana as outright collaborators and traitors.

The outbreak of civil war immediately raised the question of allied military aid to the resistance movement. This aid was normally given on the principle that the receiving guerilla organization should use the arms for fighting the Italians or the Germans. But in the conditions prevailing in Albania in 1943–44 the task of deciding who was and who was not fighting the enemy at any given moment would probably have defeated Solomon himself. As the efforts of the British liaison officers to mediate between rival groups came to nothing, and as the energies of the nationalists were gradually absorbed by the civil war itself, the policy of allied military assistance tended to favour the communist partisans rather than the *Balli Kombëtar* or the royalist guerillas. Like their counterparts in Yugoslavia, the Albanian communists knew that they had to fight on two fronts—against the Germans and against their domestic political opponents—if they were to achieve the twin objectives of national liberation and social revolution. Like the Yugoslav partisans, they were also in a strong enough position to carry on the struggle on both fronts. As a result, the communists got the larger share of the allied military supplies; more limited quantities went to *Balli Kombëtar* and to the royalists in the north, who were not yet embroiled in the civil war.

Certain important developments elsewhere also helped the partisan cause in the Balkans. The question of Yugoslavia was discussed by Churchill, Roosevelt and Stalin at their meeting in Teheran in November 1943. Shortly afterwards Britain decided to stop giving military aid to Mihailović's *Chetniks* and switched its full support to Tito's partisan movement instead. This followed the despatch of a British military mission, headed by Brigadier Fitzroy MacLean, to Tito's headquarters in September. The new policy was based on a purely military calculation: the Yugoslav partisans were thought to be in a better shape as well as more willing than Mihailović's forces to tackle the Germans. This shift in British policy in Yugoslavia also proved a source of encouragement for the Albanian communist partisans who were in the midst of a civil war. Yugoslav representatives in Albania not only kept them informed about allied policy but also advised them on how best to cope with a military and political situation which was not dissimilar to the one obtaining in Yugoslavia.

Following the Yugoslav pattern, the Albanian communist partisans held a congress at the southern town of Permet in May 1944. It set up two important bodies: an anti-fascist council of national liberation which was to serve as a parliament, and an executive committee, or provisional government. Enver Hoxha was elected chairman of the latter as well as commander of the national liberation army. The congress also voted against the return of king Zog and against the formation of any government, either in the country itself or abroad, without consulting the people first. In addition, the meeting at Permet reaffirmed the policy of pursuing a relentless armed struggle against collaborators, the *Balli Kombëtar*, the royalist guerillas and the northern clan chieftains. By this time the situation in the northern areas had become very confused, though the convulsions of the civil war had not yet reached them. The most important force there was the royalist guerilla movement of Abas Kupi. After a period of co-operation with the communist partisans, he broke with them in November 1943 and set up a political organization of his own which advocated the restoration of king Zog. Two British liaison officers—Colonel Neil MacLean and Major Julian Amery—had laboured for months to persuade Abas Kupi and other northern leaders to take up arms against the Germans. But their efforts achieved limited results. Most of the clan leaders were by then too bemused by the highly fluid and complex situation or too concerned with their own precarious position and safety to do much about fighting the Germans. Only Abas Kupi, the ablest

old-fashioned guerilla leader of them all, showed any real inclina-
tion to do so. But even he was discouraged by the turn of events.
The British had given him no indication as to what Zog's position would be after the war. And the communist partisans, who
had provoked a civil war in southern Albania, had made plain
their intention of destroying all their political opponents before
the war was over. Given these daunting facts, how could he
(Abas Kupi argued) devote his undivided attention to military
operations against the Germans?

Having defeated the *Balli Kombëtar* forces in the south by
mid-summer 1944, the communist partisans began planning to
extend their operations to northern Albania. This drive was given
a fresh impetus by two new factors : the fear that British officers
were organizing the northern groups for the purpose of preventing the communist party from gaining absolute power; the
gratification caused by the arrival of the first Soviet military
mission in Albania in August 1944. Some members of the British
mission were soon involved in a bout of frantic activity to prevent
open war between the northern guerillas and the victorious
partisan forces marching from the south. They tried to arrange a
truce between nationalists and communists, but the latter refused
to agree to it. General Wilson, the supreme allied commander
in the Mediterranean, then intervened with a personal message
to Enver Hoxha asking him to prevent the partisan forces from
attacking the royalist units in the north. Unless this was done,
allied military supplies to the partisans would be suspended, as
these were intended to be used against the Germans, not for
fighting a civil war. In his reply, the Albanian communist leader
maintained that there was no civil war of any kind in Albania,
and that his forces were merely engaged in hunting down
Germans and their collaborators. (The non-existence of civil war
was later to become a permanent feature of the Albanian official
record of the events of 1943–44.) But despite General Wilson's
warning (or perhaps because of it), the communist forces continued their offensive against the northern nationalists as well as
against the retreating German armies. Fortified by their numerical
superiority and by the ample armaments provided by the allied
command in Italy, the partisans were able to dispose of their
political rivals in a matter of weeks. In October they took certain
measures to reinforce their political control. At a meeting of the
anti-fascist council of national liberation held in Berat it was

decided to set up a provisional government under Enver Hoxha. The meeting confirmed the powers of the national liberation councils which had already been set up to act as local government bodies. A solemn declaration was also issued guaranteeing full civil and human rights to all citizens.

Underlying all this feverish political and military activity was a desperate sense of urgency prompted by the fear that the western allies might land troops in Albania. Although the communists realized that they could not obtain absolute power without allied military aid, the physical presence of British troops in the country was the last thing they wanted. Their suspicions were increased by two developments. In September the allied headquarters in Italy had asked permission to land a small force at the southern Albanian port of Sarandë. The request was refused on the grounds that no such help was required. But far more worrying from the communist point of view was the landing of British troops in Greece in October. This was followed by the return to Athens of the Greek government in exile. After recognizing that Greece came within the British sphere of influence, Stalin had asked the ELAS communist forces there not to seize power but to co-operate with the government in Athens. Although at first they agreed to this, the Greek communists were shortly to provoke a civil war, in which they were defeated. Would there be a British intervention in Albania as well? The Albanian communists could not be sure; the uncertainty made them more and more jittery and aggressive.

After a battle lasting several days in which the allied air force played an important part, the partisan armies occupied Tirana, where the provisional government was installed on 28 November. Shortly after, the new authorities rounded up and executed several hundred people from various parts of the country who had sought shelter in the capital during the fighting. When the last of the German armies had withdrawn from Albania, the partisan forces crossed into Yugoslavia where, for about 3 months, they took part in joint operations with Tito's forces in Kosovo, Macedonia, Montenegro and elsewhere.

The communist partisan forces were in control of most of Albania by the end of 1944. Their success would have been impossible without western arms and military equipment. Although, in theory, these were supposed to be solely employed to put as many Germans out of action as possible, in actual practice the partisans used allied arms to kill and maim a larger number of their fellow countrymen than they did Germans. The allied command proved incapable of getting the communists to fulfil their part of the bargain during the civil war. However, the roots of this impotence were political rather than military. In the final and critical phase of the war, the western powers still had no policy to speak of in regard to Albania, beyond asking its people to cause the nazis the greatest possible harm. When Winston Churchill went to Moscow in October 1944 to discuss with Stalin the sharing of political influence after the war, they informally agreed, in terms of percentages, that Romania would come within the Soviet sphere, Greece within that of Britain, whilst influence in Hungary and Yugoslavia would be shared equally between the western powers and Russia. Albania had no place in this grim political arithmetic. And neither did its future come up for discussion at the Yalta meeting between Roosevelt, Churchill and Stalin in February 1945. In other words, the country was nobody's particular baby when the future of Europe was discussed in 1944–45.

But perhaps Albania's political future was really settled when Britain chose to give its full backing to Tito's partisan movement after the Teheran conference in November 1943. It was inevitable that Tito's communist allies in Albania should also become beneficiaries of this choice. The roots of British policy towards Yugoslavia were revealed in a conversation that Churchill had, shortly afterwards, with Brigadier Fitzroy MacLean, head of the British military mission to Tito's headquarters. When MacLean expressed his fears that the Yugoslav partisans would set up a communist régime at the end of hostilities, the prime minister enquired whether he intended to make Yugoslavia his home after the war. On being assured by MacLean that he had no such plans, Churchill said: "Neither do I. And, that being so, the less you and I worry about the form of government they set up, the better. That is for them to decide. What interests us is, which of them is doing the most harm to the Germans?"[1] The British prime minister's glacial verdict determined the future of all those Yugoslavs and Albanians who neither belonged to the communist movement nor wished to do so.

There are no reliable figures of the losses sustained by Albania during the second world war. According to the United Nations

[1] F. MacLean, Eastern Approaches, Cape, London, 1956, pp. 322–3.

Relief and Rehabilitation Administration (UNRRA), 30,000 people were killed; 200 villages destroyed; 18,000 houses burnt down, and about 100,000 people left homeless. Albanian official figures are somewhat higher, and include the complete or partial destruction of most of the country's bridges, roads, mines and factories, as well as the loss of about one-third of its livestock. The Albanian official estimate of Italian and German casualties is about 70,000.

Chapter 5

COMMUNISTS IN POWER

W HEN ENVER HOXHA'S provisional government moved
to Tirana at the end of November 1944, it did so in a state of
elation engendered by the knowledge that the communist partisan
forces had freed the country from foreign rule largely by their
own efforts. The new régime proceeded to carry out its programme of political and social revolution buoyed by the same
sense of elation and self-confidence. Its first measures were
designed to assert its authority over the police, the courts and
other departments of state; to gain full control of the economy;
to destroy the power of political opponents, and eliminate every
vestige of western influence in Albania. The speed and ruthless-
ness with which some of these measures were put into effect were
partly due to the exhilaration of success, but also partly to a
sense of growing insecurity. As relations between the communists
and western powers were severely strained during the civil war,
the régime feared that Britain and the United States would do
their utmost to prevent it from securing full control.

Special tribunals were quickly set up for dealing with "war
criminals". This ambiguous term, which presumed guilt before
any judicial process had taken place, was initially applied to those
suspected of having collaborated with the enemy. However,
before long those who were thought to be actively opposed to the
régime or in any way unsympathetic to it had the label "war
criminals" or "enemies of the people" pinned on them. A special
people's court was set up in Tirana in January 1945 for trying
"major war criminals". Presided over by the minister of the
interior, Koçi Xoxe, the most powerful communist leader after
Hoxha himself, the court conducted a series of show trials which
went on for many months, involving several hundred former
politicians and civil servants as well as ordinary people either unwilling to submit to communist rule or generally averse to its
methods. Neither the president of the people's court nor any of

the judges sitting with him had had any legal training or experience. During the trials, spectators were encouraged to take an active part in the proceedings by expressing their views on the degree of guilt of the defendants and on the type of punishment considered appropriate in each case. Such participation was designed to impart a popular revolutionary flavour to the show trials. Under these conditions, needless to say, the very notion that justice would be fairly or scrupulously administered was a delusion. A large number of defendants were summarily sentenced to death or to long terms of imprisonment. In some cases their families, particularly those of the landed gentry and the clan chieftains, were sent to special labour camps for indefinite periods on the grounds of being potential opponents of the régime or merely undesirable social elements. These early show trials had another wider purpose: to cow the rest of the population into quick submission. The property of those members of *Balli Kombëtar* and of the royalist movement who had gone into exile was confiscated by government decree. A so-called profits' tax was also introduced which led to the confiscation of the property of many well-to-do people. Those unable to pay because the amount demanded by the government was higher than their total assets were also sent to labour camps.

Agrarian reform is another problem that was tackled at this early stage. This had been under constant discussion during Zog's rule but little or nothing had been done about it. Promised changes in land tenure remained a distant mirage in the eyes of the country's landless peasants. To win their political support, the new régime issued a decree in August 1945 expropriating, without compensation, land belonging to individuals with other sources of income. Landowners whose livelihood depended on farming and who cultivated their estates with modern machinery were allowed to retain about 100 acres. Religious bodies were limited to some 50 acres. All forests and pasture lands were nationalized. The expropriated agricultural land was redistributed among 70,000 landless or poor families, each getting twelve acres. As a result of these changes, the régime had destroyed within a year of its coming to power the class of landowners (*beys*) which had had a considerable influence on Albania's economic and political affairs since the days of the Ottoman empire.

The Albanian provisional government was first recognized by

Yugoslavia in April 1945; in November recognition was granted by the Soviet Union, Britain and the United States. But the last two countries, which had maintained special missions in Albania for some months past, made full diplomatic recognition dependent on three conditions being fulfilled : the holding of free elections leading to the formation of a truly representative government; the enjoyment of freedom of speech and of assembly by non-fascist groups and individuals; an unfettered press and provision for foreign correspondents to work in the country.

Albania's first general election under communist rule was held on 2 December 1945. A decree of the provisional government laid down that only the official candidates of the Democratic Front, a body dominated by the communist party, would be allowed to present themselves for election. Apart from a few communist sympathizers, the eighty-two parliamentary candidates on the official list were all party members. The fact that no other political groups or individuals were permitted to compete in the election campaign ran counter to the declaration the communist party had issued at Berat one year earlier promising free elections and several other civil and human rights. The violation of this undertaking was to cause a serious rift between Albania and the western powers, as we shall see later. Facing no opposition of any kind, the official candidates carried the day with a majority of nearly 90 per cent. The new national assembly met in January 1946, when it abolished the monarchy and proclaimed Albania a people's republic. It also approved a new constitution along Soviet lines.

As the régime hastened to consolidate its position at home, its relations with Yugoslavia entered a highly disturbed period. The immediate source of friction was Kosovo. When at the end of 1944 the Germans withdrew from northern Albania and Kosovo, the latter was taken over by the Yugoslav partisans. These went immediately into action against many Albanian inhabitants of the province on the grounds that they had collaborated with the enemy during the years when Kosovo was part of Albania. Official accounts of the operations spoke of meting out punishment to fascists and collaborators, whereas what in fact happened was a repetition of the hideous pre-war massacres and countermassacres between Serbs and Albanians. Albanian communist partisans operating in Kosovo side by side with Tito's forces witnessed some of these massacres, and were badly shaken by what they saw. But what was really shaken to its foundations during those months of savagery and violence was the simple belief that by working closely together Yugoslav and Albanian communists would find a Marxist solution to the problem of the Albanian minority in Yugoslavia, thereby ending once and for all the ancient feud between Serbs and Albanians. However, when the test came, the irreducible facts of nationalism proved far stronger than any Marxist theory interpreted by Balkan communists.

The province of Kosovo was formally restored to Yugoslavia early in 1945. Its restoration became a foregone conclusion after Tito forced the Albanian communist leaders in 1943 to give up their plan for applying the principle of self-determination to the province after the war. The Albanian communists' belief in the validity of this principle stemmed from a resolution passed by the fourth congress of the Yugoslav communist party held at Dresden in 1928, which laid down that Kosovo should eventually return to Albania. This was endorsed in 1940 at a party conference in Zagreb. But some time between 1940 and 1943 this policy of dealing with a difficult minority problem was reversed, probably because Tito, a Croat, discovered that only by retaining Kosovo within Yugoslavia's borders could he hope to win over the Serbs to the communist cause. Tito and his associates, however, were not content with this drastic shift in their earlier policy: they would be far more ambitious and unite all the inhabitants of Kosovo and of Albania itself into a single national community within the new Yugoslav federation. The Yugoslav communist leaders may have believed that such a radical solution would somehow make the Albanian question disappear altogether from the Balkan political scene; what it in fact did was to place a vicious explosive charge under the relations between the Yugoslav and Albanian communist parties.

Signs of trouble between the two parties first appeared at the meeting of the central committee of the Albanian communist party in November 1944, just before the liberation of the capital. A Yugoslav representative, Velimir Stojnić, who took part in the deliberations, put forward a plan for uniting Yugoslavia and Albania into one state. The proposal, which provoked a heated debate, seems to have been supported by Koçi Xoxe, one of the party secretaries, and a few others. Albanian official sources have subsequently hinted that an attempt was made at the meeting to remove Enver Hoxha from the party leadership for being an obstacle to the Yugoslav plan. Although he retained his position, the plan itself was not rejected but stayed on the agenda, acting as a dangerous political fuse. Within a short time it caused a split within the ranks of the Albanian party between moderates and militants. The former opposed union with Yugoslavia and favoured an independent foreign policy based on friendly relations with both east and west. In domestic affairs, the moderates advocated a policy of national reconciliation as well as the postponement of radical socialist measures until agriculture and industry had made some progress within the framework of a market economy. The militants, on the other hand, pressed not only that the two countries should unite without delay but that Albanian external and domestic policies should be a carbon copy of the Yugoslav pattern in both fields. Although the pro-Yugoslav faction led by Xoxe may have been in a minority, it nevertheless won the day, thanks to the powerful backing of the Yugoslavs, overcoming all opposition from other leaders, including Hoxha.

Tension between the two groups grew steadily. At the end of 1945 Hoxha himself publicly criticized the moderates, singling out Sejfulla Maleshova, who had spent several years in Moscow before the war, as one of their leaders. A minor poet himself and the official in charge of cultural affairs, Maleshova supported a fairly liberal policy in literature and the arts, one which did not involve a complete break with national traditions. By the beginning of the following year, the deep rift in the party ranks was out into the open. Maleshova was expelled from the politburo and from the central committee of the communist party. At the same time, the leadership laid down a number of rigid guidelines for future action. In foreign affairs, Albania would create close ties with the Soviet Union and its allies. At home, measures would be intensified to bring various industrial concerns under state control; further radical reforms in agriculture would also be introduced. As these measures were being implemented, Xoxe made use of his wide powers as minister of the interior and party secretary to prepare the ground for full integration with Yugoslavia by getting political leaders and officials to endorse this policy either through persuasion or outright intimidation.

A major step towards full integration was taken when Enver Hoxha, in his capacity as communist leader, prime minister and minister of foreign affairs, signed a treaty of friendship, co-operation and mutual aid with Yugoslavia during a visit to Belgrade in July 1946. The treaty envisaged the co-ordination of the economic plans of the two countries; the standardization of their monetary systems; the creation of a customs union and the unification of prices. A large number of Yugoslav experts and advisers were sent to Albania charged with the task of carrying out these decisions. They were given key positions in most government departments and the armed forces. Joint stock companies were set up for the purpose of exploiting and developing the country's oil and mineral resources. The formation of these companies, through which Yugoslavia obtained complete control of the Albanian economy, was resented by many Albanians just as much as the Yugoslavs resented the imposition of similar agencies on their country by the Soviet Union at about the same time. So in less than 2 years after its liberation, Albania found itself a vassal state perched on the brink of a very slippery slope which would lead to final absorption by its bigger neighbour.

At the same time, Albania's relations with the western powers were deteriorating fast. One of the causes of this deterioration was the communist régime's refusal to allow free elections in December 1945. The political groups, such as the monarchists and the social democrats, which were prepared to take part in the election campaign with their own candidates, were branded as foreign agents and were not allowed to do so. Attempts by other non-communist groups and individuals to take advantage of the communist party's earlier promise about free elections and freedom of expression were likewise thwarted. British and United States missions in Albania complained to the government in Tirana that this repressive policy contravened not only its own commitments but also the Yalta declaration of 1945 on liberated Europe which stated that representative governments based on the will of the people should be set up after the war. In the eyes of the Albanian leaders, these complaints were merely fresh evidence that the western powers wanted to prevent the communist party from reaping the fruits of its military victory. The antagonism that arose between the partisans and the western allies during the civil war of 1943–44 now became far more bitter. In their general feeling of insecurity and apprehension, the communists were more than ever inclined to put the blame on the western powers for all their domestic difficulties. In some parts of northern Albania, for instance, the régime met with a

good deal of opposition from people unwilling to submit to local
communist rule coupled with foreign domination. A number of
genuine small uprisings occurred in these areas during 1945–46
for which the western powers were held responsible.

Another source of tension was the communist fear that the
British army would intervene in Albania just as it had done in
Greece at the end of 1944. Linked with this were certain fairly
widespread suspicions that Britain and the United States supported the Greek government's claim to a large part of southern
Albania. Playing on these suspicions, the régime did its best to
persuade Albanians that the country's survival within its current
frontiers was wholly dependent on its own survival. A number of
developments tended to strengthen this claim as well as widen
the gap between the régime and the west. In July 1946, the
United States senate passed a resolution (the so-called Pepper
resolution) in favour of ceding northern Epirus (southern
Albania) to Greece. Although it was only an expression of opinion
which did not commit the American administration in any way,
the resolution nevertheless had an unsettling effect on Albania
and was promptly exploited by the communist régime for the
purpose of fomenting more hostility towards the western countries.
Under pressure from Greece, its territorial claim on Albania was
raised, albeit somewhat half-heartedly, at the Paris meeting of
the allied foreign ministers between August and September of
the same year. Perhaps sensing the harm that a discussion of the
matter might cause, James Byrnes, the American secretary of
state, managed to get the issue removed from the agenda. Enver
Hoxha, who represented his country at the meeting, put the
Albanian case when he said : "I solemnly declare that neither the
Paris conference nor the conference of the Big Four nor any
other gathering can review the frontiers of my country which has
no foreign territory of any kind under its jurisdiction". Even
though no decision on the frontier question was taken in Paris,
the mere fact that it was broached at all provided the communist
régime with more fuel for its domestic campaign against the
west. However, its claim to be a staunch defender of national
independence was somewhat blighted, in the eyes of the people,
by its gradual submission to direct Yugoslav rule.

The behaviour of the Albanian communists in the immediate
post-war years could be explained simply in terms of their determination to set up a government which tolerated no political or

ideological persuasion other than their own and brooked no western influence of any kind. But their aggressive attitude towards Britain and the United States had another powerful motive behind it. This was the Yugoslavs' reluctance to have western observers witness the political legerdemain they were then performing at the expense of Albania's independence. Moreover, the Yugoslavs were themselves at loggerheads with the western powers over the question of Trieste. The result was that the British and American missions in Tirana found it increasingly difficult to carry out their functions. Severe restrictions were imposed on the movements of their officials, who were accused of aiding and abetting active opponents of the régime. In April 1946 Britain withdrew its mission from Albania on the grounds that diplomatic relations between the two countries had become impossible under prevailing conditions. Some 7 months later the United States government took the same step.

Relations between Britain and Albania were further exacerbated by an incident that took place shortly after the British mission had left Tirana. In May, two British warships sailed through the Corfu channel, the narrow stretch of water between Greece and Albania. They were immediately fired upon by Albanian coastal batteries which, fortunately, failed to hit their targets. The British government sent a note of protest to Albania; the latter apologized for the incident, claiming it had been due to an unfortunate error. However, shortly afterwards the Albanian government issued an official statement which said that in future no foreign warships or merchant vessels would be allowed to navigate within three miles of Albania's coastline without its permission. As the Corfu channel is in some parts considerably less than 3 miles wide, this meant the Albanian government would, in effect, deny the ships of other countries passage through an international waterway. The British navy considered this ruling unacceptable and decided to test Albanian obduracy by means of an exercise in old-fashioned gunboat diplomacy. On 22 October four destroyers sailed south from the port of Corfu on the way to one of the Greek islands. During their passage through the straits two of the ships struck mines. One of them was wrecked, the other badly damaged. There were also heavy casualties: 44 officers and men killed and several others injured. Britain accused Albania of mining the channel or permitting it to be mined after the German mines had been cleared at the end of the war. As the Albanian government refused to accept responsibility for the disaster, Britain lodged a complaint with the Security Council of the United Nations. The Corfu channel case involved Britain and the Soviet Union during the early part of 1947 in one of the first major encounters of the cold war at the United Nations. Although the Security Council found Albania guilty by seven votes to two, its ruling was nullified when the Soviet Union, as a permanent member of the Council, decided to apply the veto. The case was then referred to the International Court of Justice at the Hague. After a series of long hearings and intricate legal and procedural wrangles, in April 1949 the Court found Albania guilty of causing the disaster and ruled that its government should pay Britain £844,000 compensation. At the same time Britain was held responsible for having infringed Albania's sovereignty when its warships carried out, shortly after the incident, a mine-sweeping operation in Albanian coastal waters without permission. It was during this exercise that the British navy recovered twenty-two freshly painted German mines from the Corfu channel.

Yet despite the verdict of the International Court, the question as to who actually laid the mines, which caused such heavy losses in human lives so soon after the second world war, has remained unresolved. Albania has never accepted responsibility for the tragedy and hence has refused to pay any compensation to Britain. The country certainly did not possess the technical resources needed for mine-laying operations. In its Olympian legal deliberations the Hague Court did not, or perhaps could not, take into account the harsh political reality that by 1946 Albania was not, strictly speaking, a sovereign state but a vassal of Yugoslavia. This being the case, whoever may have laid the fresh mines in the channel, the decision to do so could not have been taken without the authority or the knowledge of the Yugoslav government. At that time both Yugoslav and Albanian communists were equally apprehensive about British intentions regarding Albania in view of Britain's strong reluctance to countenance communist rule in neighbouring Greece. In the end, the Corfu channel tragedy became a political landmark in the Albanian régime's general drift towards greater isolation from Britain and other western countries.

In home affairs, the régime proceeded to tighten its grip on the economy. By the middle of 1946 all private industrial concerns as well as most of the country's domestic wholesale and retail trade had been brought under government control. Pressure on the peasants was also intensified : apart from being prohibited to engage in the sale or the transfer of land, they were urged to form agricultural co-operatives. Yet neither these nor any of the earlier measures made any real impact on the country's grave economic situation. In fact, its sheer survival in the early post-war years would hardly have been possible without the aid of $26,260,000 provided by the United Nations Relief and Rehabilitation Administration (UNRRA), the greater part of which came from the United States. With regard to forward economic planning, the régime was increasingly obliged to take into account the policies laid down by the government in Belgrade. And it is in this sphere that new sources of disagreement and recrimination between the two countries began to emerge. When it came to implementing the far-reaching economic and financial agreements concluded in July 1946, Yugoslavia and Albania held widely different views about their ultimate objective. The Albanian communists hoped that the financial and other aid which their allies were able to provide them with would make it possible for their country to become more or less economically independent before long. The Yugoslavs, on the other hand, thought the very scarce resources they could place at Albania's disposal, while helping to further its economic progress, should serve a far more important purpose : to achieve political union between the two countries. Economic and financial aid, in other words, was to be the handmaid of a policy of political domination. The Albanians resented this and began expressing their resentment in terms of economic grievances. They complained, among other things, that Yugoslavia paid very low prices for the raw materials it imported from its ally; that it had failed to contribute its full share of capital to the joint companies set up in Albania; that Yugoslav advisers working in government departments in Tirana were inclined to exceed their purely advisory powers and functions. By the beginning of 1947 relations between the two communist régimes had become so bad that the Albanians sent an economic delegation, headed by Nako Spiru, a member of the central committee, to Belgrade in April for the purpose of sorting out some of the difficulties that had arisen between them. Far from improving relations, the talks merely revealed the wide gap existing between the views of the two countries. The Yugoslav government refused to consider an Albanian request for aid to build an oil refinery and a number of consumer industries before the Albanian régime had taken steps to co-ordinate its economic planning with Belgrade. As a special concession, the Yugoslavs were willing to help Albania develop its mineral resources and its agriculture, but the Albanian leaders were not prepared to accept the offer because they thought it would do nothing to reduce the country's backwardness or foster its economic independence. The April talks in Belgrade, however, did perform one useful function. Like Molière's M. Jourdain, who found he had been speaking prose all his life after harbouring the illusion of having babbled in poetry, both Yugoslavs and Albanians discovered that their bitter economic squabbles were only a mask concealing sharply divergent political attitudes and ambitions. The Yugoslav leaders, for their part, were in a great hurry to foreclose their annexation of Albania before Russia or the western powers stepped in to prevent the plan for changing the political map of the Balkans from being put into force. Some of their Albanian counterparts, on the other hand, felt their nationalist feelings deeply affronted by such a plan. They knew, moreover, that if they meekly submitted to direct control from Belgrade not only would there be a great revival among their people of the old animosity towards Yugoslavia but the popularity of the communist régime itself would slump to zero.

Matters came to a head shortly afterwards when the leader of the pro-Yugoslav group, Xoxe, went into action. In his capacity as minister of the interior and police chief, he ordered the arrest of nine members of parliament suspected to be opponents of union with Yugoslavia. Among them was Sejfulla Maleshova, one of the leading moderates in the communist party. The arrests were a clear indication that Belgrade meant business; perhaps they were also a warning to other party members who might have cherished hopes of full independence. The man whom the Yugoslavs suspected of belonging to this group was Enver Hoxha, the party leader. He gave the first outward sign as to where he stood in the dispute with Belgrade when he suddenly paid a visit to Moscow in July 1947, ostensibly for the purpose of seeking Soviet economic aid. Hoxha's visit proved successful as the Soviet government undertook to set up several factories in Albania as well as to provide it with agricultural and industrial equipment. But his trip to Russia had a deeper political significance : it was Stalin's indirect admonition to Tito that he was far from pleased with the way the Yugoslav leaders were behaving towards their Albanian comrades. The Yugoslavs took the hint and held Nako Spiru responsible for the serious turn in the relations between Belgrade and Tirana. Xoxe subjected Spiru to a campaign of pressure and intimidation which led to his suicide in November 1947. From then onwards, the Yugoslav-Albanian dispute played a fairly important part in the far more serious quarrel that was developing between Stalin and Tito.

Although the Soviet Union had recognized Yugoslavia's special position in Albania in the early post-war years, Stalin had nonetheless continued to take an interest in Albanian developments and had kept a wary eye on Tito's part in these developments. When Tito visited Moscow at the beginning of 1946, the Soviet leader raised the Albanian question with him. He said there was some trouble in Albania's communist hierarchy between Hoxha and Xoxe, a thing that puzzled him. One of the Yugoslavs accompanying Tito told Stalin that several Albanian politburo members thought Hoxha was not a strong enough personality, so they had asked Xoxe to keep an eye on him. Stalin did not pursue the matter any further, but managed to convey to Tito that he was fairly well-informed about Albania's affairs and by no means uninterested in what was happening there.

The issue cropped up again when the Yugoslav deputy prime minister, Edvard Kardelj, saw Stalin in Moscow about a year later. Stalin told him on that occasion that Hoxha had been complaining about the behaviour of Yugoslav advisers working in Albania. Kardelj replied that he knew nothing about the matter; but pressed by the Soviet leader, he went on to explain Yugoslavia's views on the Albanian leadership. Although Hoxha had had a good war record, Kardelj said, he was in some ways a bourgeois intellectual lacking in proper Marxist-Leninist training. The Yugoslavs, for their part, had a higher opinion of Xoxe, a far better and more consistent political leader than Hoxha.

Shortly after Nako Spiru's suicide, Stalin asked the Yugoslav government to send a delegation headed by Milovan Djilas to Moscow to discuss Albanian developments. By that time, the Yugoslavs had taken note of two things : one was that Hoxha and other Albanian communists had been in close touch with

Moscow for some time past and had kept it informed about Yugoslav policies in Albania; the other was that Stalin intended to make Yugoslav designs on that country part of the political armoury by means of which he hoped to bring Tito to heel. During his first meeting with Djilas in January 1948, Stalin brought up Spiru's death by saying that relations between Yugoslavia and Albania had come to a pretty pass when a member of the Albanian central committee was driven to take his own life. Djilas tried to explain the circumstances that had led to Spiru's suicide, but Stalin dismissed the matter by saying that he had no objection to Yugoslavia "swallowing" Albania as the Soviet Union had no special interest in the country. Djilas objected to the term "swallowing" and maintained that the purpose of Yugoslav policy was to bring about unification between the two countries; whereupon the Soviet foreign minister Molotov, who was present, remarked that "swallowing" and "unification" were one and the same thing.

While Djilas and other members of the Yugoslav delegation were still in Moscow, something else occurred that roused Stalin's suspicions concerning the political future of the Balkan peninsula as a whole. During an official visit to Romania, the Bulgarian communist leader Georgi Dimitrov had said that he was in favour of setting up a federation comprising not only all the countries of the Balkans but also Hungary, Czechoslovakia and Poland. A few days later the Soviet newspaper *Pravda* rebuked the Bulgarian leader for making such a statement, which it considered politically irrelevant. Stalin followed up this rebuke with a request that the various federal schemes that were being bandied about should be urgently discussed in Moscow between him and the Bulgarian and Yugoslav leaders. These discussions were held in February 1948, with Stalin, Molotov, Dimitrov, Djilas and Kardelj as the main participants. The Soviet case was bluntly put by Molotov who said that certain serious differences had arisen between Moscow, on the one hand, and Belgrade and Sofia, on the other. He cited two such cases : the signing of a Yugoslav-Bulgarian alliance (November 1947) without consulting the Soviet government; Dimitrov's statement on a possible east European federation. Stalin dismissed the Bulgarian leader's idea as nonsense, and said that while a federation between Bulgaria and Romania was out of the question, one between Bulgaria and Yugoslavia should be set up as soon as possible; this should later incorporate Albania. He then dealt with certain more immediate problems concerning the latter. The Yugoslavs had already sent an air force squadron to Albania and were preparing to move two army divisions there. The official justification for these military measures was that they were meant to counter a possible invasion from Greece. But some Albanian communists suspected that this was only an excuse for tightening Tito's hold on Albania. The Soviet leader clearly thought likewise for he complained bitterly to Djilas and Kardelj that their government was planning to despatch two divisions to Albania, an independent country, without prior consultation with Moscow. When Kardelj said that the move had been agreed with the Albanian government, Stalin retorted that such a move could have serious international repercussions; moreover, he added, the Yugoslavs had made it a practice not to consult him about anything. After their talks with Stalin, the Yugoslav leaders came to the conclusion that he was utterly opposed to their policy of annexing Albania, and that his earlier suggestion that they could absorb the country whenever they wished was merely a device for gaining time and sowing confusion. His whole attitude during the Moscow talks also confirmed their suspicions that Hoxha and some of his associates had been busy undermining Yugoslav plans behind the scenes from the very beginning.

On the wider issue of a Balkan or east European federation, Stalin had made it quite plain that, as far as Soviet post-war policy was concerned, such schemes, which were a legacy of the Comintern, were as dead as the guns used to fight the Napoleonic wars. Yet federal plans and theories still had a good deal of attraction for Comintern old hands like Tito and Dimitrov. These had, after all, been the stock-in-trade of the Bulgarian, Yugoslav and Greek communist parties throughout the '20s and the early '30s. The chief preoccupation of these parties during this period had been with the highly complex problems of nationalism; the linchpin that both united and divided them was Macedonia. Each communist party had to adjust its own particular policy and propaganda to the Comintern's constantly shifting attitude to the current politcal situation in each of the countries concerned. The main objective of the Comintern bureaucracy in Moscow was to do everything within its power to undermine the right-wing governments of the Balkans by directing into revolutionary channels the grievances of the many national groups of the area. The nationalist squabbles between Bulgaria, Yugoslavia and Greece were reflected in the political attitudes of the respective communist leaders residing in Moscow. Some of them, particularly the Yugoslavs, were often rebuked, and occasionally dismissed from office, for advocating policies considered obnoxious by the Comintern at a given moment. These often conflicting policies were finally brought into line in 1935, when the Comintern laid down its general policy of a "united front" between communist and peasant parties in eastern Europe and between communists and social democrats elsewhere in order to meet the challenge of nazi Germany. It was during this period that the seeds of Yugoslavia's post-war federal schemes were sown.

After the war, Tito discovered that a Yugoslav federation, perhaps reinforced by a wider structure that included other Balkan countries, would strengthen his own position thus enabling him to withstand Stalin's policy of domination. By the same token, the Russian leader was determined to prevent the formation of any large political groupings in eastern Europe which might make it difficult for him to exert direct control over every communist régime in the area. At the same time, many Albanian communists who, like the Yugoslavs, had come to power by their own efforts, saw their country's absorption into the Yugoslav federation as part and parcel of the policy of domination pursued by Serbian and Yugoslav governments in the nineteenth century and the early part of the twentieth. Hence, as good nationalists, they would do all they could to oppose it. Like many Albanian nationalist leaders before them, they were prepared to seek help from the devil himself to preserve their country's independence. And the only devil willing to provide them with any support between 1945 and 1948 happened to be Stalin.

By the beginning of 1948 the Yugoslavs knew they had to act swiftly if they were to bring about their Albanian coup before Stalin had had time to block it altogether. One of the problems facing Tito was that the final decision about uniting the two countries had to be taken by the Albanian communists themselves. Like most communists, the Yugoslavs were sticklers for formal constitutional propriety. So they asked their principal ally in Albania, Xoxe, to prepare the ground for the event. He was assisted by Savo Zlatić, a special emissary from Belgrade who was charged with arranging a special meeting of the Albanian central committee. This was convened at the end of February.

It turned out to be the final encounter between the two communist parties, and a triumph, albeit a short-lived one, for Yugoslav policy. After being forced to admit his past errors, Hoxha joined other members of the central committee in blaming the late Nako Spiru for the serious crisis that had developed between Belgrade and Tirana. As a reward for this gesture, he was allowed to retain the party leadership. On the other hand, several of Hoxha's colleagues paid the penalty for opposing the idea that Albania should become part of Yugoslavia. One of these was Spiru's widow, Liri Belishova, who lost her seat in the central committee. So did Mehmet Shehu, the country's most successful and most ruthless wartime partisan leader. He was also dismissed from his post of army chief of staff. However, the most significant act of the meeting was to approve the proposals put forward by Xoxe for merging the economic systems and the armed forces of the two countries as a further step towards political union.

After this crucial meeting, Xoxe, working closely with the Yugoslavs, began implementing its decisions and removing from the party and government bureaucracy many officials who disagreed with them. Hoxha himself, as the main opponent of Yugoslav designs, was in grave danger of being overthrown. The party leader knew perfectly well that when the political merger between the two countries was completed Tito was likely to replace him with Xoxe. In a final spurt of frenzied action, the latter called a meeting of the politburo in April, when he proposed that Albania should submit a formal application to become a member of the Yugoslav federation. But Hoxha, probably armed with the knowledge that a clash on the issue of Albania had taken place between Stalin and the Yugoslav delegation in Moscow, managed to secure a majority against the proposal. A campaign of terror unleashed shortly after to subvert the majority vote in the politburo was of no avail. By that time the conflict between Stalin and Tito was fast moving to its climax. It was Yugoslavia's formal expulsion from the Soviet bloc in June 1948 that finally put an end to its drive to gain complete control over Albania. News of the expulsion was received with great jubilation by Hoxha and some of his colleagues. Immediately afterwards, the Albanian government repudiated all its economic agreements with Yugoslavia on the grounds that they were incompatible with national sovereignty; expelled all Yugoslav specialists and advisers, and set in motion a frantic press and radio propaganda campaign against Tito. A couple of months later an economic agreement was concluded between Moscow and Tirana by which the Soviet government undertook to make good the economic and technical aid Albania had forfeited because of its break with Yugoslavia.

The scene was not set for settling accounts with Xoxe and other pro-Yugoslav elements in the communist party. This was done in three stages. At a central committee meeting held in September, Shehu, Belishova and other anti-Yugoslav leaders were restored to their former positions. Xoxe was relieved of his functions as party secretary and minister of the interior; the latter post was given to Shehu, one of Xoxe's principal victims. Next, the whole policy of the country's involvement with Yugoslavia was reviewed at the first congress of the Albanian communist party held in November. All mistakes committed between 1944 and 1948 were attributed to the Yugoslavs acting through their agents, Xoxe and Pandi Kristo, who were expelled from the party. The congress re-elected Hoxha as secretary-general, a clear sign of Stalin's full confidence in him. It was also decided to change the name of the party to the workers' party of Albania, on the grounds that the old designation did not adequately reflect the fact that the great majority of the population and of party members were peasants. The final act of the Albanian-Yugoslav drama was played in May 1949, when Xoxe was convicted of treason at a secret trial held in Tirana and sentenced to death. The way to this dénouement may have been opened by a visit that Hoxha paid to Moscow shortly before. Xoxe's trial and execution marked the beginning of the great wave of political trials and purges that swept eastern Europe in 1949 and the early 1950s, engulfing the Hungarian Laszlo Rajk, the Czech Rudolf Slansky, the Bulgarian Traicho Kostov and many others. But there was one important difference between the case of these communist leaders and that of Xoxe. Whilst the former were convicted as Titoists and nationalists and were posthumously exonerated from these and other charges made against them, there can be little doubt that Xoxe had devoted the whole of his career between 1944 and 1948 to the policy of securing his country's union with Yugoslavia.

Having broken most links with its former ally, Albania now

joined the ranks of the other countries of eastern and central Europe—Bulgaria, Romania, Hungary, Czechoslovakia, East Germany—which were under Moscow's direct political and ideological control. During the early part of 1949 it concluded trade agreements with most of these countries and became a member of the Council for Mutual Economic Assistance (Comecon). Why was this sudden transition from Tito to Stalin welcomed with such apparent unseemly enthusiasm by many Albanians? The main reason, as was noted earlier, was that communists and non-communists alike thought that while federation might be the right solution to Yugoslavia's internal problems, its extension to Albania was a device for satisfying old imperialistic aspirations. The country's only way of avoiding this snare was to seek aid from a powerful ally. But the Albanian régime could not hope for this to come from its immediate neighbours, Greece and Italy, or from Britain or any other western country. So the initial impulse that drove the Albanian leaders into a close alliance with the Soviet Union was neither any special love for Moscow nor even an affinity with Stalin's methods of government, but nationalism pure and simple. In addition to its readiness to come to their rescue at a critical moment, Russia had the great advantage of possessing no common frontier with Albania; this, the Albanians thought, would make it more difficult for Moscow to exert the kind of direct pressure that Belgrade could.

It was Enver Hoxha who got most of the credit, in the eyes of many Albanians, for carrying out this difficult rescue operation. Although the part he had played was subsequently exaggerated by propaganda, it was nonetheless a fairly significant one. Albania was by no means the cause of Stalin's break with Tito. He had several more important grievances against the Yugoslav leader, and would have quarrelled with him regardless of the Albanian question. But if the quarrel had occurred after Albania's union with Yugoslavia had become an accomplished fact, it might have taken a more serious turn, involving the difficult, and perhaps bloody, operation of having to unscramble the union. What Hoxha managed to do was to delay the implementation of the Yugoslav plan by a policy of prevarication, procrastination and dissimulation conducted with a nerve and tactical skill worthy of the teaching of the Florentine old masters of the art of political survival, Niccolò Machiavelli and Francesco Guicciardini.

This is what Guicciardini has to say about his political experience
in the service of two Renaissance popes :

> To be open, truthful and frank is a noble and generous thing,
> although often harmful. On the other hand, dissimulation
> and deception are useful and often indispensable, because of
> the evil nature of men ... I would suggest truthfulness should
> be ordinarily preferred, without abandoning deception alto-
> gether. That is, in the ordinary circumstances of life, use truth-
> fulness in such a way as to gain the reputation of a guileless
> man. In a few important cases use deceit. Deceit is the more
> fruitful and successful the more you enjoy the reputation of
> an honest and truthful man; you are more easily believed.[1]

Hoxha knew by the end of the war that Tito was the most
powerful and the most celebrated communist leader in Europe
after Stalin. This meant that any overt and outright opposition
to him was both unproductive and dangerous. The Albanian
leader had learnt his first lesson in dealing with Tito during the
war when he had to comply with the Yugoslav request that the
future of the province of Kosovo should not be settled by a
plebiscite. So in the early post-war years he resorted to the tactics
of resisting whenever possible Yugoslav wishes and ambitions
behind the scenes, and submitting to pressures when these
threatened to upset the political apple-cart. But however serious
relations between the two countries became, he never risked
criticizing the Yugoslav régime in public. On the contrary, he
often made reassuring and soothing public statements when
differences between him and Tito became particularly acute. For
instance, this is what he had to say at the beginning of 1948,
when Stalin was preparing to stage his showdown with the Yugoslavs : "We are linked by unbreakable fraternity and unity with
the heroic people of Tito's Yugoslavia, a guarantee of the freedom, the independence and the sovereignty of our and all other
democratic peoples in the Balkan peninsula. This fraternity and
unity ensured our country unselfish and fraternal aid during the
war, and now made possible the all-round development of our
new life."

Tito, as we have seen, had never really trusted Hoxha; he

[1] Quoted in L. Barzini, *The Italians*, Hamish Hamilton, London, 1968,
p. 187.

had been aware of his secret intrigues with Stalin to the detriment of Yugoslav interests. Why, then, did he not get rid of the Albanian leader when he was in a position to do so? This was perhaps because at the end of the war Hoxha was, like Tito himself, a national leader who could not be easily replaced by a minor and comparatively unknown figure such as Xoxe, who had espoused the Yugoslav cause from the very beginning. Moreover, Hoxha had come to embody both his party's and his country's aversion to Yugoslav rule. If this rule was to be established without bloodshed or without causing an international hue and cry, Hoxha had to give his public consent to the change. This he refused to do by adopting a policy of evasion and deviousness until it was too late. In the end, by a strange stroke of irony, Tito's appearance on the European scene as the champion of his country's independence against Soviet imperialism coincided with Hoxha's emergence as the champion of Albanian independence against Yugoslav encroachments. Hoxha now assumed the mantle of earlier Albanian politicians, such as Ali Pasha Tepelena, the Bushati pashas and king Zog, who had managed to extricate themselves from similar difficult situations by some of the cunning policies described by Guicciardini and Machiavelli. Stalin's ideological campaign against Tito, in which the latter was accused of every imaginable doctrinal offence under the sun, was heaven-sent to Hoxha for it enabled him to conceal his nationalist motives and thereby claim that his hostility to Yugoslavia had stemmed mainly from doctrinal objections.

Chapter 6

FROM TITO TO STALIN

SHORTLY AFTER ITS break with Yugoslavia, the
Albanian régime was involved in a series of political trials and
purges. Hoxha seemed determined to remove from the communist party and government all groups or individuals who had
shown any sympathy towards Yugoslavia or had supported Koçi
Xoxe. But the dividing line between alleged pro-Yugoslav elements and potential opponents of Hoxha's leadership became
more and more blurred as time went on. The situation was
aggravated by Stalin's paranoid decision to rid eastern Europe of
a large number of communist leaders accused as Titoists, Trotsky-
ists, Zionists and western agents. The east European régimes vied
with one another in ferreting out victims for Stalin's gruesome
sacrificial orgy. The grisly persecution of innocent people became
a demonstration of absolute loyalty to Moscow as well as a way
of assuring the survival of some of the leading persecutors themselves. Hoxha, who was in a very vulnerable position after his
long confrontation with Tito, felt that he too had to prove his
utter loyalty to Stalin by showing that he was no less willing than
his east European comrades to ferret out alleged opponents of
the rigid control Moscow was trying to impose on eastern Europe.
All these forces working together plunged the Albanian leader
into a state of paranoia similar to Stalin's.

A radical purge of the ranks of the communist party was
carried out. Between the end of 1948 and the beginning of 1952
eight per cent of its members, some 4,000 people, were expelled.
The great majority were accused of being "enemies of the
people" or disloyal to the party. Some of them were executed
after secret trials, though their exact number has never been
disclosed. The central committee of the party lost fourteen of
its thirty-one members, and the people's assembly (parliament)
about one-third of its members. The Albanian government headed
by Hoxha was also not immune from this orgy of persecution:

Scanderbeg, a 16th century engraving

Byron in Albanian dress, a painting by Thomas Phillips

F.S.Noli

King Zog

Mao Tse-tung with Beqir Balluku and Hysni Kapo, in Peking, 1967

Enver Hoxha with Yao Wen-yuan, in Tirana, 1974

Hydro-electric scheme at Fierzë, northern Albania

May Day parade of children in Durrës, 1964

University girls parading in militia uniforms

Tirana before World War II

The Palace of Culture and statue of Stalin in modern Tirana

A forced labour camp in the Mati valley between Shkodër and Tirana. This photograph was taken from a moving bus while the communist guard's attention was drawn by other passengers, as there are strict orders against taking photographs

Peasants walking home from a collective farm

the minister of industry (Abedin Shehu) and the deputy minister of communications (Niazi Islami) were sacked.

The rift with Belgrade left the Albanian economy in a very precarious state. There was an acute shortage of food. In the immediate post-war years, the country had relied on Yugoslavia to provide it with grain and other foodstuffs in times of bad harvests. As this source was no longer available, the Soviet Union and its allies set in motion an emergency aid operation designed to prevent Albania from collapsing altogether. Food and other supplies were rushed by air from Hungary and Bulgaria, by Soviet ships through the Dardanelles, or by rail across Austria to Trieste, which was under western control, thence by sea to the Albanian ports. This improvised rescue scheme succeeded in staving off economic disaster and preventing the Albanian leadership from losing its nerve and turning elsewhere for help.

Yet despite the welcome Soviet rescue operation, the régime's sense of isolation was sharper than ever before. Having lost the ambiguous support of Yugoslavia, it was left utterly friendless in the Balkans and with hardly a friend anywhere else. The Albanian leaders had hoped that Russia would conclude a defence treaty with them, particularly after Yugoslavia repudiated its alliance with Albania in November 1949. But Stalin was in no hurry to do so. The country thus had no firm Soviet commitment to come to its defence until the signing of the Warsaw Pact in 1955. Yet the Albanian régime was actively engaged in serving the interests of Russia's foreign policy by its involvement in the Greek civil war during the late 1940s. In May 1947, a special commission of the United Nations had held Albania responsible for aiding the Greek communist guerillas. Some two and a half years later, the commission asked the general assembly to declare the Albanian government responsible for endangering peace in the Balkans and to call on both Albania and Bulgaria to stop helping the Greek guerillas. By that time Tito's régime had been evicted from the Soviet bloc and Yugoslavia had closed its frontiers with Greece. So Albania and Bulgaria were the only two countries left through which Russia could channel military supplies to the communist side during the last stages of the Greek civil war.

When civil strife in Greece came to an end, the Soviet government decided to make the best possible use of Albania in its general European defence strategy. Having lost the use of Yugo-slavia's Adriatic ports, the Russians started building a submarine base on the island of Sazan off the port of Vlorë. After an ex-penditure of several million dollars, the base came into operation some two years later with a fleet of twelve submarines and several auxiliary vessels. In addition, the Russians built a number of air-fields in Albania. A large contingent of Soviet military and naval experts was sent to supervise the construction of these and other defence projects. Apart from the wider strategic considerations, the presence of Russian naval and air power in Albania was meant to reassure Albanians who, possessing only a small ill-equipped army and no navy or air force, were thought to be easy prey to Yugoslav or western designs. However, the develop-ment of nuclear weapons and long-range missiles gradually re-duced the usefulness of the Soviet submarine base in the Vlorë bay. The Russians, nevertheless, retained it until 1960.

In 1948 Hoxha sought Stalin's support for reasons of national and personal survival; he later found Stalinist methods of rule very useful in preventing the communist régime from falling apart as well as in shielding his own position from internal or external perils. A series of dangerous developments soon drove him further along the path of Stalinist extremism. In the sum-mer of 1949 the Albanian press and radio began reporting border clashes and similar other incidents in different parts of the coun-try. Skirmishes were reported to have taken place in August along the Greek-Albanian frontier. At about the same time an Albanian member of parliament was killed by an anti-communist guerilla band operating in northern Albania. Official sources reported that there had also been provocations along the border with Yugoslavia. The Albanian government, clearly worried by these events, sent several notes to the United Nations in which it accused Greece and Yugoslavia of fomenting trouble in the frontier areas. During a tour of the northern provinces, Hoxha complained that the western powers had set up a committee of Albanian exiles whose aim it was to bring about the overthrow of the communist régime. Shortly afterwards, a military tribunal in Shkodër sentenced two people to death for having engaged in acts of sabotage. Several other defendants were given terms of imprisonment. News about skirmishes and trials continued to come out of Albania throughout the autumn and winter of 1949.

The situation took a turn for the worse the following year. In addition to stories of frontier provocations and of clashes between security forces and guerilla groups, the official news media carried reports of parachutists dropped from aircraft flying from Italy. In July 1950, Albania sent a note to the Italian government complaining that it was permitting the parachuting of agents on Albanian territory. A number of these (the Albanian note claimed) had, on being captured, confessed they had been trained in Italy and had been dropped by Italian planes. One or two other protests along similar lines were sent to Rome, but apparently without evoking any response. There were more trials of captured parachutists and other active opponents of the régime. One of these was held at Korçë, in southern Albania, in December. Of the five agents alleged to have entered the country from Greece and Yugoslavia, two were sentenced to death, the rest were sent to prison. Another major trial, which took place at Kukës, near the border with Yugoslavia, involved twelve Yugoslav agents, of whom two were given death sentences.

This highly disturbed state of affairs reached its climax in February 1951, when a bomb exploded at, or near, the Soviet embassy in the Albanian capital, killing or injuring several members of the Russian diplomatic and military staff. This signalled the beginning of an unprecedented reign of terror and repression. A large number of people were arrested and a fresh purge of the communist party was carried out. An emergency decree laid down draconian measures for dealing with the crisis : a thorough enquiry into the activities of terrorist organizations was to be carried out within ten days; their members were to be swiftly tried, with no appeals allowed against court sentences. Another decree called on citizens to surrender all their arms and weapons to the authorities. From then onwards, the trials of alleged parachutists and saboteurs came thick and fast until well into 1953. Throughout this period the Albanian government kept complaining to the United Nations about gross interference in the country's internal affairs by Yugoslavia, Greece, Italy, Britain and the United States. From time to time the western press published reports on the Albanian disturbances; these were generally ascribed to the deep discontent of the majority of the people with the repressive policies of the régime. The latter's persistent complaints about foreign intervention were usually discounted as propaganda.

Several years passed before any light was thrown on the grave disorders of 1949–53. In October 1967, the British newspaper the *Sunday Times* published a series of articles on Kim Philby's career in the British Secret Intelligence Service up to the time of his defection to the Soviet Union in 1963. These dealt, among other topics, with his transfer to Washington in 1949 as liaison official between the United States Central Intelligence Agency (CIA) and its British counterpart. Shortly after Philby's transfer, he was said to have been involved in planning and organizing uprisings in some of the communist countries of eastern Europe. Albania was selected for a number of reasons as the most suitable area where this clandestine enterprise could be tried out. Its communist régime, which was far from being firmly established, was facing fresh troubles because of its violent quarrel with Tito. The country's two immediate neighbours, Greece and Yugoslavia, would not object to, and might even welcome, (it was thought) a radical change in the government at Tirana. The next step was to recruit exiles who would take part in the secret undertaking. Britain and the United States sponsored the formation of a "national committee for a free Albania" with representatives from the different non-communist groups which had played a part in the resistance movement of the second world war. Each of these groups nominated the agents who would be sent to Albania after undergoing special training in Cyprus, Malta and West Germany. The whole operation was set in motion in the spring of 1951, when the first parachutists were dropped in northern Albania. Several other groups were infiltrated by land, air and sea at various intervals until the beginning of the following year. But in most cases, the infiltrators found the Albanian army and police forces waiting for them when they got there. Many of them were either killed in the fighting that ensued or were captured and tried. Others managed to escape to Greece where they told the painful story of the disastrous failure of the subversion. It was immediately suspected that some form of treachery had taken place, but its source could not be traced. Some years later, when Kim Philby was revealed to have been Russia's principal agent in the west, responsibility for betraying the plot to overthrow Hoxha's government was pinned on him. Philby himself admitted in his book *My Silent War* that the account of his career as a Soviet agent that had appeared in the *Sunday Times* was substantially correct.

The whole affair had certain important and possibly lasting

repercussions in Albania itself. Thanks to Philby's betrayal, the régime not only stamped out the rebellion fomented from abroad but imposed on the country, out of fear and revenge, a much harsher type of Stalinist rule than had existed before the subversion attempt was made. Great pains were taken during the next few years to persuade Albanians that the subversion had been aimed not only against the communist régime but against the country's independence and territorial integrity. The involvement of Greece and Italy in the plot, however indirectly, was used to reinforce this line of argument. Yugoslavia was also brought into the campaign of persuasion when a committee of Albanian exiles opposed to Hoxha's régime was set up there in 1951. So it can be said that all the necessary elements existed for conjuring up the old fear of partition in people's minds. And the Albanian communists did all they could to stimulate and articulate this haunting fear. They assumed the rôle of David who had slain not one but several hefty Goliaths. Another outcome of the sedition attempt was to make Hoxha and his associates obsessively, and more or less permanently, suspicious of the western countries, hence openly hostile to them.

The question whether the sedition would have succeeded if Philby had not been in a position to inform his masters in Moscow about it is an open one. But its chances of success would, in any case, have been appreciably reduced by two factors. One is the absence of any clear indication as to the type of government that would have been set up if the rebellion had swept away the communist régime. The other is the lack of evidence that a successful popular uprising in Albania would have had the necessary military or political backing from Britain and the United States. Although there are no reliable figures on the losses in human lives during the disturbances of 1949–53, the number of those killed, executed or imprisoned is believed to run into several hundred.

The second party congress was held at the end of March 1952. After taking stock of the situation, it declared that the country's main danger stemmed from Yugoslav revisionism and from the aggressive policies of the western powers. Given these conditions, the party and the people would work together in harness to bring about a socialist society, "with a pickaxe in one hand and rifle in the other". This bellicose slogan, which became the hallmark of Albanian propaganda for many years to come, was intended to engender the feeling that Albania was in a state of siege in which hardly anybody could be trusted, one that de-. manded constant vigilance. The party congress vindicated Hoxha's stewardship by re-electing him as general secretary, backed by a central committee whose members were completely loyal to him.

The other main task of the congress was to approve the country's first five-year plan (1951–55). Economic planning during the turbulent late 1940s had been on a more or less hand-to-mouth basis, with sudden changes in investment allocations and production targets. This unsatisfactory performance was due to the absence of any agreement between Belgrade and Tirana on basic economic policy, to shortage of capital, and to the Albanian communists' lack of any experience in economic and industrial affairs. The situation changed when Albania established direct links with the Soviet Union. Moscow promised to provide the country with economic aid as well as the technical expertise needed to make the best use of it. The new economic plan devoted a major part of the national budget (about 42 per cent) to the development of the chrome, copper, nickel, oil and coal industries; the building of hydro-electric plants and light industries. The funds assigned to agriculture—the country's main source of income—were much smaller (some 18 per cent), though important results were expected to be achieved through collectivization, mechanization and through increasing the area under cultivation.

But it soon became evident that these ambitious targets could not be reached. In its attempt to forge ahead too quickly in industry as well as in agriculture, the régime met with failure in both. One of the principal causes of the failure was of a political nature. After their unhappy alliance with Yugoslavia, the Albanian leaders became increasingly obsessed with the notion that the country could only achieve a measure of real independence by embarking on a programme of industrial development as quickly as possible. Such an undertaking inevitably entailed the danger of neglecting the primitive agriculture in which the great majority of the people were employed. One hope was that collectivization was the panacea that would quickly do away with the ancient backwardness of the peasants. About 100 collective farms had been set up since the end of the war, and in 1951 a panic decision was taken to introduce forced collectivization on a large scale. However, the decision was reversed shortly afterwards as being inopportune for a number of compelling reasons. Most peasants were fiercely opposed to the plan for joining co-operative farms. Their opposition came at a time when the régime faced the hazards of western subversion; that is, when it could least afford antagonizing the peasantry. Furthermore, collectivization was not a practical proposition owing to the shortage of qualified people and of the technical resources needed to make it work. So it was decided to shelve the plan for the time being and to concentrate instead on improving the private sector. Farmers' delivery quotas of grain, meat and other agricultural produces were reduced and their tax arrears for 1949–52 cancelled. A number of ambitious industrial projects were abandoned; the money saved was used to provide larger agricultural credits for purchasing more tractors and other farm machinery.

The task of lifting the country out of its economic, social and cultural backwardness was a formidable one. Some of the idealists who had joined the communist movement in its early stages had done so out of a deep sense of shame induced by this lamentable state of affairs. This shame had made them impatiently eager to wipe out within the shortest possible time the legacy of Ottoman rule and of the troubled years of independence between the two wars. However, efforts to bring this about were severely handicapped by the illiberal and intransigent behaviour of the communists during the war and the early post-war years. This lost the country the services of a small but experienced group of professional people and trained administrators when it could ill afford to do so. Figures published at the end of 1948 revealed the appallingly low intellectual level of the communist party, the motor of radical reform. Over 21 per cent of its members were either illiterate or semi-literate; 19 per cent had received only primary schooling; some 14 per cent had secondary education, whereas the figure of communists with some university qualifications was infinitesimal. By early 1952 a slight improvement had taken place, with a small increase in the number of party members who had secondary and higher education. The educational level of the party membership reflected, by and large, the state of affairs that existed in the country as a whole.

The problem of illiteracy had begun to be tackled with a good deal of enthusiasm during the war years. Many peasants, both men and women, who joined the ranks of the partisan movement were taught the rudiments of reading, writing and arithmetic together with training in guerilla warfare and elementary Marxism. Then in 1946 a systematic drive against illiteracy was launched by harnessing the idealism of the young and the experience of the older generation, through persuasion or coercion. As a result, by 1950 the illiteracy rate was reduced from 80 to 30 per cent; 5 years later it was proudly claimed that illiteracy among adults under the age of forty had been wiped out. Although this was in itself a remarkable achievement, it could hardly make a major contribution to the solution of Albania's innumerable problems.

The educational system, like everything else, was badly dislocated by the war. When peace came, Yugoslavia gave some assistance, mainly by granting university and other scholarships to Albanian students. But this co-operation came to an abrupt end in 1948. From then onwards Albania adopted the Soviet system of education lock stock and barrel, and became dependent on Moscow for the training of most of its professional people and specialists. There was an acute shortage of teachers of every type. To overcome this, several colleges were set up for training primary and secondary school teachers. A number of vocational schools were also established to meet the increasing demand for skilled or semi-skilled workers in engineering, agriculture, medicine and the social services. Russia contributed to this educational advance by providing Albanian schools and colleges with specialists and technical equipment. Some remarkable results were achieved within a relatively short time : by 1950 the number of pupils and teachers had doubled; shortly afterwards a fairly large number of graduates in engineering, agriculture, medicine and economics came out of Soviet universities.

There was also some progress in the badly neglected health and social services. New hospitals were built and an energetic campaign was set afoot for bringing malaria under control by draining some of the marshlands. Measures were also taken to reduce the incidence of tuberculosis and syphilis. As a result of these and similar other initiatives, the general health of the people showed some improvement. By 1953 the death rate had dropped from 16.7 to 13.6 per 1,000 and the infant mortality rate from 112.2 to 99.5 per 1,000. Yet despite these advances, the fearful legacy of social and cultural backwardness and widespread poverty had hardly been touched.

Although Hoxha's régime felt fairly secure, both economically and ideologically, on achieving the status of a full Soviet satellite, its troubled relations with Yugoslavia continued to be a constant source of irritation and worry. Violent propaganda exchanges became a more or less permanent feature of these relations. Tirana accused Yugoslavia of persecuting the Albanian-speaking population in Kosovo and Macedonia and of trying to foment rebellion in northern Albania. Belgrade, for its part, complained that the Albanian régime was itself stirring up trouble among Albanians living in Yugoslavia as well as harassing the Yugoslav embassy staff in Tirana. As a result of this mounting tension, the two countries withdrew their respective diplomatic missions in 1950 without, however, bringing about a formal break in their diplomatic ties. Even though some of the allegations about the maltreatment of the Albanian minority later proved to have been substantially well-founded, the welfare of these people was not the main concern of the Albanian régime in the late 1940s and the early 1950s. What it really hoped to achieve by its propaganda against Tito's government was to strengthen its own position at home by posing as a stout champion of Albanian nationalism. At the same time, fear may also have played some part in this campaign of vituperation. There was first the fear that Yugoslavia might attempt to regain control over Albania by taking advantage of the fact that the latter had failed to obtain a formal military guarantee from the Soviet Union. Then there was the fear that the infection of Tito's revisionist policies might spread to Albania and so undermine the strict Stalinist control that Hoxha considered essential if his régime was to remain in power. The second fear was to gain the upper hand during the next few years when the Albanian communists harped more and more on the grave sins of heresy that Tito was supposed to have committed against the sacred texts of Marx, Lenin and Stalin. The fear of ideological contamination claimed its Albanian victims from time to time.

The régime's worries about its own and the country's security were clearly evident when Yugoslavia, Greece and Turkey signed in February 1953 a treaty of friendship and co-operation, better known as the Balkan pact. The Albanian leaders detected in it an indirect threat to the independence and territorial integrity of their country. Shortly afterwards the three signatories of the

pact issued a declaration which said that Albania's independence was an important factor for the peace and stability of the
Balkan peninsula. But the Albanians considered this insufficiently
reassuring; they singled out the absence of any reference to the
country's territorial integrity as evidence that the Greek claim to
southern Albania remained a live issue. Some of these fears may
have been partly genuine and partly artificial but the state of
anxiety into which Stalin's death on 5 March 1953 plunged
Hoxha and his associates was starkly real. They now lost the
protector who had steered them safely to harbour in the stormy
seas of 1948. Would Stalin's successors give them the same kind
of security or would they cast them to the wolves?

Apart from providing the Albanian communists with a relatively safe haven inside the Soviet bloc when the quarrel with
Yugoslavia broke out, Stalin had rendered them another invalu-
able service, thanks to Kim Philby's extraordinary feat of espionage, when their régime was in serious trouble during the 1949–53
crisis. But their strong attachment to Stalin stemmed from other
deeper causes. He was, in their eyes, the revolutionary leader
who had transformed a vast, primitive peasant society into a
powerful, sophisticated industrial state. Some of the methods
he had employed to bring about this transformation may have
been harsh, even savage, but, given the immense problems he
faced, no other methods would have done. True, in terms of
size and population the Soviet Union and Albania were worlds
apart, but the difficulties their country had faced when the communist régime came to power (the Albanian leaders argued) were
no less formidable than the ones that Stalin had had to contend
with throughout his career. And if powerful Russia under Stalin
had to have its secret police, its labour camps, its collectivized
agriculture, its purges, its general policy of coercion, how could
a communist régime have survived in Albania, surrounded as
it was by unfriendly countries, without the help of similar
crutches? The Albanian leaders of course garnished their peculiar
attachment to Stalin and Stalinism with suitable ideological
theories, but these were barely capable of covering the nakedness
of their cold political calculations and of their obsessional preoccupation with sheer personal survival. Their blind devotion to
Stalin was, however, soon questioned by his successor, Nikita
Khrushchev, whose policies were to cause them a good deal of
trouble throughout the next decade.

Chapter 7

FROM KHRUSHCHEV TO MAO TSE-TUNG

HOXHA, LIKE MOST other communist leaders of eastern Europe, was in the dark about future trends in Soviet policy whilst the struggle for power was going on in Moscow after Stalin's death. One thing that became clear fairly soon was that there was going to be a transition from one-man rule to government by committee, or collective leadership. As a token of his acceptance of the new policy, in 1954 Hoxha gave up the premiership to Mehmet Shehu and resigned from all other government posts, retaining only the party leadership. A reduction of Soviet economic aid was the first sign from Moscow that the post-Stalin hierarchy was likely to revise its attitude to Albania. Another equally serious, though indirect, warning came in April 1955 when Hoxha's leadership and policies were challenged at a meeting of the party's central committee in Tirana. The attack was led by a deputy prime minister (Tuk Jakova) and the minister of education (Bedri Spahiu). Although both were sacked shortly afterwards on being accused as revisionists (i.e. pro-Yugoslav), it is quite probable that they were spokesmen for a fairly large body of opinion within the communist party which had decided, after the death of the Soviet dictator, that the time was ripe for staging some kind of protest against the harsh rule of his Albanian disciple.

But the event that really marked the beginning of a new time of troubles for Hoxha and for the Albanian communist party was Khrushchev's and Bulganin's momentous visit to Yugoslavia in May 1955. Speaking at the Belgrade airport in Tito's presence, Khrushchev said, referring to Yugoslavia's expulsion from the European communist bloc in 1948, "we sincerely regret what happened and resolutely reject the things that occurred". He held Lavrenti Beria (Stalin's police chief who was executed in 1954) solely responsible for disrupting the relations between the two countries and promised that the Soviet Union would do all it could to mend them. The joint declaration issued at the end of the visit indicated that reconciliation would be confined to the governments of the Soviet Union and Yugoslavia and would not affect relations between their communist parties. As a price for ending the breach with Tito, the Soviet side accepted the basic principles of Yugoslav policy : respect for national independence and recognition of every country's right to determine its particular course of political, economic and social development. In a statement he made shortly afterwards, Tito pointed out that the formal ending of hostility between his country and the Soviet Union did not mean that Yugoslavia would rejoin the Soviet bloc or give up its independence in domestic or foreign affairs.

Khrushchev's historic visit to Belgrade had a profound effect on eastern Europe, sending reverberations throughout the countries of the area during the next few years. Stalinists in Moscow and in other communist capitals were deeply dismayed by the event. They feared that the rehabilitation of a man who was a communist heretic and a nationalist would undermine the discipline and cohesion of the Soviet empire that Stalin had so laboriously built after the second world war. Those who had suffered under Stalinist rule (and they constituted the great majority of the people of eastern Europe) were encouraged by the new development; they hoped their own countries would be allowed to benefit in some measure from Yugoslavia's example. The visit's impact on Albania, on the other hand, was more complex. There both communists and non-communists feared that Khrushchev and Tito might do a deal whereby Yugoslavia would regain the ascendancy it had enjoyed in Albania between 1944 and 1948. In addition to sharing this fear with the majority of their countrymen, Hoxha and Shehu had their own special reasons to be alarmed by the new friendship between Moscow and Belgrade. As Tito's most vehement opponents, might they not be among the first leaders of eastern Europe to be sacrificed by Khrushchev as he pursued his appeasement of Yugoslavia? All they could do in their predicament was to make certain of their security at home. With Hoxha in charge of the party machine and Shehu in control of the secret police and the army, they had ample means of doing this. In 1955 they decided to extend their power over the peasantry by embarking on a policy of forced collectivization.

The régime had been somewhat cautious in this field between

1946 and 1955, apart from one or two false moves. About 150 collective farms were set up during this period. With the Yugoslav danger looming once more on the horizon, the political motives for regimenting the peasants, which had always been present in communist thinking and planning, suddenly moved to the foreground. The régime had never been quite sure of the peasants' loyalty for a number of good reasons. As most Albanian governments in the past had treated them very roughly, the peasants had for generations developed a sullen aversion, tinged with the spirit of anarchism, to all forms of authority and officialdom. During the second world war, as we saw earlier, the communists had managed to gain the support of a large number of poor peasants. However, many others had rallied to the nationalist cause and had remained faithful to it in defeat. The communist leaders feared that the general discontent of this group might be exploited for its own ends by Yugoslavia or by the new leadership in Moscow. So in 1955 it was decreed to substitute almost complete control for the policy of relative moderation in agriculture. Peasants who opposed collectivization or were simply unenthusiastic about it were promptly branded as "kulaks" or, worse still, as class enemies. In some cases, they resorted to slaughtering or selling their animals before joining the new co-operatives. In addition to causing widespread social and political turmoil, the collectivization drive was responsible for a serious decline in livestock and food production. By the end of 1959 about 83 per cent of the country's arable land had become part of the system of state or co-operative farms. This left in private hands only the poor land of the highland districts of northern Albania.

Both the theory and practice of Hoxha's rule were badly shaken, not by an anti-communist agency, but by the deliberations of the twentieth congress of the Soviet communist party in February 1956. At one of its open sessions, Anastas Mikoyan, the deputy prime minister, criticized Stalin's rule in general terms, singling out several old Bolsheviks whom he had destroyed after branding them as "enemies of the people". This was followed a few days later by the far more elaborate and severe indictment that Khrushchev, the new first secretary of the party, delivered at a secret session. He began by attributing most of the crimes committed during Stalin's tyranny to the myth which had been deliberately cultivated over many years that he was some kind of a superman endowed with infallibility and other extraordinary powers of wisdom and perception. Believing his own myth, he became intolerant of other people's opinions and incapable of putting into practice Lenin's principle of collective leadership. This had led him to classify all those who happened to disagree with him as "enemies of the people", a perverse notion which enabled him to destroy political opponents at will. Stalin had resorted to extreme repression, Khrushchev went on, long after the revolution had proved successful and the Soviet state was firmly in the saddle. The victims of this policy had been not merely some real enemies of the régime but also many individuals wholly innocent of any transgression against either party or government. When Kirov, the party leader in Leningrad, was murdered in 1934, Stalin had suspended the operations of the legal system and had issued orders that people merely suspected of having committed acts of terrorism should be speedily tried and executed. Seventy per cent of the members of the central committee, Khrushchev said, were arrested and shot in 1937 and 1938. Many thousands of other innocent communists had been likewise sent to their death after Stalin himself had endorsed lists of names submitted by his secret police. Khrushchev's main concern was with Stalin's crimes against members of the communist party, government leaders and officials; the sufferings of the Russian people under his tyranny were largely ignored. The only time he touched on the plight of ordinary human beings as opposed to privileged members of the party was when he spoke of the deportation of whole populations—the Karachai, the Ingush, the Balkars—between 1943 and 1944. Regarding Russia's quarrel with Yugoslavia in 1948, this had been artificially blown up by Stalin himself who had said, "I will shake my little finger and there will be no more Tito. He will fall." But no matter how much Stalin shook his little finger, Tito came to no harm because he had behind him a people who had been through the hard school of fighting for freedom and independence.

At the close of his speech, which was a calculated ploy in the struggle for power then going on in Moscow, Khrushchev urged his listeners not to make his revelations public : "We should not give ammunition to the enemy; we should not wash our dirty linen before their eyes". However, the enemy, in this case the countries of the non-communist world, knew far more about the horrors of Stalin's tyranny than Khrushchev had seen prudent to disclose to the secret conclave in Moscow. Nevertheless, the text of the speech was published in the western press shortly afterwards; it was also broadcast to Russia and the other communist countries of Europe. Its treatment by the communist régimes was more devious and circumspect. In the Soviet Union itself, the gist of the speech was made available to certain levels of the party machine. The Polish leaders did the same, whereas the Hungarian, Romanian and Albanian party bosses decided to play safe by censoring the document before passing it on to their underlings. Unhampered by such inhibitions, the Yugoslav press published a fairly detailed report of the speech.

The first country to react to the proceedings of the Soviet twentieth congress was Albania. This was somewhat surprising as it was generally believed that its leadership had brought the situation under control after Khrushchev's visit to Belgrade. The party organization of Tirana held a special meeting in April, barely two months after Khrushchev's speech, to review the current state of affairs. Several hundred delegates took part, among them many members of the central committee and the politburo. The meeting, presided over by the minister of defence, Beqir Balluku, turned out to be very different from the formal rubber-stamp affairs which had become such a prominent feature of Albanian public life. Delegate after delegate rose to his feet in rapid succession to attack the whole philosophy of party policy. Hoxha and his colleagues were accused of holding party members as well as the population at large in utter contempt. They were said to pursue policies without any regard for the consequences these might have for the country as a whole. Several speakers said that the time had come for the leadership to render an account of its record. Why, for instance, had there been so many purges and executions since 1949? Why was there such reluctance to restore to office the large number of communists who had been unjustly dismissed? Other delegates demanded free and full debates on such issues as the twentieth congress of the Soviet communist party, the personality cult, Koçi Xoxe's execution, relations with Yugoslavia, the absence of democratic rights within the party organization, economic policy. Hoxha was not present when this sweeping onslaught on his leadership was unleashed. But when the proceedings appeared to be getting out of hand, he decided to intervene. He began by being conciliatory towards his critics: he said the views they had expressed stemmed, not from any basic hostility to the régime itself, but from a mis-interpretation of the events of the past few years. Hoxha admitted that some mistakes had been committed but added that these hardly justified the grave allegations that had been made. But his conciliatory approach misfired. Many angry delegates reminded him that as he had not been present at the beginning he should listen to what they had to say. Sensing the dangerous mood of the gathering, Hoxha counter-attacked and demanded the immediate adoption of a resolution expressing confidence in his leadership. On securing this, the meeting was dissolved. Sharp retaliation followed soon after. All those who had addressed the meeting were expelled from the party and imprisoned. Hoxha's opponents had clearly acted without adequate preparation. They had also underestimated his considerable tactical skill and his ruthless determination to make full use of the coercive powers at his disposal when his absolute authority was threatened. The outspoken critics of the régime were branded as Yugoslav stooges. This was, to say the least, a politically convenient oversimplifica-tion. Although the Yugoslav government may have played some part in inspiring the Tirana meeting, the opposition that rose to the surface came from a very mixed bag of people : party members who were genuinely worried about the state of the country; individuals who had been encouraged by the reconcilia-tion between Moscow and Belgrade and by the more hopeful atmosphere generated by the twentieth Soviet party congress; political careerists looking for the main chance, and so on. Apart from lacking any real cohesion, the dissidents had little or no experience in the art of political organization. So their movement ended in failure, thus making it very difficult for a similar protest to be staged in the future.

There were also signs that Albania was not altogether immune from the kind of intellectual ferment that spread to Poland and Hungary after Khrushchev's speech. An Albanian literary critic published in May 1956 an article in the country's main cultural periodical in which he questioned some of the basic assumptions of Stalinism. "People [he wrote] are not all alike. They have different desires and aims; they love and hate different things. It is the duty of the writer to trace the cause of such differences and to reveal their roots. ... Members of a social group, in addition to the things they have in common as a result of their economic status, have also certain purely individual traits." He went on to say that people could not be judged merely as members of a particular social group; their equally important individual and environmental characteristics had to be taken into account as well. One or two other Albanian writers made a plea for open and free debates on national problems. But these fragile buds of intellectual freedom were soon destroyed by a new frost of political intolerance.

The Albanian leader now faced the dangers implicit in Khrushchev's friendship with Yugoslavia and in his determination to dismantle part of Stalin's apparatus of repression. Hoxha feared that both his own position (perhaps even his life) and the country's independence were put at risk by these policies. Being in no position to oppose them openly, he fell back on the device of dissimulation which he had used with some success during his involvement with Tito before 1948. At the third party congress in May 1956, he gave his full support to the decisions of the twentieth congress of the Soviet communist party and promised that he would do his best to improve relations with Yugoslavia. And taking a leaf out of Khrushchev's book, he blamed Beria for having engineered the rift between Albania and Yugoslavia in the first place. Khrushchev sent two special envoys (Suslov and Pospelov) to Tirana for the purpose of persuading Hoxha to rehabilitate Koçi Xoxe. His posthumous rehabilitation was part of the bargain struck between the Soviet leadership and Tito a year earlier. But Hoxha's attitude remained inflexible : Xoxe was not convicted for any ideological offences but for the part he had played in subjecting his country to foreign rule; his case could not therefore be reopened.

Khrushchev must have realized after the Albanian party congress that the smallest country of the Soviet bloc had no intention of making the slightest accommodation to his policies, and that its leaders were likely to cause him the same sort of trouble that Tito had once caused Stalin. All he could do in the circumstances was to keep up the pressure on Tirana and hope for the best. Hoxha, for his part, having paid formal lip-service to the new trends of the post-Stalin era, wondered how long he could withstand the steady pressure from Moscow. At home, he had taken all necessary steps to silence his critics. At the same time, he had set out to persuade his countrymen that his sole preoccupation was the defence of Albania's independence from the dangers inherent in the new amity between Moscow and

Belgrade. In an effort to secure external support for his régime, he paid a visit to China in October 1956. The foundations of Albania's subsequent alliance with Peking were laid during the visit.

The outbreak of the Hungarian revolution in October-November 1956 and its suppression by the Soviet army gave the Albanian leaders and other Stalinists of eastern Europe a valuable breathing-space. Hoxha was now in a position to say to Khrushchev, "I told you so". And he did this with all the self-righteousness at his command. Writing in the Soviet newspaper *Pravda* (8 November 1956) he maintained that Yugoslav revisionism was at the root of the Hungarian and Polish disturbances. Tito promptly denied this, pointing out that the real cause of the troubles was the pernicious system of one-man rule and the Stalinist practices wielded on its behalf. The Soviet press commended the Albanian leader's loyalty to communist principles, but rebuked him for his outspoken remarks about Yugoslavia. The fact is that the turmoil of eastern Europe made it possible for Hoxha to shift his position from local politician primarily concerned with his own safety to vigorous defender of the security of the communist bloc as a whole.

Addressing a party meeting in Tirana shortly after the Hungarian uprising had been quelled, he defended Soviet military intervention in Budapest but disagreed with those who "discounted the entire positive side of Stalin's revolutionary career and concentrated on its darker aspects". Whatever mistakes Stalin may have made, Hoxha said, he had been right on matters concerning the vital interests of the working class, on Marxist-Leninist doctrine and on the struggle against imperialism. As this constituted a straight challenge to Khrushchev's verdict on Stalin's dictatorship, Hoxha and Shehu were summoned to Moscow for consultations in April 1957. Khrushchev asked them to end the purges and to reinstate communists who had been sacked. On their refusal to do so, he accused them of behaving like sectarians hell-bent on pursuing Stalinist policies. This part of the Moscow talks was only made public several years later by Albanian sources. But as the main concern of the Soviet leader was to bring about some kind of improvement in Albanian-Yugoslav relations, he expressed his views on the matter in a blunt public statement during the visit. Despite the great difference that existed between the two countries, Khrushchev said, every effort should be made to overcome them. In the hope that a timely act of Soviet generosity might induce Hoxha to comply with its wishes, the Soviet government agreed to write off the credit of $105 million which Albania had received between 1949 and 1957. The country was also promised food supplies worth seven and three-quarter million dollars as well as more technical aid. As a result of this assistance the Albanian economy began to pick up. The government abolished food rationing and raised the wages of most workers in the autumn of 1957. On the other hand, while the Albanian leaders were quite pleased to receive gifts from Moscow, they showed no sign that they were prepared to give anything in return.

A sudden change in the Soviet attitude towards Yugoslavia came to the rescue of Hoxha's intransigence. Tito did not accept the invitation to take part in the Moscow conference of ruling communist parties in November 1957 but sent his deputy, Kardelj, instead. The Yugoslavs also refused to sign the statement issued at the end of the meeting on the grounds that it recognized the Soviet Union as leader of the international communist movement. This act of non-commitment was criticized by Russia, China and the communist régimes of eastern Europe. A meeting of the Yugoslav communist party congress in April 1958 increased still further the volume of criticism. The congress approved a political programme which contained the familiar ingredients of Yugoslav policy : rejection of bureaucratic rule; the establishment of socialist democracy based on workers' self-management; full national independence; non-alignment in foreign affairs. The programme was condemned as hopelessly revisionist by most communist countries. Albania coupled its condemnation with renewed attacks on the Yugoslav treatment of the Albanian population of Kosovo.

At about the same time an important shift to the left was taking place in China, affecting both its domestic and external policies. Greater stress was laid on the unity of the international communist movement (hence on the struggle against Yugoslav revisionist ideas) and on the need to exert stronger political and military pressure on the United States and western Europe. A new feature of the domestic scene was the setting up of people's communes in 1958. A brainchild of Mao Tse-tung, the communes were designed to provide an administrative framework for making the best use of human labour in order to offset the shortage of machinery; to tighten government control over the life of the individual; to show that the Chinese communists were capable of devising new forms of social organization that out-classed those existing in the Soviet Union and its allies. The seeds of the subsequent quarrel between Peking and Moscow germin-ated whilst these radical changes were occurring. Sensing their possible implications, the Albanians hastened to strengthen their ties with China. A delegation went to Peking in 1958 to discuss trade and economic co-operation. A few months later an Albanian minister was sent there for the express purpose of studying the new system of people's communes.

In the meantime, relations between Russia and China were deteriorating rapidly. Among other things, Mao Tse-tung had strong objections to Khrushchev's policy of co-existence with the western powers and to his failure to consult the Chinese before taking the momentous step of denouncing Stalin. Khrushchev went to Peking in August 1958 to discuss these and other matters with Mao, but his visit only served to reveal the deep gulf between them. By this time the Soviet leader knew that a sharp conflict with the Chinese was likely to erupt sooner or later and that his immediate task was to make sure of the loyalty of his European allies. In May 1959 he paid a twelve-day visit to Albania. During his stay there he made several speeches in which he warned Italy and Greece not to allow NATO to station nuclear bases on their territories. But these warnings were meant to serve as a smokescreen for the main purpose of his visit, which was to dissuade the Albanians from seeking an alliance with China. In Khrushchev's calculations, if a country as small and as weak as Albania proved successful in enlisting Peking's support against Moscow, what was to prevent the bigger communist countries of eastern Europe from making the same attempt? Khrushchev himself indicated shortly afterwards that his visit to Tirana had been unfruitful. He gave an interview in Moscow to the leader of the Greek liberal party, Sophocles Venizelos, in which he promised to take up with Hoxha the question of grant-ing greater cultural autonomy to the Greek minority in southern Albania. The interview was clearly meant to infuriate the Albanian leaders who, however, managed to contain their anger until after their break with the Soviet Union had taken place.

The first open clash between the Russians and China occurred at a meeting of communist party leaders in Bucharest in June

1960. All the leaders of the parties in power were present, with the exception of Enver Hoxha, who was represented by Hysni Kapo, a member of the Albanian politburo. The chief protagonists were Khrushchev and the Chinese delegate Peng Chen. In his opening speech, the Soviet leader launched a somewhat oblique attack against Mao's views on war and peace and the current international situation. He pointed out that it was childish to assume that a purely mechanical interpretation of Marx, Engels or Lenin could enable one to cope with the problems of the modern world. He laid stress on the destructiveness of nuclear war and on the need to make the policy of peaceful coexistence a success. The Chinese delegate's reply was mild and not very forthcoming. His main contention was that peace could only be preserved if the unity of the communist movement was not impaired by the infection of Yugoslav revisionism. But the real drama of the conference was played behind the scenes. The Soviet delegation circulated among the participants a long document in which both the policies and actions of the Chinese leadership were mercilessly criticized. Taking their cue from the Soviet brief, all delegates present, with one exception, supported Khrushchev's indictment of China. Only the Albanian delegate Kapo refused to do so. He said that Khrushchev had sprung on the meeting an important matter and demanded a decision without giving the delegates adequate time to study the highly complex issues involved. But Kapo's objection was lost in the bitter exchanges that ensued between the two main contestants. Khrushchev accused Mao Tse-tung of behaving like Stalin, "oblivious of any interests other than his own, spinning theories detached from the realities of the modern world". Although the Chinese talked a great deal about war, he said, they had little understanding of the true nature of modern war. He was also contemptuous of China's domestic experiments like the communes and the "great leap forward" : economic progress, he maintained, was achieved by carefully planned development, not in leaps and bounds. In his reply, Peng Chen said it was clear that Khrushchev had called the meeting for the sole purpose of discrediting the Chinese communist party and Mao Tse-tung. The Chinese leadership, he went on, had no faith in Khrushchev's analysis of the international situation because it rested on illusions about the true nature and strength of western imperialism. These diatribes showed that there was a serious breach between two great powers bent on pursuing and defending their own vital interests. The doctrinal arguments were a useful device for obscuring the harsh facts of power politics as well as for enlisting the widest possible support for their respective cases. As far as the Albanians were concerned, the breach meant the end of their policy of seeking Mao's help against Soviet pressure whilst remaining on friendly terms with both China and Russia. Khrushchev forced them at Bucharest to make a clear choice and they chose, somewhat sheepishly, China.

Soon after the Bucharest meeting Russia began exacting its price for the choice Albania had made. Soviet grain deliveries were stopped at a time when the country was on the verge of famine as a result of drought, floods and earthquakes. It was threatened with expulsion from the Warsaw Pact if the Albanian leaders persisted in their refusal to toe the line. The Soviet embassy in Tirana encouraged the formation of a pro-Soviet group within the Albanian party headed by two high officials (Liri Belishova and Koço Tashko) who were subsequently dismissed. In July 1960, the Albanian authorities announced the discovery of a plot to overthrow the régime in which ten members of the armed forces and government officials were said to have been involved.

The next act of the Sino-Soviet drama was staged the following November at the conference of 81 communist parties in Moscow. Before the conference opened the Soviet party distributed to all delegates a document attacking the policies of the Albanian leadership. This was followed by a private meeting between Khrushchev and Hoxha which showed that no compromise between them was possible. During the first few days of the conference itself, several delegates voiced their misgivings about China's policies and about its unwillingness to work in harmony with the Soviet Union and other communist countries. Teng Hsiao-ping, the Chinese delegate, realized that what he faced was a well-orchestrated offensive against his country's party so he decided to counter-attack. He accused the Soviet leader of stringing together a mass of arguments which misrepresented the Chinese case. Teng was particularly grieved by the highly uncomplimentary remarks the Russians had made about China's people's communes, the policy of the "great leap forward" and the person of Mao Tse-tung. Far from being a disastrous failure, as the Soviets maintained, the communes had helped to lift the people of China out of their backwardness. As for Mao, no criticism or denigration could obscure the fact that it was he who had united the people and shown them the way to revolutionary change. Coming to the heart of the matter, the Chinese delegate said that there were neither superior nor inferior parties in the international communist movement; every single party was fully independent. This meant that the decisions of the Soviet communist party, or any other, could not be binding on the rest. Teng's warning was crystal clear : the Chinese were no longer prepared to submit to Moscow's guidance, leadership or discipline but would pursue an independent course, one which best served their national interests. The next speaker, Enver Hoxha, was the only one who had a good word to say about China's case. In an effort to show that his Marxist-Leninist heart was in the right place, he went over some of the ideological controversies covered by Teng Hsiao-ping. Then he let out what was uppermost in his mind in a torrent of abuse and vituperation against Khrushchev himself. He spoke of the tremendous Soviet pressures to which the Albanian party and government had been subjected after the Bucharest meeting. Attempts had been made to undermine the loyalty of party leaders, of members of the armed forces and even of Albanian students at Soviet universities. Khrushchev himself had told the Chinese that he would deal with Albania in the same way that Stalin had dealt with Yugoslavia. The Soviet leader had been as good as his word, Hoxha said. During 1960 his country had suffered several natural calamities. There had been earthquakes, floods and a drought lasting 120 days. The people were threatened with starvation. The Albanian government had explained the critical situation to the Soviet Union and had sought to buy grain from it. But after waiting for 45 days for a reply, Albania was sent 10,000 tons of grain instead of the 50,000 tons it had requested. Khrushchev had once told him, Hoxha went on, not to worry about Albania's grain supplies : the country's annual consumption amounted to what mice ate in the Soviet Union in one year. The fact was that whilst Russia's mice were able to gorge themselves, the people of Albania were threatened with starvation unless their leaders complied with Moscow's every wish. The only crime his régime had committed, the Albanian leader added, was that it did not agree that the Chinese communist party should be summarily and unjustly condemned. For this it had been treated in a manner that was shabby, anti-Marxist and uncomradely.

Hoxha's speech had a shattering effect on the Moscow gathering. The Polish leader Gomulka said it was "a disgusting, shameful, gangsterish and irresponsible attack on Khrushchev and the Soviet party". Luigi Longo, who headed the Italian delegation, described Hoxha's outburst as "not only disloyal but also infantile". The French communist leader Thorez declared : "The members of our delegation had listened to [Hoxha's] speech with a feeling of shame. As militant communists, they had never heard such language either in party meetings or in the meetings of the international communist movement. . . . The path followed by the delegation of the Albanian party was a very dangerous one."

There can be little doubt that the Albanian leader was under severe emotional strain when he attended the Moscow conference. He was certain by then that Khrushchev was out to destroy him either by economic blackmail or by outright subversion. Feeling hemmed in and cornered, he let out a strangled cry of despair. Hoxha was at the same time a prisoner of the obfuscating technique of political discourse, with its Orwellian double-think and double-talk, which Stalin had bestowed on the communist movement. In pursuing the shadow of a highly ambiguous and flexible ideology, he, perhaps more than most other communist leaders, had missed the substance of crude power as it operated in the modern world. Consequently, when Khrushchev shattered his rather naïve belief that Russia was some kind of Marxist fairy godmother by behaving like the supreme ruler of an imperialist power which demanded utter loyalty and obedience from its vassals, Hoxha felt bewildered, frustrated, angry, and not a little frightened.

The Albanians held their fourth party congress in February 1961, the last one to be attended by representatives of the Soviet Union and the other countries of eastern Europe. There the policies of the régime were vigorously defended by both Hoxha and Shehu. The party leader said that it would be suicidal for his country to submit to the demand that its communist government should become less dictatorial. Such a move would only lead to the kind of convulsions that had overtaken Hungary in 1956. Shehu admitted that he and his colleagues were often accused of being tyrants, dogmatists and narrow-minded nationalists; he thought this was because, unlike their adversaries, the Albanian communists were true Marxists. Although the Soviet and east European delegates avoided open polemics with their hosts, they pointed out that no communist régime could afford to ignore the creative ideas of the twentieth congress of the Soviet party. China's representative, on the other hand, went out of his way to commend the great achievements of the Albanian régime and the outstanding qualities of its leader. The government announced on the same occasion the broad outlines of the country's third year plan for 1961–65. These allocated the lion's share of investments to industry (54 per cent), leaving agriculture far behind (14.6 per cent). This meant a rejection of Khrushchev's advice to the Albanians that they should give up large-scale industrial development altogether and devote the greater part of their resources (including foreign aid) to farming.

The party congress confirmed that the rift with Russia was almost complete and the alliance between China and Albania an accomplished fact. The price which the Albanian leaders were made to pay for their rebellion continued to mount inexorably. In April the Soviet and Czechoslovak governments informed them that the credits ($132 million) which they had promised for Albania's third year plan would no longer be available. At the same time, all Soviet and east European experts working in the country were withdrawn, and all Albanian students attending Russian universities sent home. The Chinese quickly came to the rescue of their new ally in Europe. They granted it economic aid ($123,000 million) which covered the greater part of the losses sustained as a result of Soviet action. Peking undertook to use these funds for building twenty-five industrial plants in Albania with the help of Chinese experts who replaced their Soviet counterparts. And finally, the Soviet Union withdrew its submarines and other warships from the naval base at Sazan near the port of Vlorë. The Russians also seized a number of Albanian ships undergoing repairs at Sebastopol.

Albania's rejoinder to these Soviet actions took the form of a show trial, held in May 1961, in which the ten officers and government officials who had been arrested the previous year faced charges of plotting to overthrow the régime. They had all confessed, it was alleged, to have been agents of Yugoslavia, Greece and the United States. Four of the accused were sentenced to death, the others to terms of imprisonment ranging from 15 to 25 years. Although everything pointed to the defendants' links with the Soviet Union, the authorities decided to shift the blame elsewhere perhaps because the unvarnished truth might have caused great disquiet inside Albania. The trial itself, which was conducted along Stalinist lines, was completely ignored by the news media of eastern Europe.

So far the discussions about the dispute between Russia, on the one hand, and China and Albania, on the other, had taken place behind closed doors. The ordinary people of these countries were hardly aware of what was going on. In October 1961, Khrushchev decided to bring the whole matter into the open. He did so for two main reasons : to let the Albanian leaders know that he was no longer prepared to have any dealings with them; to give the first public notice to the world at large that a serious crisis had arisen between Moscow and Peking. Addressing the twenty-second congress of the Soviet communist party in Moscow, he said that the Albanian leaders were, to his distress, resorting to the very same practices that Stalin had employed when he was the absolute ruler of the Soviet Union.

> We are following events in Albania with a feeling of anxiety for the destinies of the . . . Albanian people. We are pained to see that Albanian rank-and-file communists and the whole Albanian people, who are vitally interested in friendship and co-operation with all socialist countries, are obliged to pay for the mistaken line of their leaders. We are deeply troubled by this situation and have persistently sought and are seeking ways of overcoming the differences that have arisen.

Chou En-lai, speaking on behalf of the Chinese communist party, was displeased with the way Khrushchev had handled the matter.

> We hold [he said] that should a dispute or difference . . . arise between fraternal parties or fraternal countries, it should be resolved patiently in the spirit of proletarian internationalism and on the principle of equality and unanimity through consultation. Any public, one-sided censure of any fraternal party does not help unify and is not helpful to resolving problems. To bring a dispute between fraternal parties or fraternal countries into the open in the face of the enemy cannot be regarded

as a serious Marxist-Leninist attitude. Such an attitude will only grieve those near and dear to us and gladden our enemies. The communist party of China sincerely hopes that fraternal parties which have disputes or differences between them will unite afresh on the basis of Marxism-Leninism and of mutual respect for independence and equality.

And as if to underline his strong objection to Khrushchev's statement, Chou En-lai laid a wreath on Stalin's tomb and left Moscow without waiting for the end of the Soviet congress. The Chinese were angry because they considered the Soviet leader's attack on the Albanians as a veiled attack not only on their own positions but also on their right to make whatever friends and allies they chose among other communist parties.

Khrushchev took up the challenge of China's spokesman when he said :

Chou En-lai . . . voiced concern in his speech over our having openly raised the issue of Albanian-Soviet relations. As far as we can see, his statement . . . reflects alarm lest the present state of our relations with [the Albanians] may affect the solidarity of the socialist camp. We share the anxiety of our Chinese friends and appreciate their concern about . . . unity. If the Chinese comrades wish to apply their efforts to normalising [Albania's] relations with other fraternal parties, no one is in a better position to do so than the communist party of China.

The Soviet leader then went on to press his case against the Albanians. He said that for some time past there had existed within the Albanian party "an abnormal and evil situation in which any individual objectionable to the leadership is liable to meet with cruel persecution. Where are the Albanian communists who built the party and fought the Italian and German invaders? Nearly all of them have become victims of the bloody misdeeds of Mehmet Shehu and Enver Hoxha." Referring to appeals made to him by individual Albanian communists to put an end to this persecution, Khrushchev went on :

A few years ago the central committee of the Soviet party interceded with the Albanian leaders over the fate of Liri

Gega, a former member of the politburo, who had been sentenced to death along with her husband ... In approaching the Albanian leaders at the time, we were guided by considerations of humanity, by anxiety to prevent the shooting of a woman, and a pregnant woman at that. We felt and still feel that as a fraternal party we had a right to state our opinion on the matter.

Khrushchev also mentioned two other leaders—Liri Belishova and Koço Tashko—who, he said, were persecuted for supporting the Soviet-Albanian alliance. He then made what seemed like a direct appeal to the Albanian people to overthrow their leaders when he added:

... to put an end to the cult of the individual would in effect mean that Shehu, Hoxha and others would have to give up their key positions in the party and government. And this they do not want to do. But we are certain the time will come when the Albanian communists and the Albanian people will have their say, and then the Albanian leaders will have to answer for the harm they had done their country, their people and the cause of socialist construction in Albania.

Speaking in Tirana shortly afterwards, Hoxha rejected Khrushchev's accusations in forthright and even violent terms. He claimed that the people of Albania had given an answer to Khrushchev's appeal to overthrow its rulers in thousands of telegrams and letters expressing complete solidarity with them. At the same time, the Chinese press gave its full support to the Albanian leadership, absolving it from Khrushchev's strictures. The split with Moscow became final in December 1961, when the Soviet Union broke off diplomatic relations with Albania. The other countries of eastern Europe, on the other hand, withdrew their ambassadors but not their diplomatic missions from Tirana.

When Khrushchev said a few years earlier that Stalin had believed that a mere shake of his finger would precipitate Tito's downfall, he could hardly have foreseen that the same kind of impotence would attend his own efforts to unseat Hoxha. The latter was able to remain in power because he had assimilated all that Soviet experience was capable of teaching him in the techniques of political self-preservation. He also benefited from the fact that his country had no common land frontier with the Soviet Union. In other words, what had been a source of grave anxiety in 1948 became a positive asset in the 1960s. But the economic, political and social consequences of the rupture with the Soviet Union were incalculable.

The abrupt cessation of economic aid and the withdrawal of Soviet and east European experts played havoc with the third 5-year plan for 1961–65. Given that half of the country's volume of imports and exports was geared to the Soviet Union, foreign trade was badly disrupted. In order to bring the gravity of the situation home to the people, the government launched at the beginning of 1962 a national appeal to make the best possible use of available resources, to reduce costs of production, to abandon unnecessary investments and avoid waste. This was coupled with a campaign of so-called "popular consultation" in which people were asked to submit proposals for helping to make the country as self-sufficient as possible. It was claimed that within a few months thousands of individual suggestions had been put forward, of which some five thousand proved useful. These resulted in the manufacture of a large number of spare parts which could no longer be imported from abroad.

In an effort to diversify its foreign trade, Albania concluded a new trade agreement with Italy shortly after the break with Moscow. However, the country's immense difficulties were compounded by China's inability to deliver in time the machinery and equipment it had promised. This caused the postponement of work on several important industrial projects by some 3 years. The gap between the end of Soviet assistance and the actual arrival of Chinese aid also revealed some of Albania's most serious economic and industrial shortcomings: low productivity, bad planning methods, poor workmanship, great administrative inefficiency. Between 1948 and 1961 economic planning was highly centralized, with Soviet and east European advisers attached to government departments taking most major decisions. This rigid control from the centre meant that very few Albanians were trained in management or given the opportunity to think for themselves or to assume personal responsibility. Having been exhorted for years to obey higher orders without questioning, party and government officials were reduced to rubber-stamping automatons devoid of any real initiative.

The crisis of the early 1960s together with the country's close involvement with China forced the leadership to revise some of its basic assumptions and attitudes. Perhaps the principal lesson the Albanians learnt from their Chinese allies was to put their faith, not in foreign aid, whether from China or anywhere else, but rather in the Victorian virtues of self-reliance and self-help. Unlike the Soviets before them, the Chinese urged the Albanian régime to decide for itself what its economic priorities were; these should then be achieved by making the most rational and efficient use of the available domestic and external resources. Moreover, China's foreign-aid policy had certain attractive features for a poor country like Albania. It was interest-free; repayments were deferred either indefinitely or until such time as they did not impair the recipient's economic progress. Chinese experts working in Albanian industrial enterprises received the same rates of pay as local employees of similar professional standing. The income of their Russian predecessors had in some cases been as much as three times that of the highest official in the country. These things helped to foster a new kind of relationship between protective power and client state, one which Albania had rarely experienced in the past. The new relationship shook the régime out of its frozen Stalinist lethargy, releasing fresh energies in economic, political and social endeavour.

At the beginning of 1966 the authorities introduced certain radical policies which bore the imprint of Mao Tse-tung's revolutionary doctrines. The size of the Albanian government was reduced and the civil service made substantial cuts in its establishment. Plans were set afoot to decentralize political and economic bodies and to wage war on bureaucratic red tape and muddle. Party and government officials as well as intellectuals were obliged to spend part of the year working in factories and farms. Military ranks were abolished and political commissars were reintroduced in the armed forces. The communist party's fifth congress (November 1966) gave a fresh impetus to this new radicalism. Its underlying principles were explained by Hoxha. He said that class struggle should not be narrowly interpreted as one waged only against a particular social class; it should embrace bourgeois ideology, harmful alien influences as well as the whole gamut of feudal, patriarchal and bourgeois social customs and modes of thought. What the country was embarking upon was nothing less than "a struggle for the hearts and minds of men . . . a struggle for bringing about the ultimate victory of communist ideology and morality". This was to be a long-term programme embracing the accountability of officials; a radical reform of schools and other cultural institutions; women's emancipation; the eradication of religious beliefs and prejudices.

During the greater part of 1967 Albania was in the grip of a carefully planned revolutionary upheaval very much along the lines of China's cultural revolution of 1966–69. This consisted of a series of propaganda campaigns, spearheaded by members of youth organizations, designed to bring about the complete collectivization of agriculture, the destruction of religious institutions, the emancipation of women, the pruning and control of the bureaucracy. The scope and significance of these and other policies and the opposition they encountered will be discussed in subsequent chapters. But the thing that became evident from the outset was that whilst the objectives of the Chinese and Albanian upheavals were fairly similar, their political tactics were entirely different. Having come to the conclusion that the Chinese communist party was no longer capable of becoming a vehicle of his revolutionary ideas, Mao Tse-tung decided to bring about its destruction by releasing against it the fury of the youthful Red Guards as well as the power of the Chinese army. Hoxha, on the other hand, was not prepared to take any such risks. Albania's social and political campaigns were manipulated and directed by the communist party itself; its leadership and structure were immune from the tumult that followed. The armed forces were also not involved in any way. Those organizations which were involved, such as the youth and women's movements and the trade unions, remained under the control of the party throughout. In time, some of the Chinese Red Guards got out of hand and put forward demands which were contrary to Mao's ideas; by contrast, their Albanian opposite numbers hardly ever strayed from the narrow path laid down by the leadership.

Albania's diplomatic and political relations with Russia and the other communist countries of Europe were at a standstill throughout the 1960s. There was, however, one important change in its commercial ties with some of them. In 1963 trade was resumed on a yearly basis with most communist countries, excepting the Soviet Union. Although Albania benefited from the resumption of these exchanges, the motive behind them seemed to be political. After the Russian-Albanian break, the Soviet government perhaps feared that, finding itself in acute economic difficulties, the Albanian leadership might seek to supplement Chinese economic and technical aid with aid from the western countries, and so come under their political influence. The restoration of trade was one way of preventing this happening. Another more oblique change occurred in Albania's relations with Yugoslavia when Alexander Ranković, the Serbian head of the Yugoslav security police, was dismissed in July 1966. He was held responsible, among other things, of having systematically persecuted the Albanian population of Kosovo for many years. Official admission that such malpractices had in fact taken place largely confirmed some of the allegations made by the Albanian régime about Yugoslavia in the past. Even though Ranković's downfall did not wholly allay Albania's hostility towards Belgrade, it did cut the ground from under some of its later complaints about Yugoslav policies.

The Soviet invasion of Czechoslovakia in August 1968 coupled with the threat to the independence of Romania and Yugoslavia caused Albania to rethink some aspects of its foreign policy. In September it decided to withdraw from the Warsaw Pact. Although the Albanian government had not taken part in its work for about 6 years, it was still an official member of the pact, so could have been asked to allow joint military exercises to take place on its territory. As such exercises had been a prelude to the occupation of Czechoslovakia, the Albanian leaders were determined to prevent the same thing happening in their country. Withdrawal from the Warsaw Pact was immediately followed by talks on defence problems between Peking and Tirana and by the introduction of a scheme for training young people between the ages of six and eighteen to wage "a people's revolutionary war" in case of attack. These developments indicated that the Albanian leaders had taken to heart the Chinese precept that self-reliance should also extend to national defence. Another outcome of the Czechoslovak crisis was to persuade them that they could no longer afford to remain aloof from their immediate neighbours. Realizing that its very independence was at stake, Albania established full diplomatic relations with Yugoslavia in 1971, after 13 years of bitter animosity. Three decades of complete alienation between Greece and Albania were also brought to an end when they exchanged ambassadors in the same year.

Albania's utter dependence on a rising great power like China brought its own special worries and troubles. One of these was the policy of reconciliation between Washington and Peking in the early 1970s. There were fears that Albania might sooner or later become a pawn in China's *realpolitik* as had often happened with other powerful protectors in the past. The Albanian press and radio expressed their displeasure at China's new friendship with the United States by ignoring altogether president Nixon's visit to Peking in February 1972. There were also differences between Peking and Tirana over the enlargement of the European Economic Community after the adherence of Britain, Eire and Denmark. The Chinese saw it as a counterweight to the immense power of the United States and Russia; the Albanians as merely another large grouping of avaricious capitalist states. On the other hand, both countries were opposed to the conference on European security and co-operation. Albania refused to take part either in the preparatory work of the conference or in its final session at Helsinki in July 1975. It was the only European country to do so.

China decided to come to Albania's assistance in the early 1960s not merely on grounds of ideological affinity but also (and perhaps mainly) because the latter was prepared to stand up to Soviet pressure. Mao and his associates hoped to encourage and cultivate the latent anti-Soviet nationalism of some of the other communist countries of eastern Europe by turning Albania into a base from which China's political and ideological message could spread to them. But this hope proved illusory. After taking Albania under its wing, Peking attempted to induce Romania to pursue a more openly anti-Soviet policy. The Romanian leadership, however, refused to take the plunge and proceeded to evolve a knife-edge policy of neutrality in the quarrel between Moscow and Peking. Nevertheless, the quarrel itself did help to strengthen to some extent Romania's defensive nationalism vis-à-vis the Soviet Union. In its quest for friends and allies in Europe China changed its earlier attitude to Yugoslavia. When the Yugoslavs indicated, after the Soviet occupation of Czechoslovakia, that they would oppose by force of arms if necessary any Soviet attempt to subjugate their country, Peking abandoned its doctrinal objections to Tito's régime and resumed diplomatic relations with Belgrade in 1970. Throughout this time Albania was

China's only fully committed ally in Europe. Several powerful radio transmitters were built on Albanian territory during the 1960s for the purpose of spreading Mao's philosophy far and wide. But apart from inspiring or encouraging a few small Maoist groups scattered here and there, their message fell on deaf ears or on ears plugged with the cotton-wool of fear and prudence.

Chapter 8

AGRARIAN AND INDUSTRIAL
REVOLUTIONS

THE PERIOD BETWEEN 1961 and 1965 (which covered
the third 5-year plan) was, according to Hoxha, the most difficult
that Albania had experienced since the second world war. For
this he blamed Russia's decision to deprive the country of economic and technical aid as well as of the service of its experts. The
serious situation that resulted was reflected in the failures of the
economic plan. The projected increase of industrial production
by 39 per cent and of agricultural production by 72 per cent fell
short by 13 and 36 per cent respectively. National income increased by 32 per cent instead of the planned 56 per cent. The
serious drop in food production could not, however, be wholly
ascribed to the vagaries of Soviet policy. It was mainly due to
local causes which have plagued Albanian agriculture, in one
form or another, ever since. These are primitive farming methods,
bad planning, inefficient management of labour and resources,
lack of investment.

After the breach with Moscow the Albanians revealed some of
the economic disagreements which had helped to bring it about.
The Soviet leaders, Hoxha said in November 1966, wanted to
turn Albania into a flourishing agricultural community concentrating on the cultivation of vegetables, fruit and plants for industrial use. The country, they argued, lacked the necessary
natural resources for a programme of full industrialization. But
this conclusion, according to Hoxha, was based on misleading
reports by Soviet experts stationed in Albania who had either
underestimated or deliberately minimized the extent of its mineral
wealth. Under the pretext that members of the communist bloc
should adopt the principle of the international division of labour,
with each country producing the things for which it was best
suited, the Soviet Union was determined to turn these countries
into useful sources of raw materials and food as well as into

markets for Russian industrial equipment and manufactured goods. The Albanians considered the adoption of such a policy tantamount to national suicide.

The organization of the Albanian peasantry was one sphere in which China's cultural revolution has had a marked effect. The first collective farms, as we saw earlier, were set up shortly after the second world war, whereas large-scale collectivization did not come into force until the mid-1950s. By the end of the decade over 50 per cent of the arable land had been placed under either state or co-operative administration. This left in private hands the poor land of the mountainous districts of the north which, besides being of minor economic significance, was not particularly suited to consolidation into large agricultural concerns. Nevertheless, in 1967 it was decided to bring this land too under public ownership, thus making Albanian farming the most thoroughly collectivized in the whole of eastern Europe. The motives behind this final spurt were political and ideological rather than economic. The highlands possessed certain special features that rendered them untrustworthy in the eyes of a hard-pressed revolutionary régime. Just as in the past they had been centres of resistance to Turkish domination, they were one of the last strongholds of opposition to communist rule. The clan system with its extended families, its special loyalties and its ancient social customs had managed to survive in these areas, largely inhabited by Roman Catholics, who had been some of the most determined opponents of the régime from the very beginning. The collectivization campaign was carried out in various stages. At first each village constituted a single co-operative farm; then several villages were amalgamated into a larger unit; finally these units were joined to the nearest and more prosperous collective farms of the lowlands which provided them with credits, technical equipment, seeds and fertilizers. The hilly farms were given the task of growing potatoes. By the early 1970s about half their annual income derived from this crop. A number of secret trials which were reported to have been held in 1967 indicated that the collectivization drive in the highlands had encountered strong opposition.

The general policy of the government was to form larger units by amalgamating collective farms wherever possible. By 1970 there were 805 collective farms compared with 1,484 in 1960. The average farm covered some 2,220 acres and comprised four to five villages. In addition, there were forty large state farms which cultivated one-fifth of the country's arable land. Private plots had been reduced to a minimum and were clearly destined to be abolished altogether. They had only managed to survive because they looked after the greater part of the livestock. One of the earliest and most successful collective farms is located at Këmishtaj in the fertile plain of Myzeqe. In 1950 it consisted of 550 acres of land cultivated by fifty families. Within 20 years its size had grown to 2,650 acres and the number of working families to five hundred. The farm maintains three primary schools, one secondary school, an agricultural college, as well as various welfare and social services. Women make up nearly 60 per cent of its labour force. They also occupy many executive positions. Following the example set by Tachai, the production brigade of an agricultural commune in the Chinese province of Shansi, Këmishtaj became the model to be emulated by all other Albanian collective farms.

The government had tried for a number of years to make the country self-sufficient in grain. Although the gap between consumption and production was gradually narrowed, Albania had to make up its grain deficit throughout the 1970s by imports. There were also almost endemic shortages of meat, eggs and milk. Far from helping to solve any of these problems, total collectivization had tended to aggravate them. Under the new bureaucratic system, peasants had less incentive to work harder than was strictly necessary. Slackness was also encouraged by poor organization. In 1964, for instance, one-third of the agricultural labour force did between 200 and 220 days' work; 4 per cent did no work at all.

Petroleum is Albania's oldest industry. Bitumen mining flourished at Selenicë, near Vlorë, under the Romans. This was developed by various foreign concerns during the nineteenth century. But the real beginning of the country's oil industry dated from the first world war when the Italian army, which then held the greater part of southern Albania, discovered oil deposits at Drashovicë, also in the vicinity of Vlorë. As independent Albania was incapable of developing its oil resources between the two great wars, exploratory concessions were granted to British, Italian, American and French oil companies. However, when fascist Italy secured a dominant position in the country, the petroleum industry, like other mining concerns, became an

Italian monopoly. From 1926 onwards production was concentrated in the oil fields of Patos and Kuçovë (later renamed Stalin). Between 1926 and 1936 annual production rose from 1,000 to 48,330 tons. Lacking fuel resources of its own, Italy was prepared to invest capital and technological skill in the Albanian oil industry even though such investment brought modest returns. The Italians built a 49-mile pipeline linking the Kuçovë field with the port of Vlorë. As most of the crude oil went to Italy for processing, Albania was reduced to buying from Romania all the finished oil products it required, paying as much as thirteen times the price it received for the crude oil it exported. This form of exploitation was made possible by Italy's military, political and economic predominance.

The Italian fascist régime intensified oil production during the second world war, raising it from 126,800 tons in 1938 to 250,000 tons by 1942. In the years immediately after the war the industry was managed by an Albanian-Yugoslav joint company. But owing to lack of investment and technical expertise, output dropped in 1948 to one-fifth of the figure it had reached 6 years earlier. After the break with Tito the situation was completely altered. The industry passed under the management of the Soviet Union which provided the necessary capital and technical assistance. Production gradually increased and Albanian crude oil was exported to some of the countries of eastern Europe where it was refined; Albania got in return the finished petroleum products it needed. Two developments occurred in 1957 which were of crucial importance not only for the future of the oil industry but also, indirectly, for the country's relations with the Soviet Union. A refinery, built at Cerrik with Russian aid, came into full operation; a new source of crude oil of higher quality than hitherto was discovered at Patos. Output was almost doubled and plans were made to raise production to 2,300,000 tons by 1960. However, the Russians were not prepared to finance this expansion on two grounds: at that time they were themselves looking for world markets for their own large surplus of oil; the Albanian leaders had already begun to show the first signs of rebellion against Moscow. So they were bluntly told by Khrushchev that further investments in the oil industry were a waste of money. The Chinese, on the other hand, took a much more sanguine view of Albania's industrial development. They were willing to provide financial and technical aid for expanding oil production and for developing other mining concerns. As a result of this aid, the output of crude oil rose steadily to 2,700,000 tons, the figure claimed for 1975.

Albania's coal deposits consisted of comparatively high quality lignites or brown coal. The first coal mine was established at Memaliaj, near the southern town of Tepelenë, in 1918. Although a number of other deposits were discovered later, Memaliaj remains the chief source of supply. Coal production was negligible before the second world war, but has since continued to rise in order to meet the country's growing industrial needs. The average annual output for 1964–67 was 362,000 metric tons and reached 668,000 metric tons in 1970.

One of the major successes of the post-war period has been the harnessing of Albania's rivers and waterfalls to the generation of hydro-electric power. Its potential has been conservatively estimated at 2.5 million kilowatts. Work on the first hydro-electric plant at Selitë was begun by the Italians during the second world war and was eventually completed by the communist régime. It supplies the capital, Durrës and Elbasan with electric power. Several other medium-sized plants were constructed subsequently, partly with Soviet and partly with Chinese aid. Chinese capital and technical assistance have been solely responsible for the erection of two large hydro-electric installations in northern Albania : the "Mao Tse-tung" at Vau i Dejës with a capacity of 200,000 kilowatts, the other at Fierzë planned to produce 400,000 kilowatts. In 1967 it was decided to create a power network covering the whole country; within three years rural electrification was completed. In view of the fact that Albania's village and hamlet communities (some 2,550 of them) had never had modern power supplies of any kind, this was no mean achievement. As a result of this development, in 1974 the Albanian government concluded an agreement with Yugoslavia for supplying a number of industrial concerns in Montenegro with electricity.

Great strides have also been made in the exploitation of metal ores. Albania is the largest producer of chrome ore in Europe (barring the Soviet Union) and the sixth largest in the world. Chrome mining, which is located at Bulqizë and Kukës in the north and at Pogradec in the south, was developed on a modest scale between the two great wars. Between 1964 and 1975 production expanded from 307,000 to 900,000 tons a year. Copper mining in the northern districts of Rubik, Kukës and Kurbnesh had also shown a marked upsurge during the post-war years. Output rose from 145,000 tons in 1964 to 600,000 tons in 1975. A copper wire and cable factory was built at Shkodër.

Unlike most other branches of the mining industry, iron-ore extraction only began in the late 1950s. The country evidently possessed sufficient resources to warrant the building (with Chinese help) of its first steel works near the town of Elbasan. When it became fully operational the plant was anticipated to process 800,000 tons of iron-nickel and yield 250,000 tons of steel products a year. At the inauguration of the steel works in October 1971, the deputy prime minister Adil Carçani said :

The plant marks the beginning of a new stage in Albania's industrial development : the creation of a metallurgical industry with proper facilities for smelting and processing iron-nickel ore, one of the country's greatest resources. In addition to helping us become less dependent on imports, the plant will increase our means of production, thus enabling the various branches of industry, particularly engineering, to advance much more rapidly.

The decentralization of the economy and the general improvement of planning methods were widely discussed throughout the 1960s and the early 1970s. The first steps were taken in 1966 to dismantle the old structure of central planning and control. Individual enterprises were made independent, at least in theory, and were placed under the supervision of local government bodies which were granted some of the powers formerly exercised by the central planning authorities. For instance, the only obligation collective farms had was to hand over to the state certain specified quantities of their produce; otherwise they were free to plan their production and regulate the incomes of their members as they saw fit. Industrial enterprises were likewise encouraged to produce goods which the economy needed and consumers were prepared to buy, regardless of any global production targets. In other words, a somewhat half-hearted attempt was made to introduce the first principles of a market economy in place of the old system of abstract production targets laid down by planners who had no time for the demands of ordinary consumers. But the task of changing direction in economic planning and management proved an extremely difficult one. In the first place, bureaucratic habits and the reluctance to assume responsibility had become so ingrained that few officials were prepared to try out new ideas and methods. Secondly, economic reforms of any kind, however mild, were unpopular with some of the party diehards. They feared that the more independent enterprises would in time give rise to a new class of bourgeois-minded technocrats that was thought to have emerged in some of the other communist countries of eastern Europe. Such fears were expressed in June 1974 by Hysni Kapo, a member of the politburo, when he said: "The bitter experience of the Soviet Union and other revisionist states showed that by exaggerating the rôle of specialists and underestimating that of the working class, the intelligentsia, although composed of the sons of the people, became the main strata of a new bourgeoisie and a powerful supporter of the restoration of capitalism". Young economists and managers were in the forefront of the drive for more efficient and less bureaucratic economic planning. Enver Hoxha himself tried to steer a middle course between the conservative hardliners and the more progressive wing of the party. About 4 years after the first decentralization measures were introduced, he was complaining that the central planning authorities were still engaged in settling minor issues and so were either delaying or ignoring altogether the major policy decisions that should concern them. He thought there was a real danger that local party and government organizations would try to dominate agricultural and industrial enterprises in much the same way as the central authorities had done in the past. From statements made by Hoxha and other official spokesman it became clear that the struggle against the old system of bureaucratic control would be long and arduous and that economic reforms (the use of the term itself was taboo) would continue to be hamstrung by ideological and political inhibitions.

The change in the pattern of Albania's foreign trade that took place in the later 1960s reflected the progress made in industrial development, particularly in mining. Whereas during the early post-war years the country's export trade had been restricted to mineral, petroleum and farming products, a certain degree of diversification had occurred by 1970. Chrome, iron-nickel, oil, bitumen, copper and copper wire constituted 55 per cent of the total volume of exports; the remaining 45 per cent was covered by tobacco, cigarettes, dairy produce, fruit, vegetables and various light industry goods. The volume of imports was shared between machinery and industrial equipment (80 per cent) and grain and consumer goods (20 per cent). However, despite these achievements, Albania has had a permanent foreign trade deficit since the end of the second world war; this was first covered by the Soviet Union and subsequently by China.

One of the numerous problems facing the communist régime in 1945 was the lack of an adequate system of transport and communications. The foundations of a road network were laid by the Austro-Hungarian military authorities during the first world war. This was improved and extended, mainly by the Italians between 1925 and 1943. When Italy's occupation ended in 1943 there were about 2,370 kilometres of roads potentially capable of handling heavy motor traffic and 370 kilometres of secondary roads. But a substantial part of the road system was either badly damaged or destroyed during the second world war as a result of guerilla operations and counter-measures by the armies of occupation. After the war great efforts were made to repair and enlarge the system by pressing into service young people and political prisoners, very misleadingly classified as "volunteers" by official sources. This meant, in effect, relying heavily on unpaid and unskilled labour. A labour force of this type had also been largely responsible for building Albania's railway system stretching (270 kilometres by the mid-1970s) from the capital to the centres of three industrial areas : north to Laç (chemicals), east to Elbasan and Prenjas (metallurgy), south to Fier (oil). There are plans to link Laç with Shkodër and Fier with the port of Vlorë.

Albania's population had slightly more than doubled since the end of the war, reaching 2,378,000 in 1975. The annual rate of population growth had varied from 19.9 per thousand in pre-war years to an average of 29 per thousand in 1951–65. The birth rate rose to its highest point in 1955 with 43.8 per thousand; during the following two decades it showed a gradual decline, dropping to 30.6 per thousand at the end of 1974. The death rate fell from 11 to 7.2 per thousand in the same period. This rapid rise in population brought about a parallel increase in the number and size of urban centres. Tirana, which before the war was a small town of 25,000 inhabitants, became one of the country's leading industrial cities with a population of 180,000 which continued to rise. Other main towns with 50,000 to 60,000 inhabitants are Shkodër, the ports of Durrës and Vlorë, Elbasan and Korçë. However, despite this port-war urban expansion, 66 per cent of the population still lived in fairly small and widely dispersed villages and hamlets in the mid-1970s.

No other country in Europe has had a more formidable housing problem to contend with since the war than Albania. Not only had housing been badly neglected for many generations but the shortage was aggravated by the destruction of several thousand houses during the war years. The attempts of the communist régime to cope with the problem were almost continually hampered by its determination to devote the greater part of the country's resources to the development of both heavy and light industries. According to official sources, 185,000 new flats and houses were built between 1945 and 1970. However, the building of an average of 7,400 dwellings a year completely failed to meet the country's requirements at a time when the annual population growth was between 40,000 and 50,000. (The shortage was further aggravated by a number of earthquakes that took place in 1967, 1969 and 1975.) Indeed, the problem became so serious that it was aired in the press and in public speeches. For instance, Hoxha admitted in December 1967 that the country as a whole, but especially the cities, faced an acute housing crisis. He spoke of cases in which as many as five people shared one room. Although he deplored this state of affairs, for which he blamed the industrialization programme and the rate of population growth, he had no real solution to offer. In a newspaper article published in April 1971, a senior local party official warned the authorities that if serious social problems such as poor housing were not openly and frankly discussed in order to discover their root causes, a situation might arise in which people's submerged discontent could break out into violence.

Albania's incomes policy was subjected throughout the post-war period to an intense tug-of-war between egalitarianism on the one hand and productivity and efficiency on the other. At the beginning it was hoped that so-called "moral" incentives would serve to make the very low level of wages acceptable to industrial and agricultural workers. But such incentives proved hollow and the very principle of egalitarianism was severely criticized by party leaders during the early 1970s. The monthly wages of industrial workers varied from 400 to 1,500 leks (5 leks to one US dollar, according to an artificial rate of exchange) depending on their qualifications and experience as determined by a seven-grade system. But there were practically no differentials in the incomes of collective farmers whose average monthly wage was about 400 leks. Party and government leaders openly admitted that there could be no real advance in agriculture so long as the marked discrepancy between the wages of industrial workers and collective farmers persisted.

A new incomes policy—an odd mixture of egalitarianism and an attempt to remedy some of its past excesses—was introduced in April 1976. The salaries of party and government officials and of commanders of the armed forces were reduced by 4 to 25 per cent; those of university teachers and members of research institutes by 14 to 22 per cent. All royalties and special bonuses paid to writers, artists and scientists were lowered by 30 to 50 per cent. The grading system which regulated the remuneration of agricultural specialists working in state and collective farms was replaced by a single rate applicable to all of them. University graduates were to receive during their first two years of employment the rate of the highest-paid workers in the same enterprise. The main beneficiaries of the new policy were state and collective farm workers whose wages were increased by 50 per cent. As a result of these changes, the differentials between average wages and higher salaries were narrowed to a ratio of about one to two. The pensions of farm workers were also raised, bringing them into line with those paid to industrial workers. The official reasons put forward for reducing higher salaries were to bring the living standard of the privileged strata of officials, technocrats and professional people closer to the general level of the majority of the population; to discourage the pursuit of careers in the ranks of the bureaucracy; to "enhance the feeling of proletarian modesty" among members of the professional classes. The improvement of farm workers' wages was intended "to raise their revolutionary drive so as to bring about an increase in the production of bread grain and other crops as well as in the number of livestock". But whilst such an improvement was overdue and could in time help increase the efficiency of agriculture, the drastic reduction in the higher salaries appeared to be an ideological nod in the direction of egalitarianism. At about the same time the question of more or less equal remuneration for all employees was espoused by Chinese radicals in their public debates with the moderates after Chou En-lai's death in January 1976. Although the official statement on the new Albanian incomes policy dismissed the notion that it had anything to do with what it called "petit-bourgeois egalitarianism", this argument is unlikely to have proved very convincing to those people whose standard of living was brought down so abruptly. Caught between the urgent need to increase food production and the chimera of an egalitarian society, the régime may well have antagonized a political, military and professional élite with which it could ill afford to be on bad terms for long, and so risk turning it into a source of festering social and political discontent.

The first three decades of communist rule could be described as a period utterly dominated by Marx's theory of primitive accumulation. This maintains that the capitalist system of production had resulted from the dispossession of peasants and craftsmen and the creation of a mass of wage labourers at the mercy of a new ruling class. By the same token, the labour and privations of Albania's peasants and industrial workers—their long hours of work, their low incomes, their wretched housing and poor living conditions—were harnessed to the highly centralized and capricious planning methods of a tyrannical communist régime. One of the reasons that the latter had been so reluctant to allow any foreign press correspondents or tourists in large numbers to visit the country was its desire to prevent the outside world from observing at close quarters these unpleasant features of Albanian life. This desire for seclusion was reinforced by the great turmoil inspired by the Chinese cultural revolution, which is the subject of the next chapter.

Chapter 9

IDEOLOGICAL AND POLITICAL TURMOIL

AFTER HAVING SURVIVED the rift with his two major opponents, Tito and Khrushchev, Enver Hoxha must have realized by the early 1960s that the policy of Stalinist repression he had pursued for so long had led to stagnation and widespread apathy. There was a wide gulf between the communist party (with a membership of about 60,000) and the ordinary people. This was particularly true of the countryside where party members were very thin on the ground. So it is not perhaps surprising that his first encounter with Mao Tse-tung's revolutionary doctrines hit him with the force of a blinding revelation. He embraced them eagerly and decided to adapt them to the conditions of his own country. Mao's social and political ideas appealed to the Albanian leader's dogmatic and fanatical cast of mind as well as to his desire to get larger sections of the population, not just the communist minority, directly involved in party and government affairs.

The political concept of the so-called "mass line", which the Albanian communists took over, has been defined by Mao in these esoteric terms:

all correct leadership is necessarily from the masses, to the masses. This means: take the ideas of the masses (scattered and unsystematic ideas) and concentrate them (through study turn them into concentrated and systematic ideas), then go to the masses and propagate and explain these ideas until the masses embrace them as their own, hold fast to them and translate them into action, and test the correctness of these ideas in such action. Then once again concentrate ideas from the masses and once again take them to the masses so that the ideas are persevered in and carried through. And so on, over and over again in an endless spiral, with the ideas becoming more correct, more vital and richer each time.[1]

Closely allied to Mao's belief in the need to forge lasting links between the majority of the people and the communist party was the determination he had shown throughout most of his career to ensure that the bureaucratic machine was subjected to constant control in order to prevent it from achieving an independent, all-powerful position in Chinese society. Among the methods he had employed from time to time to exercise such control were so-called political re-education and rectification campaigns. During the cultural revolution, however, these methods gave way to the violence of the Red Guards which was directed against the bureaucracy of the communist party itself.

But perhaps the tenet of Mao's philosophy which has had the most profound and abiding influence on Albania's internal development is the theory of permanent or uninterrupted revolution. One of the lessons that Mao sought to drive home with his agitation of 1966–69 was that the transformation of China's society, the renewal of the patterns of thought and behaviour of its people, could only be brought about by means of a prolonged and intricate revolutionary process. The Albanian communists not only accepted this precept with alacrity but found themselves in complete agreement with the claim of the Chinese Maoists that the revolutionary practices of the Soviet Union and its European allies were hardly the vehicle for achieving the kind of radical changes their two archaic peasant societies had to undergo if they were to become thoroughly modernized communist societies.

Albania's own cultural revolution was officially set in motion by an "open letter" which the central committee of the party addressed to all communists, workers and members of the armed forces in March 1966. Its main theme was the evils of bureaucratic methods. The type of bureaucracy which had arisen in the Soviet Union, the letter pointed out,

had been of great help to Khrushchevian revisionists in their seizure of power. The creation of a privileged stratum of party

---

[1] Quoted in S. Schram (ed.), *Authority, Participation and Cultural Change in China*, Cambridge University Press, Cambridge, 1973, pp. 29–30.

and government officials, economic managers, artists, scientists and cultural figures, who received large salaries and enjoyed a far higher standard of living than the working class, had made possible the fostering of a revisionist outlook . . . Such tendencies must be eliminated in Albania to enable it to avoid the pitfalls of the Soviet experience.

The document then enumerated the measures that would be taken to rid the country of the evils stemming from an over-inflated bureaucratic machine. All laws and regulations in force would be revised and simplified in consultation with the people. The people's assembly (parliament) and the elected local councils would exercise stricter control than hitherto over central and local government departments. A ruthless campaign would be waged against such malpractices as "white-collar mentality", administrative arrogance, favouritism and nepotism. Great stress was also laid on the need to get people more actively involved in the actual processes of government at every level.

Certain steps were immediately taken to put some of these ideas into practice. Twelve leading party and government officials, among them several politburo members and cabinet ministers, were transferred to the provinces for an indefinite period to supervise the impending revolutionary changes. The number of ministries was reduced from nineteen to thirteen; the number and size of departments within each ministry were also drastically curtailed. (One of the ministries which ominously disappeared altogether was that of justice.) Several thousand party and government employees who were made redundant were switched to what is called productive work; this meant manual labour in most cases. Many writers and artists were also sent to work in factories and collective farms.

In trying to cope with the growth of bureaucracy the régime faced a situation reminiscent of the Circumlocution Office in Charles Dickens' *Little Dorrit* :

No public business of any kind could possibly be done at any time, without the acquiescence of the Circumlocution Office. Its finger was in the largest public pie, and in the smallest public tart. It was equally impossible to do the plainest right and to undo the plainest wrong, without the express authority of the Circumlocution Office. If another Gunpowder Plot had been discovered half an hour before the lighting of the match, nobody would have been justified in saving the parliament until there had been a score of boards, half a bushel of minutes, several sacks of official memoranda, and a family vault full of ungrammatical correspondence, on the part of the Circumlocution Office.

The government which had brought this monster into being finally decided to do something about dismantling it because it had become unwieldy and inefficient and because it was thought to provide a comfortable shelter for complacent careerists inherently opposed to radical change of any kind. The ensuing upheaval caused general confusion as well as consternation among those directly affected. But the authorities were prepared for some such reaction. The minister of the interior, Kadri Hasbiu, spoke of political intrigues and fierce propaganda against the new measures perpetrated by "anti-socialist elements and their allies". This opposition was regarded as merely another aspect of the perennial class struggle. The press rebuked several officials who were reluctant to vacate their posts on the grounds that they were being unjustly dismissed or demoted after years of devoted service to the party and government. But these cases were only the tip of an iceberg of discontent which went on seething for many years to come.

The next stage of the revolutionary agitation opened with a speech by Hoxha in February 1967 in which he announced the beginning of other campaigns against bourgeois attitudes, religious practices, the unequal status of women and the pervading spirit of individualism. These campaigns were to be carried out under the direct supervision of party organizations whose members were made accountable for their performance. Hoxha criticized several officials for condoning the practice of arranged marriages between children and the sale of religious icons in their districts. He said that such behaviour would not be tolerated and that communists who infringed the party's revolutionary principles would suffer the same fate as other political opponents had done in the past.

The campaign against religious beliefs and practices throughout 1967, culminating in the closure of all the country's places of worship, was hailed as one of the greatest achievements of

Hoxha's régime. But before this dénouement was reached religious persecution had passed through several fairly distinct phases. In the immediate post-war years, when it felt insecure and beset by numerous difficulties, the régime pursued a relatively moderate policy in its dealings with the Moslem, Orthodox and Roman Catholic communities. However, between the late 1940s and the early 1950s its attitude hardened. The Moslem community (whose membership represented about 70 per cent of the population) was the first to be subjected to direct state interference and control. Instruction in the Moslem faith and mosque attendances were first discouraged, then severely restricted. This was followed by a gradual closure of mosques. The regimentation of the Orthodox church, the next largest religious body embracing roughly 20 per cent of the population, was brought about by replacing independent-minded bishops with bishops who were both loyal to the régime and willing to establish close relations with the Russian Orthodox church in Moscow. Although Roman Catholics formed the smallest religious group in the country, they had perhaps suffered the most savage persecution of all. As the Catholic church had played an important rôle in keeping alive the Albanian language and cultural traditions during the period of Ottoman rule, the régime may have decided to obliterate from popular memory all traces of its historic contribution. The church's links with the Vatican were also seen as dependence on an outside body regarded as intrinsically hostile to communist doctrine. The fact that some of the stiffest opposition to the establishment of communist rule had come from Catholic areas may have helped to reinforce the régime's determination to destroy the Roman Catholic church root and branch. This was done in stages, beginning with the execution or imprisonment of the more influential bishops and members of the clergy. Others were systematically discredited in the eyes of the people by means of crude and vicious propaganda. The independence of the Catholic church was finally made null and void by government decree in July 1951. This severed its links with Rome and established a "national" church completely subservient to the state. Pressure on all religious communities was kept up for several years by such methods as closure of places of worship, persecution of the clergy, endless propaganda against all forms of belief. Harry Hamm, a West German correspondent who visited Albania in the summer of 1961, reported on the state of decay into which many of the country's churches and mosques had been allowed to fall. The faces of the remaining clergy, he noticed, were "full of despair and resignation". Yet he found that despite the merciless persecution, many people, particularly in the northern Catholic areas, were defiantly faithful to their religion and continued to attend church services on Sundays.

Persecution of varying degrees of intensity had been the fate of most religious communities in the Soviet Union, Czechoslovakia, Hungary, Poland and the other communist states of Europe. Yet in the end, their régimes had managed to reach some sort of *modus vivendi* with the weakened Christian and other hierarchies, once these had subscribed to the main policies of the government. Only the Albanian régime was not prepared to accept such a compromise. Its final onslaught on all religious institutions became part of the cultural revolution of 1967. Teams of young agitators were sent out on a national crusade for the express purpose of persuading, cajoling and ultimately forcing people to give up their religious beliefs and practices altogether. The authorities claimed that by the end of the year more than two thousand churches, mosques, monasteries and other religious institutions had been shut down. A special decree revoked the charters under which the three religious communities had operated and proclaimed Albania "the first atheist state in the world". The government had thus violated article 18 of the 1946 constitution which says: "All citizens are guaranteed freedom of conscience and of faith. The religious communities are free in matters of their belief as well as in their outer exercise and practice." This extinction of religious life exemplified the régime's unwillingness to tolerate the existence of extraneous institutions of any kind, however weak, obedient or subservient they might be. Such unparalleled intolerance in matters of personal freedom and conscience was at least partly an outcome of the fanaticism generated by Mao's cultural revolution.

It was admitted that this savage persecution had met with a good deal of opposition. In one northern Catholic district communist campaigners were told that the authorities should make a clear distinction between the policy of removing politically unreliable clergymen and the fundamental human right to believe in God. In a province of central Albania, elderly villagers, among them members of the communist party, objected strongly to the conversion of their mosques into warehouses. The mosque, according to them, was a holy place of silent meditation and prayer; the decision to make it serve a purely secular purpose was tantamount to raising man's hand against God. Beyond reporting that the mosques were eventually closed down, leaving the faithful badly shaken, the official account of the incident does not record what happened to the protesters in the end. But the propagandists did not confine themselves to the art of rational persuasion. According to the Vatican newspaper *Osservatore Romano* (11 July 1967), four Franciscans were burnt to death when a Roman Catholic church and a convent were set on fire at Shkodër in an outbreak of anti-religious violence during the cultural revolution.

However, the claim that the ancient religious beliefs of a whole people could be wiped out by a single exercise in mob agitation and violence proved somewhat premature, to say the least. Hoxha himself realized that the euphoria created by the naïve declaration that Albania had become the world's first godless state was based on a dangerous illusion which could lead to complacency in the ranks of the communist party. In September 1967 he said that the struggle against religious morality and traditions was by no means over and would require prolonged efforts in persuasion and education. This became the central theme of official propaganda during the next few years. What the régime had in fact done was to drive religious practices underground. The new situation became increasingly baffling and intractable for many plodding, doctrinaire party officials. One could deal with overt religious practices by the simple device of outright suppression. But how was one to cope with the tricks and subterfuges to which believers resorted in their daily lives at home or outside it? For instance, during religious feast days the sales in retail shops rose sharply, as did absenteeism. Both Christian and Moslem festivals continued to be celebrated at home in secret. Defrocked priests went on visiting the families of their parishioners; people took part in regular pilgrimages to closed or destroyed places of worship and sites of religious shrines.

Religious persecution in Albania attracted world-wide publicity in December 1972 when Pope Paul VI spoke for the first time in public about the plight of the Roman Catholic church there in an address to the College of Cardinals in Rome. The Pope said the church "seems relegated not only to the peace of silent suffering but to the peace of death. With the shepherds stricken and the flock dispersed one cannot see what human hope remains there for the church". Paul VI referred again to the problem during the Easter celebrations the following April when he declared: "There is still a church which is forced to live, even survive, in the shadow of fear, in the asphyxiating and paralysing obscurity of artificial and oppressive legality". These remarks were prompted by the news that the Albanian Roman Catholic priest Father Stephen Kurti had been executed for the offence of baptising a child in secret. The Albanian news media later confirmed his execution but maintained that the priest had been sentenced to death not for conducting a secret baptism but for spying on behalf of the Vatican, the United States and Great Britain. Father Kurti was first sentenced to 20 years' imprisonment on a similar charge in 1946. On being released in 1962, before completing his sentence, he had carried on, it was claimed, with his earlier religious and political activities. The event led the authorities to take a closer look at the whole strategy and tactics of their anti-religious policy. It was openly recognized that religious beliefs of one kind or another extended not only to the older generation but to young people as well. The blame for this unsatisfactory state of affairs was laid squarely on party organizations which were urged to intensify their atheistic propaganda. One such campaign was mounted throughout the greater part of 1973.

One of the strangest by-products of the régime's anti-religious policy was its concern with the question of people's Moslem and Christian names. Parents were actively discouraged from giving their children names that had any religious association or connotation. From time to time official lists were published with pagan, so-called Illyrian or freshly minted names considered appropriate for the new breed of revolutionary Albanians. But apparently most people took no notice of these lists and continued to give their children the traditional names of their own choosing. So in 1976 the government decided to deprive people of even the freedom of this human personal choice by issuing an order which made it obligatory for children as well as adults to assume non-religious names.

The struggle to achieve women's emancipation was perhaps the most constructive enterprise of the revolutionary tumult of 1967. In this field the communist party had already scored some successes, given the size and complexity of the problem. Before the second world war 90 per cent of the women of Albania were illiterate. They were second-class citizens; in rural areas they carried the heaviest burden of work both at home and in the fields. Although king Zog's government had introduced legislation which in theory prescribed full sex equality, the ancient tribal laws and customs which held women to be chattels still prevailed in some parts of the country. The communist régime made women's liberation from this bondage one of its prime and most urgent tasks. In addition to the motives which had inspired many liberal-minded Albanians since the beginning of the present century, the communists had a number of practical reasons for removing as quickly as possible the cultural and social barriers to the emancipation of women. Having played an important part in the communist resistance movement of the second world war, more and more women demanded full recognition of their legitimate rights in society when peace came. If the régime was to carry out its comprehensive programme of cultural, social and economic reforms, women, who constituted roughly half of the country's population, had to become active members of the general labour force. The cause of their emancipation was greatly enhanced by the prominent position that the wives of the three leading communist politicians—Enver Hoxha, Mehmet Shehu, Hysni Kapo—achieved during the post-war years. Apart from being members of the central committee, each of them held other influential officials posts. That the régime was deadly serious about the problem was made plain by this dire warning that Hoxha issued in February 1967 : "The entire party and country should hurl into the fire and break the neck of anyone who dared trample underfoot the sacred edict of the party on the defence of women's rights". He and his associates did not of course believe that a propaganda campaign lasting a few weeks or months would instantly remove the backward attitudes and customs of many centuries. Their intention was to shock the country into making the cause of women's liberation a burning national issue by mobilizing the largest number of people on its behalf, particularly in the more conservative areas. Official spokesmen laid great stress on the tremendous obstacles that had to be overcome and on the fact that the struggle to secure complete sex equality would have to go on for years, if not generations. Young men and women were given the task of spreading the party's message on women's rights among the more conservative and benighted members of the older generation throughout the land. And as many of these harbingers of revolutionary change were also engaged in the anti-religious campaign, they managed, by a good deal of intellectual sharp practice, to make Christianity and Mohammedanism responsible, among other crimes, for keeping women in perpetual bondage.

Intellectuals were another target of the cultural revolution. After subjecting them to persecution, torment and humiliation of every description for many years, Hoxha's régime sent most of the country's leading writers and artists to work in factories and collective farms ostensibly to enable them to get closer to ordinary people. This was in fact an act of sheer desperation designed to cow the intellectual community into submission. It was the climax of a long, bitter and often muddled clash between the voracious thirst of the young generation for more freedom of thought and expression and the inflexible determination of the communist leadership to throttle such aspirations at their source. The party's fears and suspicions about the rôle of intellectuals and educated people in general had grown with the progress and expansion of education. In the early post-war years, an attempt was made by Sejfulla Maleshova, then president of the writers' union, to work out a moderately liberal cultural policy based on a compromise between Marxist doctrine on the one hand and some of the creative values of national and western traditions on the other. But, as we saw earlier, both this policy and its architect were soon overthrown. Between 1948 and 1961 Albania's intellectual life was dominated by Stalin's doctrine of socialist realism. This meant that writers and artists became mere instruments of government policy and purveyors of official propaganda. Soviet art and literature were held up as exemplars of excellence. Other foreign books and works of art were only made available if they bore Moscow's imprimatur. This rigid system was only marginally affected by Khrushchev's more liberal policies whose influence was quickly contained by the Albanian authorities. The break with the Soviet Union induced Hoxha to take a far more extreme position than hitherto in cultural matters. Now not only western but Soviet and east European cultural influences of every kind were condemned as ideologically dangerous and politically unacceptable. The régime thus created a parched intellectual desert enclosed by a zariba especially erected for the purpose of preventing one of the oldest peoples of Europe from being contaminated by European civilization itself. In this wasteland of arid parochialism, writers and intellectuals found themselves at the mercy of the fluctuating personal opinions, whims and prejudices of the party boss and of his small circle of mediocre aides. Whereas under the Soviet system they at least knew more or less where they stood, the new ideological and cultural landscape offered them very few recognizable signposts to guide their steps.

The Chinese-inspired cultural policy was laid down in October 1965 by Ramiz Alia, Hoxha's mouthpiece on questions of ideology. As his statement is perhaps a unique totalitarian document of our time it deserves to be more widely known than it is. The chief function of literature and art, according to Alia, is to provide young people with the necessary immunity against the poisons of both bourgeois and revisionist ideologies. Foreign literary and artistic theories, based on abstract humanism, classless objectivity, and attachment to pure form, were to be shunned as a real threat to the country's creative endeavour. Special care had to be taken in the selection of western and Soviet books for translation. Alia criticized Albanian radio and theatre orchestras for paying more attention to foreign pop and light music than to national folk music; he said a better balance should be struck between the two genres. Films imported from the west and the Soviet bloc should also be closely scrutinized as they were all steeped in an alien morality. Albanian writers and artists should look inwards and concentrate on the life and work of the "heroes of our time", i.e. the country's industrial workers, farmers and members of the intelligentsia. This meant giving their undivided attention to purely national themes as interpreted by the party. The first open clash between this policy of suffocating control and the intellectual community's devotion to a modicum of freedom and truth occurred in June 1966. The newspaper of the communist party published a highly critical review of a novel called *The Tunnel* by the young writer Dhimiter Xhuvani, based on his personal observations while working at an hydro-electric construction site. He was accused of portraying it as a place where workers faced a life of hardship, dreary monotony and sudden death, after being either forced to go there or else lured by high wages. The only relief from this miserable existence was drunkenness, brutality and sleep. The paper condemned the book as a tissue of lies and distortions inspired by decadent aesthetic values. After this severe reprimand, Xhuvani's novel was banned and the official responsible for its publication sacked.

What the novelist had tried to convey was that life for many Albanian workers was "solitary, poor, nasty, brutish and short". But the party reminded him and his fellow writers that they were quite mistaken if they thought that their job was to depict reality exactly as they saw it. Their job was to paint a glamorous picture of society in glowing primary colours, one that could inspire people to accomplish great heroic feats, rather than help them understand the world around them or increase their self-awareness.

Xhuvani's banned novel was not the only sign of dissent during the early stages of the cultural revolution. Manush Myftiu, a member of the politburo, disclosed in a newspaper article that both active and passive resistance to the new wave of intellectual repression were widespread. He wrote that many intellectuals complained in private that the party leadership was utterly opposed to the classics of world literature, art and science, that it banned foreign books and films, and was unwilling to permit the slightest degree of cultural freedom. Places where these and other forms of dissent existed included the editorial offices of several newspapers and periodicals, the national theatre, the school of dramatic art, some of the faculties of the university of Tirana. Myftiu added that special measures would be taken if this dangerous intellectual agitation did not come to an end soon.

Alexander Dubček's reform movement in Czechoslovakia in 1968 and the student riots against Gomulka's régime in Poland introduced a new disturbing element in the Albanian situation. Hoxha himself expressed his alarm about developments in Prague and Warsaw when he said shortly afterwards: "I call on the party and the working class to view these events with deep concern and not to think they are only happening in revisionist countries and therefore have nothing to do with us". He had good reasons to be alarmed. The Czechoslovak and Polish disturbances had struck sympathetic chords even in beleaguered Albania. At one industrial enterprise several workers were reported to have claimed the right to criticize and, if necessary, oppose the decisions of the local party organization. Other reports spoke of sharp clashes at another concern as well as of the dismissal of several enterprise managers, collective farm directors and trade-union officials. Intellectual ferment inspired by the Czechoslovak reforms also spread to the university of Tirana. A correspondent of the Italian communist newspaper

L'Unità (21 July 1969) reported that thirty university students had been expelled for demanding more freedom of thought and discussion.

The whole intellectual scene and the effect that the cultural revolution had had upon it were reviewed at a meeting of the union of writers and artists in April 1969. Its president, Dhimiter Shuteriqi, openly admitted his own and his colleagues' failure to implement the policies of the régime in literature and art. Albanian literary and artistic works no longer reflected the country's "socialist reality" and therefore made no real contribution to the revolutionary changes that were taking place. There had even been a serious decline in the number of translated foreign books. What Shuteriqi was in fact saying in a roundabout way was that greater repression had bred indifference and mediocrity. Yet despite these acknowledged failures, there was no sign whatever that absolute party control would be relaxed.

The last major campaign of the agitation of the 1960s was the so-called workers' control movement. This was theoretically meant to serve a twofold purpose : to function as a more or less permanent check on the bureaucracy, particularly on its technocratic élite; to train workers in the rudiments of participation in management. At the beginning of the cultural revolution, party, government and co-operative employees were encouraged to use wall posters for the purpose of criticizing errant or inefficient officials and for airing grievances. But this Chinese device proved ineffective and even ludicrous. The posters degenerated into sordid graffiti for settling personal scores and ventilating spicy local gossip. The system of workers' control was an attempt to divert genuine grievances and complaints into more constructive channels. At the same time, the mere notion of spontaneity or freedom of action on the part of the workers was completely ruled out. When a team of workers was asked to inspect an industrial enterprise, a trading association or a government department, its duty was to find out whether the party directives were being complied with. The whole procedure of inspection and control was kept under the strict supervision of the authorities. This drive, too, caused a good deal of confusion in the minds of a people inured to the harsh discipline of obeying orders, working hard and generally minding their own business. The theory, if not the practice, of workers' control was therefore kept alive by means of repetitive propaganda throughout most of the 1970s.

Albania's cultural revolution was formally brought to a close towards the end of 1969, when Mao's own revolution, which had set the pattern, was also wound up. The régime had several good reasons for changing direction when it did. After four years of bitter social and political strife and intense ideological regimentation, the people were exhausted, bewidered and resentful. There was a great deal of restlessness and discontent among intellectuals and young people in general—two groups which Hoxha's régime could least afford to drive into a huddle of permanent opposition, especially as those under the age of thirty made up nearly 60 per cent of the population. Furthermore, the Soviet invasion of Czechoslovakia in the summer of 1968 and its aftermath caused as much alarm and fear in Tirana as it did in Bucharest or Belgrade. This was a time for healing domestic wounds, not exacerbating them.

Perhaps the most tangible outcome of four years of incessant turmoil was a purely destructive one : turning the country's churches, mosques and other religious institutions into public recreation centres, sport palaces, offices, storehouses and so on. On the other hand, the policy of pruning the vast bureaucratic establishment, by which the régime had set such great store, turned out to be a failure. By 1972 it was clear that far from contracting in size, the bureaucratic monster had gone on growing merrily since the heady days of 1966. No sooner had one set of tentacles of Albania's creaky, top-heavy Circumlocution Office been lopped than new ones sprouted in rich profusion. The press was full of accounts of this unhealthy growth For instance, the number of officials employed by the local-government adminstration of the Tirana district had increased by 2,300 between 1966 and 1971. Other local government bodies showed similar increases. The tendency to proliferation was also present in central government departments. The staff of the ministry of education had increased by 80 per cent during the same period. What worried the authorities, apart from the sheer rise in the number of civil servants, was the fact that most of the new recruits were members of the communist party. This meant that the gulf separating the régime from the mass of the people was wider than ever. In an attempt to remedy the situation, the leadership fell back on the hoary routine of more propaganda and more empty rhetoric. But the effort was wasted. Some 3 years later it was disclosed that the expansion of the central bureaucracy, in particular, was proceeding remorselessly.

Although the large-scale revolutionary campaigns were over by 1969, they continued to have important repercussions and ramifications for several years to come. The sullen rebellion of young intellectuals became a constant source of anxiety to the government. Books, plays, radio and television programmes were continually subjected to criticism and abuse on the grounds that they had strayed from the orthodox party line. Writers were rebuked for falling under the influence of Freud, Jean-Paul Sartre and Albert Camus. Poets were exhorted to stop contemplating trees, flowers or their own souls and concentrate instead on the problems and aspirations of the working class. Young people were told that their attachment to long hair, mini-skirts, narrow trousers and pop music amounted to abandoning the desperate struggle against bourgeois and revisionist decadence. When theatre managers complained in private that the leadership had forgotten that Albania was part of Europe and that its people could not be permanently cut off from Europe's civilization, the infinite self-righteousness of the party reasserted itself. Geography or no geography, Albanians had to be protected from the wicked influences of Europe. This was a matter of life and death as it concerned the very survival of socialist society. The leaders' constant harping on the dangers of uninhibited experimenting in the arts showed that they were under strong pressure to pursue a somewhat less repressive cultural policy.

In the summer of 1973 the régime passed from rhetoric to action. Most of the officials of the writers' and artists' union were sacked, including its president, Dhimiter Shuteriqi, who had held the post since 1956. The leadership of the youth movement was also radically overhauled. Two members of the central committee of the communist party, Fadil Paçrami and Todi Lubonja, were expelled from the party for unspecified grave offences against official policy. Paçrami had for years combined the function of chairman of the people's assembly with that of hack propagandist of the régime. Lubonja was a former youth leader and director of the Albanian broadcasting service.

During the next few years the purges spread to the higher ranks of the party and government. In October 1974 Beqir Balluku, minister of defence since 1953, was dropped from the government without any official explanation. He also ceased being a member of the party's politburo. Balluku's removal from the political scene was accompanied by changes in the military and political leadership of the armed forces. About a year later three other ministers were sacked under equally mysterious circumstances : Abdyl Kellezi, deputy prime minister and chairman of the state planning commission; Koço Theodhosi, minister of industry; Kiço Ngjela, minister of trade. Although there was no hard evidence for the motives behind these dismissals, they seemed to reflect serious disagreements within the communist hierarchy over important issues of domestic and foreign policy. The removal of Kellezi, one of the country's leading technocrats and the man responsible for negotiating several economic agreements with China, was preceded by the inspection of his department carried out by a workers' control team. After thanking the members of the team for pointing out his shortcomings, Kellezi told them that if they took a close look at other central government departments they would find that many of them were at fault too.

Albania's upheavals of the 1960s and 1970s bore, as we have seen, the strong imprint of Mao's revolutionary doctrines. Yet Hoxha took great pains not to admit in public the immense debt he owed to the Chinese leader. Both his vanity and his extreme nationalism may have prompted him to claim that the revolutionary campaigns he had inflicted on the country since the mid-1960s were his own contribution to the theory and practice of modern communism. Yet there is no doubt that had it not been for Mao's cultural revolution, Albania's internal development would have taken a very different course. What Hoxha had learned from Stalin were the basic techniques of achieving and holding on to power as well as the most effective methods of carrying out certain specific political, economic and social changes. Mao's philosophy had helped to modify his Stalinist thinking in the sense of making it much more ambitious in its revolutionary objectives and less dependent on purely coercive methods. The effect that this modified thinking had had on the Albanian communist party and on the country as a whole was somewhat paradoxical. As the crude, uncompromising Stalinism of the earlier years had tended to recede into the background, ideological, political and social fanaticism had simultaneously increased both in scope and intensity. When Albania was part of the Soviet empire only members of the communist party and of its immediate subsidiary bodies were directly involved in political and ideological agitation. The rest of the population were, by and large, either victims or passive onlookers of party and government policy. After the alliance with China all this changed. Not only did the thinking and general outlook of Hoxha and the other leaders become overweeningly utopian, arrogant and unyielding but most, if not all, sections of the community were systematically injected with ever-increasing doses of ideological fanaticism and political intolerance.

China's millions had, from Mao's point of view, two desirable characteristics : they were both poor and blank (in other words, backward). Their poverty made them highly receptive to revolutionary change whereas their blankness meant that they could be treated like empty sheets of paper ready to be filled with brave revolutionary theories. Taking a leaf out of Mao's book, Hoxha decided to scribble his own revolutionary hieroglyphics on the blank sheet of Albania's poor and backward peasants. But he was to discover that there was all the difference in the world between the abstract theory (Maoist or any other) and the actual feasibility of moulding the minds and hearts of human beings as if they were inert putty. The dissent to which the repression of the various phases of the cultural revolution gave rise revealed that three decades of one of the most tyrannical and bigoted rules in the world had not been able to kill the spirit of intellectual and political freedom.

Following the example set by China in 1975, Albania adopted a new constitution the following year; this replaced the one that had been in force since the end of the second world war. Its purpose was to codify the political, economic and social changes that had occurred during the preceding decade as well as some of the methods which had made these changes possible. In addition to being longer than the Chinese constitution (115 articles as against 30) the Albanian constitution is a more elaborate and uncompromising document.

The country's official designation is changed from the people's republic to the people's socialist republic of Albania. Articles 10 and 11 prescribe that workers exercise direct control over government departments, economic and social organizations as well as participate in regular campaigns against bureaucracy and liberalism. The development of the country's socialist economy is based on the principle of self-reliance, reinforced by aid from other socialist states. However, the constitution forbids granting concessions to companies or institutions belonging to capitalist and revisionist states (i.e. Yugoslavia, the Soviet Union and its allies) or obtaining financial credits from them (article 26). The preamble states that the foundations of religious belief have been abolished, whilst article 36 asserts that the Albanian state does not recognize any religion and actively supports atheistic propaganda. This is in sharp contrast with the Chinese constitution which includes religious freedom among fundamental human rights. On the question of these rights the constitution is far more rigid and restrictive than most other communist constitutions. Although it states that "citizens enjoy freedom of speech, press, organization, association, assembly and freedom to take part in public demonstrations" (article 52) this is flatly contradicted by the assertion that "rights and duties of citizens are dependent on reconciling the interests of the individual with those of socialist society, giving priority to the general interest. The rights of citizens are inseparable from the fulfilment of their duties and cannot be exercised in opposition to the socialist order" (article 38). But as the communist régime itself decided what the interests of society were at any given moment it thereby also determined what rights individuals can or cannot enjoy. Articles 92, 93 and 94, which deal with national defence, lay down that the country's armed forces are directed by a defence council headed by the first secretary of the communist party who is also commander-in-chief. All agreements accepting the capitulation or occupation of the country are made treasonable acts. The stationing of foreign military bases and troops on Albanian territory is also forbidden. These provisions brought Albania into line with Romania and Yugoslavia which adopted similar constitutional devices after the Soviet invasion of Czechoslovakia in 1968.

The 1976 constitution could be interpreted as Hoxha's political testament by means of which he hoped to make sure that his successors would preserve intact the whole structure of his own régime. It thus reflected his great fear that the leader or leaders who came after him might tamper with Albania's self-centred economic system by inviting foreign investments or even endanger the country's very existence by capitulation or by allowing foreign troops or military bases to be established on its territory. However, just as the highly ambiguous constitutional provisions on human rights are declaratory and theoretical and hence always liable to be violated, as they had often been in the past, so there could be no guarantee that the written safeguards designed to perpetuate Hoxha's régime in its pristine form would not be violated in the future.

Chapter 10

CULTURAL AND SOCIAL CHANGES

ALBANIA'S SINGLE MOST impressive post-war achievement was the expansion of its educational facilities. This had
taken place in the face of enormous difficulties and obstacles,
ranging from the heritage of illiteracy, the acute shortage of
teachers, of financial and technical resources, to almost complete
dependence on foreign aid and the communist régime's patho-
logical concern about the political reliability of the generations
that would benefit most from the new opportunities. After the
break with Moscow it became fashionable for the Albanian
leaders to play down the assistance they had received from
Russia in many fields, but even they found it difficult to deny
the valuable Soviet contribution to the development of education
between 1948 and 1961.

The Soviet system of education was adopted shortly after the
second world war when seven-grade schools (four primary, three
lower secondary) were made compulsory. In secondary education
an attempt was made to combine some of the pre-war grammar
schools (gymnasiums) with new professional and technical colleges
along Soviet lines. These provided 3- or 4-year courses in agriculture, engineering, economics, oil technology and medicine.
Special schools for the rapid training of teachers were also set up
and an impetus given to adult education. The Soviet Union provided Albania with textbooks, technical equipment as well as
with teachers and educational experts. Russian became the main
foreign language taught in secondary schools. Great efforts were
also made to teach it on a wider national scale. The foundations
of the country's higher education were laid during this period
with the setting up of several institutes and colleges. In 1957
these were merged to form the state university of Tirana,
Albania's first university. University colleges were later set up in
some of the main towns.

The 1958 reform of Soviet education, with its greater stress on

7—TA * *

technology and on the need to link academic training with practical experience in industry, presented the Albanian government with a difficult choice. Could an under-developed agricultural country afford to follow the pattern of a highly industrialized great power which was in the process of moving to a higher stage of technological sophistication? This and other related questions were eagerly debated by Albanian educationists, some of whom had serious misgivings about the feasibility of transplanting Russia's new system of education to their country. However, in the end the government decided to follow the Soviet example by adding an extra year to the seven-grade schools of general education and by gearing schools to the production requirements of agriculture and industry.

In 1967 educational reform became part of the cultural revolution when Hoxha announced the broad principles of future development. He admitted that the uncritical adoption of the Soviet system had been a mistake in view of the great disparities between the two countries. Radical changes were therefore needed to create a truly national system of education. This could only be done if the communist party assumed a much stricter control over educational policy than it had done in the past. As vocational and professional schools had been unable to meet the country's growing needs for skilled workers, new ones would be set up; measures would also be taken to make these schools more effective. Hoxha said that teaching at all levels would be firmly anchored to the doctrine of Marxism-Leninism after it had been purged of all deleterious Soviet traces. This would involve the revision of textbooks. A stricter ideological scrutiny would also be applied to both national and foreign works of literature. Special expurgated and bowdlerized editions of Albanian non-communist and foreign bourgeois authors would be published whenever it was thought that complete editions ran counter to official policy.

A school reform along lines that were far more radical than those suggested by Hoxha was finally introduced in 1970. Its basic components are academic study, production work and military training. Boys and girls from six to eighteen attending eight-grade schools, secondary or vocational schools, devote six and a half months to academic study, two and a half months to productive work, one month to military training and the remaining two months to holidays. Military training based on the theory and practice of partisan or guerilla warfare takes place first within the school itself and later in conjunction with units of the armed forces. The system gives pride of place to professional and vocational schools, bringing them closer to China's so-called "half work half study" schools. One of the criticisms made against Soviet vocational training was that it tended to favour the cities at the expense of the countryside. The Albanian leaders believed that Mao's educational theories were far better suited to their country's needs and would help to reduce the existing disparities between town and village, industrial worker and farmer, mental and physical labour.

Although higher education is in theory open to all those who have completed secondary school, irrespective of sex, social, economic or political status, a formidable barrier prevented young people who were even remotely thought to be politically unreliable from passing through its gates. Those wishing to attend university on completing their secondary education must spend one year working in industry or agriculture. This is in effect a probationary period during which their political and general behaviour is kept under close observation. The pupils who passed this test may include some true believers; but those who set greater store by opportunity to receive higher education than by ideological rectitude were only likely to get through by simulating a willingness to conform to party doctrine. Such hypocrisy is fairly widespread in many communist countries, but perhaps nowhere is it as pervasive as in Albania. Before the reform was introduced, schools, colleges and other educational establishments were administered by the ministry of education, with the communist party exercising its authority in the background. This somewhat loose arrangement was brought to an end in 1968 when the politburo set up a special commission, under the chairmanship of the prime minister, whose function it is to see that educational policy is carried out in accordance with party directives.

Yet despite the shortage of trained teachers and many other technical shortcomings, despite its extreme political and military regimentation as well as ideological discrimination, the Albanian educational system has been remarkably successful in terms of the actual numbers benefiting from it. In 1975 it was claimed that the total number of enrolled pupils and students was 700,000, or about one-third of the country's population. The corresponding figure for 1938 was 56,000.

The cultivation of literature and the arts was gravely handicapped by the régime's determination to make them mere servants of its policy and by its overriding ambition to devote the
greater part of the country's human and material resources to
industrial and agricultural development. At the same time an
attempt was made to preserve a measure of cultural continuity
by publishing the works of some of the older non-communist
writers. Selection had proved fairly easy and straightforward
in the case of the leading figures of the nationalist movement
of the nineteenth century such as Naim Frasheri. But when
it came to later writers, the communist régime has tended to
resort to the safe policy of simple suppression. This has been the
fate of Father Gjergj Fishta, Albania's greatest poet. As his poetry
is chiefly concerned with the social values of the old peasant
society and with religious themes, his books have been banned
altogether. To the post-war generations he is thus merely a name
which occasionally crops up in textbooks of literary history or in
anti-religious propaganda. The works of most other writers who
had been active during the period between the two wars have also
disappeared. In the case of Ernest Koliqi, the poet and short-
story writer who had collaborated with the Italians during the
second world war, the régime took a purely political attitude to
his work, condemning it as outright fascist. Koliqi continued his
literary career until his death in Italy, where he had emigrated
shortly before the communists came to power. His eminent contemporary Lasgush Poradeci remained in Albania, where he was
not allowed to publish any poetry even though he is completely
non-political. The work of this fine lyric poet was judged as too
mystical or too sophisticated to serve any useful social or political
purpose. His only important publication after the war is an
Albanian translation of Pushkin's *Evgeni Onegin*.

Two non-communist writers who were quite early taken to
heart by the régime as veritable masters and forerunners of the
post-war generation are Fan Noli (1882–1965) and Millosh
Gjergj Nikolla (1911–1938) who wrote under the pen-name
Migjeni. The communists felt a certain political affinity with Fan
Noli because during his brief premiership in 1924 he had tried
to introduce a programme of radical reforms which he was
unable to carry out. But he is also a considerable literary figure :
poet; author of biographies of Scanderbeg in both English and
Albanian; translator of plays by Shakespeare and Ibsen, of

Cervantes' *Don Quixote*, of Omar Khayyam's *Rubaiyat* and several other European and American works of poetry and prose. He wrote a number of trenchant satirical ballads on Albanian events and personalities of the 1920s and 1930s. In some of these his chief targets are the misdeeds and abuses of king Zog's rule. Migjeni, who died of tuberculosis at the age of twenty-seven, was the first poet of social protest in modern Albanian literature. Unlike some of the romantic writers of the nationalist movement whose vision is essentially heroic, he takes a more realistic and gloomy view of the political, social and economic backwardness of his countrymen and of the historical factors that had led to it. His pessimism is, however, laced with compassion and a utopian vision of national regeneration in ideal conditions of freedom. But neither Migjeni's mode of expression, which often verges on the dithyrambic, nor his belief in freedom of thought and experiment in literature, would have made it possible for his talent to develop, or even survive, had he worked within the straitjacket of communist cultural policy.

This straitjacket has spelt the death of Albanian poetry in the post-war period, which was dominated by a host of poetasters busily engaged in purveying the official party message on every possible subject. But, miraculously, true poetry was kept alive behind prison walls by Arshi Pipa who spent 10 years (1946–56) in some of Albania's most notorious communist prisons and labour camps. Shortly after finishing his sentence, Pipa fled from the country and emigrated to the United States where he published *The Prison Notebook* (1959), a collection of poems either conceived or written during those 10 years. They are works of art as well as harrowing documents of great brutality and inhumanity. Some of the poems contain graphic and moving descriptions of torture, hunger, humiliation, degradation, sickness and death. But in his work, which is informed by savage indignation and vehement protest against barbarous political persecution, Pipa maintains an extraordinary sense of artistic detachment coupled with deep compassion. One of his recurring themes is the great gulf that separates people in the throes of immense suffering from those living normal, humdrum lives :

Our sisters and daughters are grown up and now have children of their own. They come to visit us with their sons, daughters and babies in mothers' arms : living icons come to the grave of the living dead. Some look at us in fear, others in sheer horror. To them we are relics of another world, strange specimens carefully preserved in zoological cages. We're all forsaken and forgotten. The pity of our womenfolk, kept alive by love which no suffering can destroy, our only link with the real world; the smile of the child in its mother's arms a solitary ray of hope falling upon our tombstones.

Pipa has published two other books of verse since he left the country—*Rusha* (Munich, 1968) and *Meridiana* (Munich, 1969). The first work, written while he was at the labour camp in Burrel, is an epic poem of love and revenge between Albanians and Serbs set in the second half of the fourteenth century. Rusha is an Albanian Juliet who falls in love with, and gets secretly engaged to, Melisdrav, a Serbian Romeo. The story of the young lovers and of the intricate tribal intrigues that lead to their deaths is skilfully interwoven with lore on the social customs and modes of behaviour of medieval Albania and Serbia. Pipa handles this strange, archaic theme with a sober and sparkling simplicity, in a poetic language that is appropriately somewhat remote from modern Albanian usage. The fact that the work was conceived and written in a labour camp is a testimony to the artist's power of transcending human degradation and suffering in their most extreme form. *Meridiana* is a collection of poems of his literary apprenticeship written between 1936 and 1956. Many of these are romantic in both feeling and mode of expression, with echoes of nineteenth-century Italian poetry, particularly the poetry of Leopardi. The poems have nevertheless some of the traits and virtues of his later work: familiarity with both the classical and modern poetry of Europe as well as with the ancient oral traditions of his native country; a gentle though never despairing melancholy. *Meridiana* includes several poems from *The Prison Notebook*, some of which have either been radically revised or made more concise. Pipa, who is now professor of Italian literature at the university of Minnesota, has also published a critical study in English of the modern Italian poet Eugenio Montale (*Montale and Dante*, Minneapolis, 1968).

If the true voice of poetry was silenced inside the country, prose had fared only slightly better under communist rule. A number of reasonably good novelists and short-story writers like Dhimiter Shuteriqi, Petro Marko, Sterjo Spasse and Fatmir

Gjata had worked within the tight rules of socialist realism. They had occasionally tried, with little success, to break out of its iron-clad barriers. For several years their work was obsessively concerned with the anti-fascist struggle of the second world war and with the civil war. The fact is that whatever gifts these and other writers may have possessed were mercilessly ground down by the totalitarian Moloch of the communist state.

One writer who has been able to transcend both the rigidities of socialist realism and the harsh official censorship is Ismail Kadare. His novel *The General of the Dead Army* met with a good deal of press criticism when it was published in 1963. This is not surprising as it not only marks a complete departure from the strict canons of socialist realism but carries no simple political or ideological message. The story concerns the gruesome adventures of an Italian general and an army chaplain sent to Albania to recover the bones of Italian soldiers killed there during the second world war. Shortly after their arrival they discover that a German general is also busy digging up the graves of his fellow-countrymen who had perished fighting in the ranks of the nazi army of occupation. Albania is depicted in the novel not as a country where a tremendous social revolution is taking place, but as a brooding, nightmarish landscape strewn with the bones of Albanians, Italians, Germans, and haunted by the revived memories of recent great-power savageries, persecutions and injustices. The bizarre task of sorting out the remains of several nationalities serves as a grim counterpoint of comic lunacy and absurdity. The Italian general is portrayed with a good deal of understanding and sympathy as being himself a victim of his country's policy of conquest and plunder.

Translations of Kadare's novel have been published in France and Britain. The BBC has broadcast a successful radio dramatization of the book. Perhaps this international recognition may have helped to save him from persecution and ultimate silence. Kadare has published three other good novels which are not quite as ambitious or experimental as *The General of the Dead Army*. His second book, *The Wedding*, is centred on the post-war changes that have taken place in the status of women in Albanian society and on the problems that their emancipation has created for the conservative members of the older generation. In the hands of a lesser writer such a theme would have been treated in terms of crude, complacent propaganda associated with the fly-blown theory of socialist realism. Although the novel gives power-ful support to the reforms promoted by the communist party, it does so with subtlety and an acute awareness of their social con-sequences and cultural ramifications. In his next novel, *The Citadel*, Kadare has gone back to Scanderbeg's long, unequal struggle against the Ottoman Turks in the fifteenth century. The work is an impressive historical novel based on contemporary sources used with insight and imagination. If it has any implicit political and nationalist message, it is that the Albanians had fought single-handed for survival against desperate odds through-out the greater part of their long history. It was left to com-munist journalists and propagandists who reviewed the novel to draw a slick parallel between Scanderbeg's epic resistance to Ottoman domination and Enver Hoxha's rebellion against the Soviet Union in 1960. Kadare's fourth novel, *Chronicle in Stone*, is the story of his own childhood in the southern town of Gjirokas-tër during the second world war. The story begins with the simple, arresting statement: "It was difficult to be a child in this town". There was foreign occupation and civil strife. Foreign armies alternated with one another in bewildering succession: Italians, Greeks, then Italians again; finally Germans. The town was also the scene of many sharp clashes between local com-munist and nationalist resistance groups. The small boy observes these strange events, and the great suffering and unhappiness they bring to the inhabitants of his native town, in wonder and fear. He is in turn baffled by the actions of the foreign and Albanian protagonists of the incomprehensible drama unfolding before his eyes, and distressed by the wanton cruelties accompanying these actions. The high peak of the drama is reached when most of the inhabitants evacuate the town as the German army moves in to occupy it. The boy, who joins the straggling mass of refugees, reckons that this must be the third time in its history that the town had been abandoned. The other two occasions were when a plague had broken out in the tenth century and when the Turks had occupied it some 500 years later. It certainly was a difficult time and place in which to grow up. And when Kadare describes the painful process with the perception and feeling of an artist he speaks for many members of his own generation. Yet in the context of Albanian post-war writing his whole work is something of an aberration—a rare sturdy flower growing, inexplicably, in a largely barren patch.

Like literature and the arts, the press, radio and television operated under the strict control of the communist party and served as its principal instruments of political indoctrination and mass education. Their exploitation and control have become far more intense since the cultural revolution of the 1960s. Albania publishes some twenty newspapers and thirty-four periodicals of various kinds. Of these the most important are *Zëri i Popullit* (The Voice of the People), the official organ of the communist party; *Bashkimi* (Union), the government newspaper; *Puna* (Labour), published by the trade unions. In addition to its daily newspaper the party publishes the theoretical monthly *Rruga e Partisë* (The Party Path). The literary and cultural scene is dominated by two monthly reviews issued under the auspices of the writers' and artists' union : *Nëndori* (November) and *Drita* (Light).

The Albanian press is one of the dullest and least informative in the whole of eastern Europe. Its general tone is preachy, exhortative, patronising and self-righteous. The coverage of domestic and foreign news is highly selective and tendentious. Important internal events such as government and party reshuffles, purges and political trials are hardly ever reported, consequently people are left in the dark about what goes on in their own country. Coverage of international news is relegated to the back pages of newspapers, with carefully selected items heavily slanted to suit the current official attitude to the events being reported. The main features of the press consist of long, dreary, repetitive articles on agriculture, industrial or educational questions, and blatantly propagandistic commentaries on international affairs. Decades of this intellectually indigestible fare could only evoke boredom and apathy on the part of many readers, particularly the better educated young. Hoxha was aware of the problem and had spoken of the need to make newspapers and periodicals more readable, attractive and lively. Some attempts have been made in recent years to tackle certain important social problems such as housing, health, welfare and leisure in a slightly more intelligent and frank manner. But the blockage to any real improvement in press standards remained. The régime's chronic unwillingness, inspired by fear verging on terror, to allow any freedom of thought or expression had encouraged the persistence of mediocrity and dull conformity in the press as in many other spheres.

The development of broadcasting has been rapid since 1945 when the country possessed only two radio transmitters. By 1969 there were fifty-two transmitters, most of them shortwave, and six radio stations located in Tirana and other large towns. The number of radio sets rose from 150,000 in 1968 to double that figure in 1974. As the régime saw domestic broadcasting as a quicker and more effective instrument than the press for spreading its propaganda, it devoted considerable resources to the medium. An experimental television service transmitting programmes three times a week was introduced in 1960. Daily television broadcasting came into full operation at the beginning of 1970. The number of television sets in private use was estimated at about 35,000 in 1974. Yet despite the development of the press, radio and television, Albanians are almost totally deprived of reliable news and information about the outside world. As they have no access to foreign newspapers or periodicals, the only way they can hope to keep in touch with international events (sometimes even with what goes on in their own backyard) is by listening to foreign radio stations or by watching foreign television programmes. These practices are not specifically forbidden by law, though they are severely discouraged as acts liable to expose one to pernicious imperialist (western) or revisionist (Soviet and Yugoslav) influences. That people are nevertheless prepared to risk such contamination was shown by an official campaign launched in 1973 against external broadcasts that could either be watched or heard in the country. Television viewers living in a northern district near the border with Yugoslavia were ordered to remove from their sets aerials capable of receiving programmes from the Yugoslav television service at Skopje. Efforts were also made to curtail the reception of Italian television programmes in other parts of Albania.

One of the most unusual developments of the 1960s in the field of international broadcasting was the great expansion of Albania's foreign language radio services with considerable Chinese financial and technical assistance. Within less than 10 years broadcasts from Tirana had risen from a daily output of 7 hours in as many languages to 76 hours in seventeen languages. As a result of this expansion, by the mid-1970s Albania transmitted more programmes in foreign languages than any other communist country, with the exception of the Soviet Union and China. About one-third of these programmes, which carried China's views and propaganda on current affairs, were beamed to the communist countries of eastern Europe. The rest radiated the same message to Africa, Asia, north America and Latin America. What was bizarre and paradoxical about this huge effort to convert the whole world to Mao's (and to some extent Hoxha's) doctrines of social revolution and national liberation was that it emanated from a beleaguered, xenophobic régime which had turned its back on most other countries and was determined to prevent the people under its control from being infected by outside influences of any kind.

To mark the twenty-fifth anniversary of the régime in 1969, the Albanian institute of Marxist-Leninist studies organized in Tirana a special conference on social, economic and ideological problems in which a large number of specialists in various fields took part. The publication of its proceedings shortly afterwards led to a somewhat more realistic general approach to the country's past achievements and future prospects. One of the topics discussed at the conference was the great changes in the social structure that had taken place since 1945. Until then, for many Albanians, especially for those living in rural areas, loyalty to the family and to larger kinship groups such as the clan and the tribe had been the mainstay of social cohesion. In some parts of northern Albania the extended family was the most powerful social unit. It was composed of one couple, the wives and off-spring of their married sons, and their unmarried daughters. The head of the family, its eldest male, exercised patriarchal authority and was responsible for the wellbeing and safety of some twenty to seventy people or more. The extended families of the northern highlands were welded into clans and tribes. The same social organization existed in southern Albania too, though in a substantially modified form. There such agents of social and cultural change as the semi-feudal power exercised by the big landowners, higher educational standards, emigration to the United States and other countries had gradually reduced the cohesion and authority of the patriarchal family and all but destroyed the clan and tribal structure.

The old marriage customs of the north and south had also certain salient differences. In the northern highlands marriage was regulated by a number of well-defined and fairly strict conventions. A young man from a given clan was usually engaged in his infancy by his parents to a girl from another clan belonging to the same tribe. The breakdown of such arranged betrothals had often led to bitter quarrels and blood feuds between families and clans. In the southern areas, on the other hand, marriages were in most cases arranged by parents or go-betweens in accordance with the religious beliefs and social conventions of the families concerned. Ancient traditions and customs had largely lost the power to influence marriage ties.

The whole social structure of the country, with its family, tribal, regional and other loyalties, was gradually undermined by the post-war policies of the communist régime. The collectivization of agriculture; the industrialization programme; the increase in educational opportunities; migration from the countryside to urban and industrial centres; greater labour mobility; the constant rotation of bureaucrats; the suppression of religious practices—each of these major policies had made its own special contribution to the continuous process of erosion. The large patriarchal family, in particular, was under constant pressure and was fast disappearing. In those rural areas where it continued to survive, its head had lost most of his former power, prestige and respect. Marriage customs had also undergone radical changes and still continued to do so. The régime was fiercely opposed to arranged betrothals between infants. One method employed to end the practice was to send out teams of young propagandists who were given the task of persuading (or ultimately forcing) parents to dissolve child betrothals. Yet despite the progress that had been made in this field, in the late 1976s most marriages were still being arranged by parents or non-professional go-betweens after getting the consent of the young people concerned. At the same time, intermarriage between Moslems and Christians, always a rare occurrence in Albanian society, had made little or no headway during the first three decades of communist rule.

The Albanian communists had been aware from the very beginning of the need to sever the traditional bonds of loyalty to family, clan and tribe if they were to implement their revolutionary programme. Their alliance with China had served to sharpen their perception of the nature of the problem as well as fortify their determination to find a solution to it. At an early stage in his political career Mao Tse-tung had made the rejection of the three bonds of the Confucian ethical code—those existing between ruler and subject, father and son, husband and wife—one of the cardinal principles of his revolutionary philosophy. Hoxha was quick to see a close parallel between the conservative traditions of the Chinese and Albanian societies, and to discover that unless his régime, too, managed to break the ancient ties between subject and clan, father and son, husband and wife, the modernization of the country along communist lines could hardly be undertaken, let alone accomplished. So the drive against traditional loyalties and the campaign for women's liberation became, as we saw in the previous chapter, the main planks of the Albanian cultural revolution of the 1960s and of its subsequent manifestations.

As a result of the cultural revolution and various other social and economic policies, certain profound changes had taken place in the status of Albanian women. By the early 1970s nearly half of the pupils attending secondary schools and 40 per cent of university and college students were girls. In 1973 women made up 40 per cent of the country's labour force. They played a dominant rôle in schools, the health service and the administration of collective farms. Women's participation in active politics, however, had not kept pace with their advance in other fields. As they had been poorly represented for several years in the communist party and the people's assembly, steps were taken to increase their numbers in both these bodies. Consequently by 1973 women constituted about one-fourth of the party membership and just under one-third of the country's parliamentarians.

The family is the basic unit of socialist society; the small nuclear family the ultimate goal of government policy. Although divorce is recognized by law it is only granted when adultery or the irretrievable breakdown of the marriage has been proven. Great pains are taken by party organizations to bring about a reconciliation between partners seeking divorce. As a result of these and other pressures aimed at preserving the family unit, Albania's divorce rate is one of the lowest in Europe. Abortion is illegal and is only permitted in cases where the mother's life is endangered.

However, Hoxha had reminded the communist party on numerous occasions that the successes already achieved in such

fields as women's emancipation and the dismantling of the patriarchal family with its many complex tribal ramifications did not
automatically lead to the disappearance of the ancient habits of
thought and behaviour which had been the bedrock of the pre-
communist social system. These would only be uprooted in the
course of time through education and the intensification of the
revolutionary process. Sex discrimination would continue until
the conservative outlook had been completely eradicated.
Women, for instance, enjoyed a great deal of personal freedom
at school, university and at their places of work, whereas at home
they frequently came across many of the old male prejudices. In
many cases they were not allowed to entertain men friends or
colleagues at home. Ties outside the close family circle were
frowned upon. Many members of the older generations dis-
approved of the views of young people on love and marriage.
Girls, in particular, were often prevented by their parents from
choosing their own partners. But whilst Hoxha was highly critical
of such attitudes he was equally opposed to pre-marital sexual
relations, which he condemned as belonging to the pattern of
decadent bourgeois morality. What he espoused was the ideal of
"pure proletarian love between men and women, followed by
marriage based on mutual consent". When he spoke about such
matters he often tried to do so not so much as party leader but
as a wise and far-sighted teacher of his people, closely following
Mao's example. The fact that both Hoxha and Mao had once
been schoolmasters may have had something to do with the ease
with which they slipped into such a rôle.

Some of the bad traits of the old Albanian society had managed to penetrate the citadel of the communist party itself, mas-
querading under new shapes and guises. An extreme example of
this was the open admission by an influential party member in
a remote northern district that he was in the habit of beating his
wife. His expulsion from the party was given great publicity in
the national press. But abuses sometimes took more insidious and
subtler forms. Nepotism and favouritism, for instance, were fairly
widespread within party organizations. Members of a given clan
often reserved the best jobs and other special privileges for their
close relatives and other members of the same clan, irrespective
of their qualifications or experience. There had been cases in
which communists who were at heart opposed to the policy of
collectivization had done everything within their power to

obstruct the modernization of farming methods. The party was also said to harbour men who were opposed to women becoming party members or assuming responsible positions because they saw them as dangerous rivals. In some cases, husbands tried to prevent their wives from joining the party. When such open sex discrimination proved unsuccessful and women were able to achieve their political and professional ambitions, attempts were occasionally made to discredit them by means of malicious gossip about their personal or professional lives. What Hoxha's and the other leaders' repeated admonitions amounted to was a recognition of the simple fact that the communist party was merely a replica of Albanian society with all its general backwardness, its social prejudices and its other shortcomings. But they eagerly anticipated that when all traces of this legacy had been removed, given a good deal of time and effort, the proper conditions would be created for the emergence of an ideal type of communist citizen.

Like most other communist countries, Albania was usually reticent about prevailing trends in crime and punishment. However, after the cultural revolution the authorities and the press had been slightly more prepared to provide a certain amount of information about such matters. This was partly due to a general desire to encourage more open debates on social issues, partly because there was a marked increase in certain types of offences. Official sources claimed that there had been a steep decline in murders caused by blood feuds. Only twenty such crimes, according to Hoxha, were committed between 1966 and 1970. This seemed fairly plausible in view of the great changes the industrial, agricultural and educational policies of the régime had brought about in the lives of the people, particularly of the peasantry. A powerful deterrent to such offences was also the knowledge that, given the régime's determination to stamp out their tribal breeding ground, it would deal especially harshly with those who perpetrated them. Yet judging by the number of newspaper articles on crime that appeared in the early 1970s, it looked as though the authorities were still worried by the persistence of modes of social behaviour that gave rise to blood feuds as well as by the increase in other types of crime. Stealing and damaging socialist property were said to have become fairly widespread. The blame for these was attributed to people's attachment to the bourgeois notion of private property and to lack of vigilance on the part of government and party authorities. But perhaps a more reasonable explanation would be that when people who had been stripped of almost all personal possessions were forced to subsist on very inadequate wages, laying hands on property belonging to the state may sometimes be the only way they could make ends meet. Hoxha said in May 1971 that there had also been more political offences against the state. Although his remarks were kept deliberately vague and circumspect, he claimed that these offences had taken the form of agitation and propaganda fomented by domestic and external enemies of the régime who had wilfully distorted the nature and purpose of its radical reforms. He spoke of acts of terrorism and espionage committed by western and Soviet intelligence organizations. This is a sphere in which the régime had for many years maintained absolute secrecy. Political trials were invariably held behind closed doors, with no reports on court proceedings appearing in the press and other news media. So the only reasonable conclusion one can draw from Hoxha's misty disclosures is that the various campaigns and mass movements unleashed during the cultural revolution had met with a good deal of either active or passive resistance. And in the eyes of the Albanian authorities, all forms of resistance, however mild, to party decisions were serious political offences, hence punishable as such. Another disquieting development, from the régime's point of view, was the fact that some 2 per cent of those who went before the courts in 1970 were convicted of rape and other sexual offences. The blame for these was laid at the door of the pernicious influence of the western countries where, it was claimed, sexual promiscuity had become an integral part of the general philosophy of mass consumption.

Leisure, or rather the lack of it, is one of the social problems that was frequently discussed after the cultural revolution. Factory and collective farm employees were often asked to work overtime in addition to their normal 48-hour week. At the end of their day's work they also had to attend party meetings lasting several hours, leaving them little or no time for family life or recreation. There were complaints in the press that in many cases such meetings were either concerned with trivial matters, which could easily be settled by the managers of enterprises and the trade unions, or else with routine political lectures which only served to irritate and bore people to death. Managers and party officials were blamed for paying little or no attention to the task of providing recreation opportunities for their employees. The problem had evidently become so acute that Hoxha himself decided to lend his weight to these criticisms in April 1971. He said that young people, in particular, should be allowed to choose their own leisure activities and should not be pushed around or forced to do things they disliked. There were far too many formal and useless political meetings. He suggested that radio and television should broadcast more music that appealed to the young generation, and that people in general should be allowed greater freedom to read foreign books and see foreign films, relying on their innate capacity to reject harmful bourgeois or revisionist influences. Even if there was no sign that Hoxha's remarks heralded any change in party policy, they nevertheless indicated that there was a good deal of discontent among workers and young people who felt that they were not only being overworked but also unduly harassed during their nominal spare time.

But if the régime had been very reluctant to loosen its firm control over the political and intellectual life of the people, it could claim with some justification that it had done a good deal to improve their health and social welfare. Free medical treatment is in theory provided for everyone. The plans that were introduced in the 1950s to improve the health service were energetically pursued during the 1960s and 1970s. More hospitals, maternity homes, sanatoria, clinics and health centres were built. Although efforts were made to extend these services to the remote mountainous regions, the gap in medical facilities between towns and villages still persisted. After the quarrel with Russia, doctors received their basic medical training in Albania; a small number of graduates attended special courses at Italian and French universities. The doctor-patient ratio dropped from one to 3,400 in 1960 to one to 1,200 in 1970. Average life expectancy rose from 53 years in 1950 to 66 years in 1970. The shortcomings and inadequacies of the health service have been more frankly admitted and discussed in recent years. The head of the pathology department of the university of Tirana pointed out in August 1970 that medical research, for instance, was badly neglected owing to poor organization and lack of support from the ministry of health and other government departments.

A comprehensive social insurance scheme was first introduced in 1947. It was administered by a number of government departments and covered medical treatment, family allowances, disability payments, old-age pensions, rest and recreation facilities. The scheme had undergone a number of changes since its inception. In 1953 Albania adopted the Soviet prototype of social insurance. Several welfare benefits were at first placed under the supervision of the general council of the trade unions, but by 1965 the state had assumed almost total responsibility for them. An amendment introduced two years later provided new social benefits for industrial workers, state and party employees. In the case of peasants working in collective farms, their benefits were derived from the budgets of their particular concerns. The state pension scheme, however, covered employees of all types, including collective farmers.

Communist régimes throughout the world claimed that their authority and power stemmed directly from the will of the people. Perhaps nowhere was this hollow claim made quite so stridently or insistently as in Albania. This was particularly true after the Maoist theories on the "mass line", workers' control and uninterrupted revolution had been assimilated by Hoxha and his close associates. Yet Albania is the only communist country in Europe which has rejected even the vague concept of collective leadership which was practised, at one time or another, by the Soviet Union and its allies, and has adopted instead the system of one-man rule in its most extreme form. Enver Hoxha had been for the greater part of the post-war period the absolute ruler of his country. It was difficult to ascertain with any degree of certainty the extent to which he had been prepared to share his power with the other eleven full members of the politburo. All the available evidence suggested that his closest collaborators throughout most of this period were two members of this body: the prime minister Mehmet Shehu and the party secretary Hysni Kapo. So if Hoxha had divided his authority with anyone at all it would have been with these two. At the same time, by making it possible for their wives to belong to the central committee as well as hold other important posts, Hoxha, Shehu and Kapo were themselves guilty of the very clannishness and nepotism of which they had so often accused humbler members of the communist party. Nexhmije Hoxha has served for many years as director of the Marxist-Leninist institute; Fiqrete Shehu as director of the party school; Vito Kapo as leader of the women's union. Next in the political hierarchy are the other members of the politburo; the party secretaries; the members of the central committee; the commanders of the security and the armed forces; the members of the government. The lower levels of the communist élite consisted of people who, though they wielded no real political power as such, had great influence in their own particular fields and enjoyed considerable privileges. These are party and state bureaucrats; managers of industrial and agricultural concerns; technocrats and professional people; rank-and-file members of the communist party. The main function of these groups is to carry out the decisions of the supreme ruler and his small circle of henchmen. They are, in short, faithful administrators, not originators, of policy.

We shall next take a closer look at some of the other features of the totalitarian régime that Hoxha had managed to set up in the course of his eventful, blood-stained political career.

Chapter 11

TOTALITARIAN ISOLATION

T HE ALBANIAN COMMUNIST party, like the other communist parties of eastern Europe, is a minority or élite political organization which has succeeded in imposing its will on the majority. But the numerous purges it has undergone has made its élitist status much more unstable and vulnerable than that of any other communist party. The Albanian leaders could not be sure that the party membership was thoroughly cleansed of pro-Soviet and pro-Yugoslav elements or of communists whose loyalty to Mao's revolutionary theory and practice, as interpreted by Hoxha, was either half-hearted or else downright spurious. Given this uncertainty, the party's need to make the best possible use of its auxiliary social and political agencies, officially known as mass organizations, was correspondingly greater. In the other countries of eastern Europe the trade unions, the youth and women's organizations are largely dormant bureaucratic bodies which perform certain important routine functions prescribed by the party and only come to life on such special occasions as elections or propaganda campaigns designed to achieve certain specific objectives. This state of affairs also prevailed in Albania when it was part of the Soviet bloc. But a radical change occurred when the country moved into China's sphere of influence after its expulsion from the bloc. Then the mass organizations were given a new lease of life and became more or less permanently active extensions of the communist party.

Their rôle was clearly defined by Hoxha in 1967, when the cultural revolution was at its peak. He said then that the mass organizations were essential components of the dictatorship of the proletariat as well as instruments by means of which the party made sure that its directives were properly understood and carried out by all sections of the population. Hysni Kapo, one of the secretaries of the party, amplified this statement when he pointed out that the subsidiary agencies enabled the party to exercise direct control over the lives of the people because whereas not every Albanian family had a communist in its ranks, all families had several members who belonged to one mass organization or another. Consequently every family was indirectly, though nonetheless firmly, linked to the party itself.

The largest political organization and the most powerful after the communist party is the Democratic Front, a successor to the national liberation front of the second world war. All Albanians, including party members, over the age of eighteen belong to it. Its membership card is the most valuable document, after the communist party card, that an Albanian citizen can possess. Without a Democratic Front card he cannot obtain work, get a ration book (when one is required), make a purchase at government stores and so on. The original purpose of the organization was to serve as a forum for the country's various shades of political opinion which the communist party had to take into account when it worked out its policies. But in practice its chief function is to enlist the widest possible support for the party's programme and its revolutionary enterprises. The Democratic Front also performs certain other duties: it organizes parliamentary and local-government elections; it disseminates the teachings of Marxist-Leninist ideology beyond the narrow circle of the communist élite, it campaigns against political, social and other attitudes regarded as harmful or reactionary by the party leadership.

If the Democratic Front is the watchdog of the political and ideological behaviour of the country as a whole, the youth organization is the repository of the party's revolutionary hopes for the future. The foundations of the communist youth movement were laid in 1941 when the communist party itself came into being, and was the outcome of the campaign to recruit young men and women in large numbers into the partisan units of the second world war. Throughout most of his career Hoxha had devoted almost as much care and attention to the regimentation and indoctrination of the young as he had to the running of the party machine itself. The youth movement, embracing about a quarter of a million members aged between fifteen and twenty-five, has a central controlling body and local branches throughout the country, which are under the direct supervision of the respective bodies of the communist party. In addition, children between seven and fourteen are also placed under its general guidance. The youth organization is not only the main recruiting ground for future party members but also a convenient source of activists for revolutionary campaigns as well as of so-called volunteers for road and railway building, for work in industrial and farming schemes. Between 150,000 to 200,000 young people at a time are often engaged in such work. Most of the country's roads and railways and some of its factories have been built by this type of labour. Large concentrations of young people in labour camps during the summer months served an additional purpose. They acted as convenient training centres where captive audiences, far removed from the influence of their parents —particularly of those living in the more conservative areas— were exposed to daily indoctrination and propaganda. Yet despite the great amount of thought and energy that the leadership had lavished on the policy of brain-washing the younger generation and despite the major rôle the youth movement had played in the cultural revolution of the 1960s, there was an underlying pessimism in the party's general attitude to the problems of young people. This is seen in the many changes that have been made in the leadership of the movement, in the constant pressures as well as the endlessly repetitive propaganda to which its members were subjected. Perhaps this pessimism stemmed from Hoxha's fear that young people will in time succumb to all the temptations of other modern societies—careers, money-making, personal fulfilment, travel, generally having a good time, etc— and thus give up the selfless, arduous task of creating the utopian communist society of Mao's and his own frenzied dreams.

The trade unions are the largest and most important mass organization after the Democratic Front. They were set up in 1945 on the pattern of the Soviet trade unions with a membership of 30,000. By 1970 this had risen to 400,000. Throughout their existence the unions have been, for all practical purposes, an appendage of the party machine, performing such set tasks as fulfilling the government's economic plans, maintaining labour discipline, spreading the official gospel among their members. The lack of any strong national traditions of labour organization had enabled the régime to impose the tightest possible control over the unions with impunity. However, with the expansion of industry, with the increase in the number of skilled workers and with the development of agriculture, this control became increasingly cumbersome and inefficient. Certain tensions within the trade union movement became apparent from about the mid-

1960s. One source of discontent was the fact that wages continued to be fixed by the central authorities. This deprived the Albanian unions of the limited bargaining powers which their counterparts had won for themselves in Poland, Hungary and Czechoslovakia. The Albanian régime continued to cling to the fiction that the rights and obligations of the communist party were identical with those of the trade unions, and consequently was reluctant to permit the latter to assume even the purely theoretical function of improving the living standards and generally safeguarding the interests of their members. In an address to the congress of the trade unions in May 1972, Hoxha himself referred to their many shortcomings and, by implication, to the shortcomings of his own policy. He spoke of low productivity, of unprofitable enterprises, of the manufacture of unmarketable goods, of bad management and widespread bureaucratic inefficiency. He singled out in particular the unfair system of wages in operation. It was unjust, Hoxha pointed out, that a youngster leaving school should be paid the same rate as older workers with fifteen or twenty years' experience. The absence of pay differentials had led to low productivity, bad workmanship and to a general disincentive to acquire higher qualifications or skills. But apart from bringing such grievances into the open, he failed to suggest any constructive remedy. Perhaps the régime may have hoped that the introduction of the policy of workers' control would help remove some of the discontent by giving trade unionists a greater sense of participation in party and government affairs. But as the workers' control movement is itself manipulated by the party leadership for its own ends, it is unlikely to appear as anything but a palliative in the eyes of those who are asked to take part in it.

The women's union, the fourth weapon in the party's political armoury of mass organizations, was founded in 1943 for the purpose of recruiting women in the partisan movement. During the final phase of the second world war some six thousand girls were fighting in its ranks. After the war the union became closely involved with the recruitment and training of women in industry, agriculture and the professions. From 1946 to 1955 it was led by the party leader's wife, Nexhmije Hoxha. She was succeeded by Vito Kapo, wife of the third most powerful man in the country. During the cultural revolution the union was in the vanguard of the campaigns against sex discrimination, religious practices and social and political traditions of the pre-communist period.

If the mass organizations had helped Hoxha's régime to exercise political and ideological control over all sections of the community by propagating its special brand of Marxist-Leninist ideology and by seeing that its policies were carried out, the internal security forces had maintained it in power and ensured its survival. The ministry of the interior, the government department which controls these forces, had been headed since 1954 by Kadri Hasbiu, who was trained in Russia and has been closely involved with internal security throughout the greater part of his career. His marriage to Mehmet Shehu's sister made him part of the tight family pattern which was woven into the fabric of the Albanian communist hierarchy. Hasbiu's domain has four main branches: the secret police, the counterpart of the Soviet KGB known as *Sigurimi*; the frontier guards; the people's police; the auxiliary police.

Like the secret police of other communist countries, *Sigurimi*'s principal tasks are to eliminate all forms of opposition to the party and government and prevent counter-revolution. It has special departments dealing with political affairs, censorship, prisons and labour camps, counter-intelligence, visiting and resident aliens. Although there are no reliable figures about the real strength of the Albanian secret police, one estimate puts it at some 13,000 uniformed men. The whole country is also covered by a *Sigurimi* network of plainclothes agents and informers. The ubiquity and omnipotence of its members have given *Sigurimi*, in the eyes of most Albanians and visitors from abroad, the fearful reputation that Haiti's Tontons Macoute had during Doctor Duvalier's rule. Harry Hamm, the West German newspaper correspondent who visited Albania in the summer of 1961, noted the presence of the secret police wherever people assembled in any large numbers and their determination to prevent Albanians from having any contact with foreigners. Whenever Hamm tried to talk to people in the streets or in other public places, *Sigurimi* agents suddenly appeared on the scene, sending the Albanians he had approached scurrying away in fear. The Swedish reporter Björn Hallström, who went there in 1966, found the secret police much more in evidence than they had been during a previous visit seven years before. He and other tourists were forbidden to talk to local people or to photograph anything the authorities chose to label "backward" or "reactionary", such as Albanians dressed in their national costumes. When people ran away from him as he sat on a bench in a public park, Hallström says he was made to feel like a leper.

Even though Albania's frontier guards are organized along military lines, they come under the jurisdiction of the ministry of the interior and have far closer ties with *Sigurimi* than with the regular armed forces. The official duties of the guards are to protect the country's borders and to deal with foreign agents, smugglers and infiltrators. But perhaps their principal, if unspoken, function is to prevent Albanians from leaving the country. No reliable figures exist on those who have managed to escape but they are believed to run into several thousands. An official balance sheet of the activities of the frontier guards from 1945 to 1969, published in 1970, maintains that their units had coped with 340 groups of Greek and Yugoslav agents. In the course of many border clashes 148 had been killed and 3,600 captured. Albanian casualties during the same period are said to have been 150 men killed in action. Another claim made in the report is that after 1961, the Soviet Union had embarked on an active campaign of subversion against Hoxha's régime, infiltrating hundreds of agents into the country.

The people's police, Albania's ordinary police force, maintains branches concerned with crime detection; guarding government buildings, factories, construction sites; protecting railways and bridges; looking after prisons and labour camps. One of the duties of the people's police is to see that every Albanian possesses an identity card, a kind of internal passport which enables him to travel from one part of the country to another. This essential document makes it possible for the police to exercise effective control over movements of population. The people's police are assisted by an auxiliary force made up of able-bodied civilians who are obliged by law to serve for two months a year in their own districts. The auxiliaries are unpaid and wear a red armband to distinguish them from members of the regular police force.

Despite the lip-service which the 1946 constitution (amended in 1950) and the 1976 constitution pay to the independence of the courts and to the rule of law, Albania's judicial system and administration of justice can only make sense if they are considered in conjunction with its security services. In 1951 even this constitutional pretence was torn to shreds by the special government decree which was issued shortly after the explosion that occurred at the Soviet embassy in Tirana. This prescribed the death penalty for all those "engaged in terroristic activities" without recourse to the due process of law. A special tribunal was authorized to deal with cases in a summary fashion. Defendants were denied the right to appear when their cases were heard or to appeal against the verdict. The minister of the interior responsible for issuing the decree described it as "profoundly revolutionary". Albania's legal system and the philosophy on which it rested were revolutionary only in the sense that they were taken over from the Soviet Union lock, stock and barrel. Judges of the supreme court and of the people's courts, who are not required to have any legal qualifications, are elected in much the same way as members of the people's assembly (parliament). Judges sit in court together with assessors, or assistant judges, who have no powers to act independently as jurymen. Both the 1946 and 1976 constitutions recognize the right of defendants to obtain legal aid; this right has, however, been in suspension for several years. Whilst many inprovements have taken place in the Soviet legal system since Stalin's death, its Albanian counterpart has become even more ideological by being brought under strict party control. A law on the reorganization of the courts passed in 1968 states that the "people's courts will be guided in their activities by the policy of the party. In carrying out their responsibilities, they must strongly rely on the working masses and submit to their criticism and control." The doctrine underlying the system of justice is enunciated in article 105 of the 1976 constitution : "the courts protect the socialist juridical order, strive to prevent crime, and educate the masses of working people to respect and implement socialist law, relying on their active participation".

Sigurimi, supported by the people's police, is in charge of Albania's prisons and labour camps. Forced labour was first introduced by a government decree in August 1947 which laid down that all those who had served the pre-war régimes would be mobilized and employed in construction schemes. Shortly afterwards this policy was embodied in a labour code which gave the authorities wide powers to conscript into the labour force all able-bodied Albanians between the ages of sixteen and fifty. In September 1952 an amended version of the code made the penal system an integral part of the government's plan to organize forced labour on a large scale. The Albanian minister of justice explained that this policy was based on the Soviet principles of "class warfare and revolutionary justice". Offences such as producing low-quality goods, failure to fulfil official production quotas and absenteeism were liable to terms of from 6 months to 4 years in forced labour or corrective camps.

Among the first labour camps to be set up were those of Tirana, Valias, Burrel, Kavajë, Berat, Porto Palermo, Tepelenë and Vloçisht. The two most notorious of these are Burrel, where some of the régime's staunchest political opponents are held, and Vloçisht, where a large and constantly fluctuating labour force was engaged, during the late 1940s and early 1950s, in draining the nearby lake Maliq. Vloçisht has passed into folk memory as Albania's extermination camp. Official sources have never provided any information about the camps or even admitted their existence. Our present knowledge, unavoidably scrappy and incomplete, is based on the testimony of survivors who had left the country.

One of the most lucid and coherent accounts of camp life is to be found in the appendices of *The Prison Notebook* by Arshi Pipa, the Albanian poet and scholar who, as we saw earlier, had spent ten years in several prisons and labour camps. He was arrested in October 1946 and was sent to the prison at Durrës where he was employed, together with other political prisoners, in local road building. While he was there he learnt that his brother (Muzafer Pipa) had been executed at Shkodër after being arrested in September 1946 as an opponent of the communist régime. Pipa witnessed in the prison at Durrës an unusual form of torture known as the "waistcoat torture". This consisted of forcing the prisoner into a hefty peasant waistcoat, binding him hand and foot, then hanging him up, like trussed poultry in butchers' shops, by means of a wooden pole passed through the tight-fitting garment. Such torture by suspension often lasted several days. In July 1948 Pipa was moved to the labour camp at Vloçisht. Its inmates, whose numbers varied from 1,300 to 1,600, lived in three wooden huts covered by tarpaulin which was far from weatherproof. Sleeping accommodation consisted of rows of narrow two-tier wooden bunks with very little space between them. Owing to overcrowding and the lack of proper washing facilities, the stench in the dormitories was permanently overpowering. As political prisoners lived and worked together with ordinary offenders the camp guards were in the habit of stirring up trouble between the two groups. Acting on the theory that political prisoners were members of the exploiting classes whilst ordinary criminals belonged to the working class, the latter were actively encouraged to steal from the former. As complaints about such behaviour got them nowhere, many political prisoners were forced to sleep with their meagre rations and other personal belongings under the pillow. The daily food ration was made up of 800–850 grams of bread, potato soup and tea with a minute amount of sugar. Hunger drove some prisoners to pilfer beetroots or cobs of maize from fields on their way to and from work. The camp guards beat them up on the spot for doing so. Indeed, beatings were a daily occurrence in the camp. Such treatment was meted out at the end of the day's work to those who failed to fulfil their quota of work. The victims almost invariably included the old, the sick and people whose physical strength had been sapped by earlier tortures. During Pipa's confinement at Vloçisht at least three inmates were shot by the guards for getting too near the barbed wire fence of the camp. Several others hanged themselves after prolonged tortures. He also witnessed a particularly harrowing incident at a hospital in the nearby town of Korçë, where he was sent for treatment. One day a prisoner suffering from acute starvation was admitted and was immediately given a plate of spaghetti to eat. After taking only a couple of mouthfuls he dropped dead and was left lying on his deathbed for some time, with wisps of spaghetti hanging over his chin.

In July 1950 Pipa was moved to the prison of Gjirokastër which is located inside the walls of the town's ancient fortress. There political prisoners were segregated from ordinary convicts and were housed in underground cellars. Three hundred and fifty of them were crowded into two very dark, airless and damp rooms. These squalid living conditions together with malnutrition (the daily bread ration was reduced to 650 grams) caused the death of many prisoners. After spending nearly two years in Gjirokastër, Pipa was finally transferred to the labour camp at Burrel, in northern Albania, which at one time had the macabre inscription "This is Burrel where people enter but never leave" hanging over its gate. A large number of political prisoners perished at Burrel as a result of tortures and inhuman living conditions. Among those who died there were Koço Kotta, a former prime minister and Kristo Kirka, who in the early part of this century had lived in the United States, where he was active in the Albanian nationalist movement. A young prisoner (Gasper Çuni) died in the camp from acute appendicitis through sheer lack of medical care only four months before he was due to be released. Apparently such deaths were fairly common. Pipa himself contracted tuberculosis at Burrel and spent several months in a small room set apart for patients suffering from the same disease. They all slept on a concrete floor with thin straw mats for bedding. When patients died their bodies were moved to a corner of the camp by the dustbins. From there they were later taken outside the camp perimeter and buried beneath a splendid cherry tree. Hence the saying "he has gone to the cherries" came to carry its own grim message for the inmates of Burrel.

Another glimpse of conditions prevailing in Albanian labour camps was provided in a report published in the British newspaper the *Sunday Times* (7 July 1974) based on the personal experiences of Yousef Valyrakis, a young Greek who escaped to Albania in 1972 after taking part in the underground resistance movement against the colonels' régime in Greece. He was sentenced to three years' imprisonment for entering the country illegally but was released after he had done one year and allowed to go to Sweden. Valyrakis was held in the camps of Burrel and Ballsh. He spent a winter at Burrel where not only was no heating of any kind provided but the windows of the cells were all broken, letting the snow drift in. Food was scarce and of poor quality. From there he was moved to Ballsh, a labour camp in southern Albania, where a special section (No. 309/3) was reserved for some fifty foreign prisoners, most of them Yugoslavs and Greeks. The camp, which contained about 1,000 political prisoners altogether, was ringed by a high electrified wire fence, interspersed with searchlights and watch towers manned by soldiers armed with machine guns. The inmates lived in concrete barracks which were as freezingly cold in winter as they were unbearably hot during the summer months. Food consisted of bread, beans, macaroni, vegetables, rice and a little meat. But Valyrakis says it was all of such poor quality as to be almost uneatable. Bread was made of maize and potato flour, occasionally of sawdust. He also reports that many prisoners in Ballsh were mental and physical wrecks, some of them having been there for over 10 years : "It was awful to listen to their bawlings in the nights".

According to an estimate made by Amnesty International in January 1976, there are some eighteen labour camps for political prisoners in Albania. These are situated near mines, industrial centres, building sites, large irrigation and agricultural schemes. The total number of political prisoners is thought to be approximately 12,000, of whom 9,900 are dispersed throughout the labour camps and the remaining 2,100 throughout the country's seven large prisons. With the development of industry and agriculture, there had been a general overhaul of the labour camp system. This had brought into being new camps and caused the disappearance, among others, of the ill-famed camp at Vloçisht and the one at Tepelenë, which had some 8,000 political prisoners in the late 1940s.

Peter Mali (this is not his real name), a farm worker who escaped from Albania in September 1975, was interviewed 4 months later by an official of Amnesty International at a centre for refugees in Latina, near Rome. He was arrested in July 1961 on the charge of having criticized the government's collectivization policy. During the 12 months when he was awaiting trial, Mali was subjected to numerous tortures in order to get him to sign a prepared statement confessing his guilt. These took several forms. The most common torture was the application of electric shocks to different parts of the anatomy. Another was placing sharp axes under each armpit, then tying a rope around his body. Two other brutal refinements were burning with hot irons and inserting splinters of hard wood under his nails. Yet another form of torture which, according to Mali, is practised in Albanian labour camps and prisons is to place fleas on the prisoner's shaven head whilst his hands are tied up to prevent him scratching himself. Within a few hours of such treatment most people are driven berserk and will do almost anything that is asked of them. Mali was sent for trial in July 1962 but was not allowed a defence counsel or given legal assistance of any kind. He was sentenced to 16 years' hard labour. He spent 4 years on a construction site near Tirana; 6 years at Spaç, a labour camp in a northern mining area; 2 years in another camp near Shkodër, where he did no work but was kept in solitary confinement. Mali's sentence was reduced by 4 years for "good performance in the mines" and he was released in 1974. He lost his civil rights during the next 4 years when he had to report to the police every day after work. As a result of overwork and malnutrition his weight had dropped from 82 kilogrammes to 38 kilogrammes by the end of his second year in a labour camp. Mali's wife was allowed to visit him just once a year when she could take him a small food parcel. They saw each other for only 5 minutes in the presence of a camp guard.

Mali also provided Amnesty International with information about general conditions in Albanian camps. During his incarceration two to three prisoners died every month through lack of rudimentary medical care. He found that a large proportion of political convicts, particularly those doing life or long sentences, were either mentally ill or insane. These people frequently threw themselves onto the wire fences of the camps where they were instantly machine-gunned by the security police. In May 1973 there was an uprising of prisoners working in the mines near Spaç who were protesting about bad and inadequate food. The army was called in to quell the revolt. Four ringleaders were sentenced to death by an *ad hoc* tribunal. They were executed on the spot in the presence of all the inmates. A second uprising took place shortly after; some 170 prisoners were tried and had their sentences increased. In one camp Mali met three brothers (Pashko, Dod and Gjergj Dreshaj) who had been sentenced to terms of imprisonment ranging from 10 to 25 years for having escaped to Yugoslavia. After detaining them for 17 days at Titograd in Montenegro the Yugoslavs handed them back to the Albanian authorities who later paraded them through the streets of Shkodër *pour encourager les autres*. (The Amnesty International report says that fifty-six Albanian families, comprising at least 150 individuals, who had escaped to Yugoslavia during 1975 were believed to have been handed back to the Albanian frontier guards by their Yugoslav counterparts.) Mali also came across several victims of religious persecution. He met in the camp at Spaç two Roman Catholic priests (Fathers Nikoll Hasi and Tom Doçi) and a Moslem imam (Haxhi Hafizi). Another Catholic priest (Father Rrok Gurashi) died while he was there. The interviewer of Amnesty International found that refugees from Albania were unwilling to testify before an impartial commission on torture because of "an almost apocalyptic fear of repercussions affecting their next of kin". But these accounts are only fragments of the great human tragedy of Albania's communist labour camps and prisons. Their full story will perhaps be told one day by another survivor like Arshi Pipa who might do it some of the justice that Alexander Solzhenitsyn has done to Stalin's Gulag Archipelago.

By exercising complete control over the communist party, its subsidiary bodies and the secret police, Hoxha was able to operate in a situation in which no recognizable sanctions of any kind—moral, ethical, religious, political or judicial—were allowed to function. Following the example of his master Stalin, his own embodiment of the party's will became the supreme law of the land, an absolute *raison d'état*. All moral and human values, including the code of personal honour and fidelity which lay at the heart of the ethics of Albania's peasant society, were contemptuously swept aside to make room for the dogma of infallibility of the communist party and of its leader. This maintains that both strive to achieve certain ultimate scientific objectives which might take many years or generations to come to fruition. Therefore any mistakes or crimes which the leader or the party happened to commit along the tortuous path to final victory are trivial and unimportant as both leader and party are, by definition, incapable of being wrong about long-term, scientific objectives. The party was thus elevated to the position of a tribal deity which was not only infinitely wise, far-sighted and benevolent but also implacable towards its enemies. If these were also the enemies of the leader this was because he incarnated all the party's wisdom and utopian aspirations. But behind this façade of ideological mythology lay the stark coercive power of *Sigurimi*, the chief instrument of Hoxha's personal rule of terror. After Stalin's death the powers of the secret police were circumscribed to some extent in the Soviet Union and the other communist countries of eastern Europe. But this did not happen in Albania, where Hoxha was unwilling to pay even lip-service to the notion of "socialist legality" or the rule of law. He justified his continued reliance on police terror by the claim that the Albanian communist régime had too many powerful external enemies to afford dropping its guard. Although there was a grain of truth in the argument of external danger, this was deliberately exaggerated for the purpose of cloaking the principal motive for relying on terror. This is Hoxha's firm belief that without the instrument of the secret police he would have been unable either to rid the party of his numerous real or imaginary opponents or carry out the complete collectivization of agriculture, the suppression of organized religion, the regimentation of writers, artists, young people and of other sections of the community. The need to maintain the rule of terror may also have been reinforced by a purely personal whim. By a process of transference, Hoxha may have tried to vent on his own people—whose backwardness, poverty and spirit of social and political anarchy he despised—some of the frustration, resentment, bitterness and spleen that his dangerous confrontations with Yugoslavia, the Soviet Union and the western powers had engendered in him.

Albania's historic legacy of maladministration had played some part in making Hoxha's system of government what it was. His predecessor, king Zog, had inherited many of the police and administrative methods of the Ottoman empire. Under his rule police brutality, for instance, had persisted despite the efforts made by the British advisers to stamp it out or bring it under control. Nevertheless the abuse of authority by the Albanian police and gendarmerie had stemmed as much from sheer inefficiency caused by inadequate training as from the special occasions when the king felt that his own authority was seriously threatened. Being an old-fashioned right-wing autocracy, Zog's rule was mainly concerned with implementing certain limited political and social reforms provided these did not upset the *status quo*. As it possessed no real ideology of any kind, its administrative harshness was largely unplanned, incidental and sporadic. The king's government was at the same time responsible for introducing the rudiments of the rule of law. Not only was the independence of the judiciary recognized in constitutional theory but many judges upheld the rule of law in practice, though there were others who, because of political pressure, failed to do so. It would therefore be true to say that the communist régime had taken over the country's Ottoman political and administrative heritage with both the improvements and abuses for which the monarchy was responsible. On the other hand, in terms of consistent repressive performance Zog's intermittently harsh rule is related to Hoxha's totalitarian régime as a ramshackle ox-cart is to a Rolls Royce.

Some of the roots of the communist régime's policy of isolation from the rest of Europe must also be sought in Albania's geography and past history. The absence of adequate internal communications and the lack of railway and motor-road links with other countries had bred in many Albanians the feeling that they lived on an island off Europe which had for centuries been surrounded by a world that was either hostile or merely indifferent to their interests and general welfare. The long isolation together with the awareness of hostility or indifference, greatly strengthened by their bitter historical experiences, had in turn engendered in many of them similar feelings towards other countries. Such sentiments had in time tended to produce a somewhat self-centred and apathetic attitude to what went on beyond their borders. This outlook is fairly closely related to the view some Sicilians took about the political union of their island with the Italian mainland in 1860 described in Giuseppe di Lampedusa's novel *The Leopard*. Shortly after Garibaldi's landing on the island at the head of 1,000 volunteers, Don Fabrizio, the Sicilian prince of Salina, the main character of the novel, is visited by Chevalley, an official of the government of united Italy, who offers him a seat in the new Italian senate. The prince declines the offer, pointing out that after 25 centuries of colonial rule, imposed on their island by numerous foreign conquerors, he and his fellow Sicilians felt they had had their fill of external interference.

> The Sicilians [he says] never want to improve for the simple reason that they think themselves perfect; their vanity is stronger than their misery; every invasion by outsiders, whether so by origin or, if Sicilian, by independence of spirit, upsets their illusion of achieved perfection, risks disturbing their satisfied waiting for nothing; having been trampled on by a dozen different peoples, they think they have an imperial past which gives them the right to a grand funeral.

Lampedusa could have expressed, through his character Don Fabrizio, what many Albanians also felt about themselves, their own country and the world in general, making due allowance for the different historical traditions of the Sicilians and Albanians.

Feelings of helplessness and near-despair were also fostered by Albania's inability to secure for itself a dependable, powerful protector during the nationalist revival of the nineteenth century and the first four decades of the present century. As we saw earlier, the only power which was at all prepared to give it any consistent support was the Habsburg empire. Its collapse in 1918 left the country practically friendless, hence at the mercy of Italy, Greece and Yugoslavia. For a brief vital period immediately after the first world war Austria-Hungary's place was taken by the

United States and president Wilson's doctrine of national self-determination. Without Wilson's intervention Albania would probably have been partitioned between its neighbours. Wilsonian idealism was also largely responsible for the valuable relief and educational work that several American organizations undertook there during the 1920s and 1930s. However, shortly after the war the country came under the exclusive political influence of Italy which retained it almost to the end of the second world war. The Albanian communist régime's subsequent involvement with Yugoslavia and the Soviet Union was brought to an end, for reasons we have already discussed, in an atmosphere of bitterness and vituperation which helped to strengthen the country's isolationist propensities. The post-war failure to establish diplomatic relations with Britain and the United States had the same effect. This was due to several interlocking causes : the intransigence of the communist régime; the 1946 Corfu channel naval disaster and Albania's refusal to accept the verdict of the International Court of Justice; the American and British attempt to subvert the régime in 1949–53. Later neither side made any real effort to overcome these obstacles and reach an agreement. For his part, Hoxha showed himself unwilling to improve relations with either Britain or the United States partly because he feared their diplomatic presence in the country, partly because he found it useful to continue making them targets of his relentless domestic and external propaganda against the west in general. Britain and the United States, on the other hand, had no strategic, political or economic interests in Albania that were sufficiently important to surmount their instinctive reluctance to have any dealings with an extremist and unpredictable leader like Hoxha. Their general indifference played straight into his hands enabling him to generate, by press, radio and television, a veritable psychosis of siege in the minds and hearts of his fellow countrymen. They were constantly told that most of the western powers, together with the Soviet Union and its allies, were opposed not only to the communist régime but to the national interests of Albania itself. Of the major countries of western Europe, France and Italy were the first to establish relations with the Albanian government.

Hoxha's attempt to escape from total isolation and from the grave dangers this entailed for his régime was his alliance with China. In some respects China is the best protecting power

Albania has had after Austria-Hungary. It is thousands of miles away, it has no special interests in the country and is relatively free from any desire to dominate it unduly. However, motivated as it is by ideology, China's continuing protection is contingent on the expectation that the Sino-Soviet hostility will go on indefinitely. This shaky assumption renders the alliance somewhat precarious and untrustworthy. Moreover, China's failure to conclude a military agreement with Albania had left the latter defenceless, particularly after its withdrawal from the Warsaw pact. Peking's official views on the broad question of giving military assistance to other countries were clarified in the summer of 1971 when the Soviet government appeared to fear that a new unity with an anti-Soviet bias was about to be forged between Romania, Yugoslavia and Albania, with Chinese prodding and encouragement. Soviet objections to this possible development took the form of joint military exercises which were held throughout that summer in East Germany, Poland, Czechoslovakia and Hungary. At the same time, the Hungarian press issued veiled warnings to Romania and Yugoslavia on the dangers of forming closer ties with China. The two Balkan countries objected to these moves which were interpreted as political pressure intended to restrict their national independence and freedom of action. When the Peking correspondent of the Yugoslav newspaper *Vjesnik* (28 August 1971) asked Chou En-lai, the Chinese prime minister, what he thought of these developments he replied: "We will never betray our friends. We sympathise with small and medium-sized countries. We sympathise with them and we shall extend as much support to them as we can. However, we are very far away from Europe and, as you know, one of our popular proverbs says 'distant waters cannot quench fire'." This gnomic but unmistakable warning carried a message that seemed specially relevant to the case of Albania.

In view of its general insecurity, Hoxha's régime had paid great attention to the country's armed forces, devoting large resources to them. The people's army, which is made up of ground forces, navy and air force, comes under the minister of defence who normally serves as one of the deputy prime ministers. Military service is compulsory, with two years in the ground forces, three years in the navy and air force. According to a Yugoslav estimate (*Rilindja* 19, 20 and 21 September 1972), the strength of the ground forces is about 35,000 men organized in six infantry brigades and one tank brigade equipped with 100 Soviet medium tanks. The same source puts the strength of the navy at 3,000 men and 45 small ships of various types; of the air force at 4,000 men and 75 planes. Until 1961 Albania's armed forces were completely dependent on the Soviet Union for military equipment as well as for methods of training and organization. After the break with Moscow, China became the only source of supplies, though there is no reliable information on the form these had taken or on the quantities involved. The most serious gap in Albania's defence system was caused by the withdrawal of the Soviet submarines from the naval base at Vlorë. But if China's aid in terms of military hardware is an unknown quantity, its ideological influence on Albanian military thinking and planning has been overt and pervasive. The abolition of all military ranks was a simple act of obeisance to Mao's cultural revolution that was followed by more significant changes. The party's slogan "pickaxe in one hand and rifle in the other" came to signify that just as the armed forces were to give a hand in the building of factories, hydro-electric plants and in the opening up of new farmland, so the civilian population was to be mobilized and trained in the art of military defence. When the régime became fully aware that no outside power was likely to come to its rescue in a national emergency, it made the doctrine of guerilla warfare the main ingredient of its defence arrangements. Apart from its sheer political necessity, this doctrine had the great advantage of dovetailing with national traditions as well as with Hoxha's philosophy of total political, social and economic control.

Chinese and Albanian official statements made during the commemoration of the twenty-fifth anniversary of the people's army in July 1968 provided certain important clues about the new trends in defence planning. In a message that Lin Piao, the Chinese minister of defence, sent Beqir Balluku, his Albanian opposite number, he pointed out that just as the Albanian communist party had been victorious in its struggle against both fascists and nazis in the second world war and later against the Yugoslav and Soviet revisionists, so it would prove successful in the future by turning its armed forces into "a fighting detachment as well as a production brigade". This would be achieved by responding to Enver Hoxha's appeal to place politics in the forefront of national defence. If the Albanian leaders hoped that

Lin Piao would use the occasion to provide them with something more substantial than mere ideological and political advice, they were to be disappointed. In the absence of a Chinese pledge to come to Albania's aid in case of attack, Balluku tried to reassure the people, somewhat unconvincingly, with the claim that the country was by no means alone : "It has friends and supporters throughout the world. Marching shoulder to shoulder with us are 700 million Chinese led by . . . the communist party of China headed by . . . comrade Mao Tse-tung. Marching with us are likewise all the peoples fighting for freedom, independence and progress." The chief of staff of the army, Petrit Dume, said on the same occasion that the barriers dividing the armed forces from the people would be pulled down thus making it possible to bring the Maoist principle of the "mass line" in the sphere of national defence. This involved arming the whole population and subjecting it to intense military and political training.

Who were the potential aggressors for whom preparations for a people's war were intended? Official sources maintained that both the western powers (the imperialists) and the Soviet Union and its allies (the revisionists) were involved. But after the invasion of Czechoslovakia by the Soviet army in 1968, there were signs that what the Albanian leaders feared most of all was that Russia might make an attempt to regain its former control over the country. Moscow had, after all, pretty good grounds for wanting to get rid of Enver Hoxha. After allying himself to China, he had done everything in his power to annoy and irritate the Soviet government by his abusive and vitriolic speeches and by the anti-Soviet tirades of Albanian representatives at innumerable international gatherings. Having failed to dislodge him by subversion in the early 1960s, would the Russians try to do so by resorting to other more direct means? If the answer was in the affirmative, Hoxha perhaps hoped to deter them by making it clear that they would have to face the fierce resistance not merely of the armed forces but of the whole nation in arms. The press began talking of preparations to wage the kind of people's war the North Vietnamese communists were then waging in South Vietnam against the American and South Vietnamese armed forces. Self-reliance, not foreign aid, it was pointed out, was the key to success in such a war. The army and the "volunteer defence forces" were said to be fully equipped with modern weapons and hence able to cope with any emergency.

If these warlike noises were designed to serve as a possible deterrent to a would-be aggressor, they were also meant to enlist the widest possible public support for the régime's defence and other policies. As the country was said to be menaced by external aggression, it was the duty of all sections of the community—men and women, young and old—to rally to its defence. The foundations of the so-called "volunteer defence forces" were laid in an atmosphere of national emergency stimulated by propaganda. Secondary school pupils, as we have seen, must undergo one month's and university students two months' military training a year. Training includes drill with firearms, hand-to-hand combat, storming techniques and instruction in guerilla tactics. Theoretical instruction is supplemented by marches and excursions providing field practice in guerilla warfare in which girls as well as boys take part. Newspaper photographs of the 1969 May day parade in Tirana showed girls marching fifteen abreast carrying submachine guns.

These measures may have to some extent helped to strengthen the country's military security, but they did nothing to diminish its isolation. If anything, they may have increased people's fears that they were cut off from the outside world more than ever. The type of foreign policy that Hoxha pursued after his country's expulsion from the Soviet bloc was not particularly helpful in reducing the isolation. The limited improvement that took place in Albania's relations with Greece and Yugoslavia in 1971 was not followed up by any marked reconciliation between them. The Greek claim to a large chunk of southern Albania was for many years the stumbling block to normal relations between Athens and Tirana. This was removed when a Greek official spokesman (Xanthopoulos-Palamas) said in November 1971 that "the Greek side wishes to restore confidence and co-operation with Tirana, especially because Greece harbours no territorial designs on Albania". Apart from the resumption of diplomatic and trade relations, this gesture failed to bring the two countries any closer to one another. The Albanian government declined the invitation of the Greek prime minister, Constantine Karamanlis, to attend the Athens conference on technical and economic co-operation between Greece, Bulgaria, Romania, Turkey and Yugoslavia in January 1976. Albania's official reason for not taking part was that it set greater store by the improvement of bilateral relations between the countries of the region. Similarly, there was little advance in its reconciliation with Yugoslavia. The obstacles here were ideological as well as political. The gulf between Yugoslavia's system of self-management and Hoxha's undiluted dictatorship of the proletariat widened following Albania's decision to combine Stalinism with Mao's revolutionary theories. This in turn increased Hoxha's fears that sooner or later his people might find some of Yugoslavia's social and political ideas attractive and thereby undermine the foundations of his own tyranny. Shortly after the invasion of Czechoslovakia he made an attempt to curb his public attacks on Yugoslavia's political system and to pursue towards Tito a policy that was less ideological and more in tune with the danger of a possible Soviet incursion in the Balkan peninsula. This half-hearted policy was, however, complicated by the revival of nationalism and irredentism among the one million Albanians of Kosovo from 1968 onwards. As this revival was stimulated by Hoxha's own extreme nationalism as well as by official cultural exchanges between Kosovo and Albania, the Albanian leader may have felt that a closer friendship with Tito would have been a betrayal of the cause of his fellow Albanians across the border. So the potent mixture of ideological aversion and nationalist calculation induced him to revert to his former anti-Yugoslav policy, albeit in a more cautious and restrained form.

After Khrushchev's fall from power in 1964, the Soviet press and radio made numerous suggestions about resuming diplomatic relations with Albania. But these were invariably turned down with a good deal of passion and venom. In 1970 Hoxha said that as "they were not able to bite our hand the Soviet revisionists now wanted to kiss it. But they owed the Albanian people, who were their sworn enemies, great political, ideological and economic debts." Four years later he maintained that neither the party nor the people would ever make peace with the Soviet leadership. Such fierce intransigence perhaps concealed an awful apprehension that a Soviet embassy in Tirana might become a focus of political intrigue and possibly subversion.

The Albanian leaders sometimes tried to refute the widespread belief that their government pursued an isolationist policy by pointing to the establishment of diplomatic and trade ties with over sixty countries. Such an opening to the outside world had in fact taken place in the sense that purely official links were established with many of the smaller European countries, such as Austria, Turkey, Switzerland, Belgium, the Netherlands and the Scandinavian countries as well as with several countries in the Middle East, Africa and Latin America. Yet the esssential immobility that had plagued Albania's foreign policy since the early 1960s becomes apparent when one compares it with the active foreign policies that Romania and Yugoslavia, for instance, had conducted during the same period. Whilst remaining a member of the Warsaw Pact, Romania had done its utmost to counteract the danger of Soviet expansionism by broadening its political, diplomatic and economic contacts and by having friendly relations with all the countries of the west, the third world and China. The constant exchange of official visits between Nicolae Ceausescu and the political leaders of these countries was one of the striking features of this complex diplomatic and political endeavour. Yugoslavia, too, had made its policy of non-alignment with any of the power blocs a springboard for the widest possible co-operation and involvement with most parts of the world. Ceausescu and Tito had divested foreign policy of some of the cramping inhibitions of ideology, making it serve the short- and long-term interests of their two countries. Hoxha, on the other hand, became a prisoner of his cranky ideology and of his quixotic search for the absolute security of his régime. Moderation in action or speech was for him a form of betrayal of his system of government whose survival was inescapably linked in his own mind with the country's turbulent history of national survival. His rejection of the precept that politics is the art of the possible coupled with a good deal of diplomatic and political ineptitude in the conduct of foreign affairs had left Albania almost friendless and perhaps more vulnerable than ever before. The régime's real test will come if the Balkan peninsula were to face another crisis such as the one that beset it in the wake of the invasion of Czechoslovakia in 1968.

Albania's human exchanges with other parts of the world have also been on a very small scale since the end of the second world war. The country was practically untouched by the tides of mass tourism which had swept over Italy, Greece, Yugoslavia, Romania and Bulgaria. The régime's deep concern about its political and ideological safety had overridden its desperate need for the valuable revenue in foreign exchange which could be derived from the tourist industry. Although tourism is encouraged to some extent, it is deliberately kept on a small scale and restricted to tightly controlled package holidays. The Albanian authorities generally preferred Maoists and other sympathizers of the régime to politically uncommitted tourists bent on pleasure, recreation and all the other attractions of travel abroad. Young tourists, in particular, were annoyed and discouraged by the stringent, puritanical regulations which disallowed entry to men with long hair, beards and sideburns and women wearing short skirts or flared trousers. The government's tourist policy was explained by Hoxha when he said the country was closed "to enemies, spies, hippies and hooligans, but open to friends (Marxist or non-Marxist), to revolutionaries and progressive democrats, to honest tourists who did not interfere in our affairs. Socialist Albania was not a hotbed of bourgeois degeneration, nor was it dazzled by dollars or roubles." But while a limited number of foreign travellers were allowed to enter the country, there has been no Albanian tourist traffic in the opposite direction. Only Albanian subjects on official duty are permitted to travel abroad. There is also a general ban on visits by Albanian ex-patriates. This was very occasionally lifted for those who had left the country before the second world war. If Edward Gibbon's complaint of 200 years ago that although Albania was within sight of Italy it was less known than the interior of America has since become outdated, it has only become so in the sense that the interior of America is no longer a mystery. Albania itself still remained a *terra incognita* for most people, just as the rest of the world was for the vast majority of Albanians.

One problem that poses itself concerns the place that Hoxha's régime occupies in the ranks of contemporary totalitarian governments and the features that distinguish it from some of them. The most comprehensive study of modern totalitarianism that has appeared so far is Carl Friedrich's and Z. K. Brzezinski's *Totalitarian Dictatorship and Autocracy*, (New York, 1965). It lists six distinctive features that modern totalitarian governments have in common : an all-embracing ideology; a single political party led by one man; a highly developed secret police; monopoly of mass communications; control of military weapons; central control and direction of the economy. These are obviously fairly broad characteristics, some of which are to be found in old-fashioned dictatorships, in despotic and even in democratic governments. Governments of all types exercise control over military weapons and equipment; many non-totalitarian military and despotic régimes dispose of secret police forces. These also control the media of mass communications, just as democratic governments try to do in times of war or national crisis. In a review of Friedrich's and Brzezinski's work, Professor Hugh Seton-Watson has suggested that modern totalitarian régimes operated when four specific conditions were present. These are the concentration of political, economic and spiritual power in the same hands; the denial of any moral or spiritual authority independent of the will of the ruler; the denial of any autonomy to private and personal life; the availability of most modern means of publicity, communication and coercion.

Albania has certainly had in power since the end of the second world war a single political party which had in the course of time subjected its people to the full rigours of an overriding ideology. It has also had in Hoxha a durable leader who was in complete control of the party machine and of its ideology. A good deal of his authority and prestige rested on the fact that he was one of the founders of the communist party, the commander-in-chief of the partisan forces during the second world war, and later supreme leader, doctrinal high priest as well as chief propagandist of the régime. This is how the official history of the Albanian communist party (English edition, Tirana, 1971) sums up his stewardship :

> He is the founder of the PLA [i.e. the workers' party] and has led it since its creation through all the historical stages of the revolution. He has made the greatest contribution to working out its Marxist-Leninist revolutionary line. With his wisdom, determination, far-sightedness and revolutionary courage, comrade Enver Hoxha has ensured the consistent revolutionary implementation of the Marxist-Leninist norms of the party, has never allowed it to be diverted into a blind alley and has always brought it forth triumphant from all the difficult and complicated situations (*sic*). In his works, comrade Enver Hoxha has made a Marxist-Leninist theoretical generalization of the revolutionary experience of the PLA, thus making an invaluable contribution to the treasury of Marxism-Leninism.

The Marxist legitimacy of his rule was badly shaken when Albania was driven out of the Soviet bloc, but he soon recovered by constructing a local ideological bridge between Stalinism and

Maoism. Hoxha's continued dependence on the power of the secret police more than 30 years after the communist revolution set Albania somewhat apart from most of the other communist states of eastern Europe, where the police had been brought under stricter political and judicial supervision. With the full collectivization of agriculture, the régime exercised greater control over the economy than was the case in Poland, Hungary or Yugoslavia, where large numbers of peasants were not collectivized. The existence of a huge, ever-expanding army of party and state bureaucrats in a small country like Albania, with its comparatively unsophisticated population, served as an additional prop to totalitarian rule. Therefore in terms of sheer power and doctrinal authority Hoxha was nearer to Stalin in his heyday or to Mao Tse-tung throughout most of his career than to any of the other contemporary rulers of eastern Europe.

Friedrich and Brzezinski have made another important contribution to the study of modern totalitarianism with their concept of the "islands of separateness". These are those areas of society not completely under the thumb of the régime, where dissent and even opposition to its authority could spring from. Such "islands" include the family, churches, universities and institutes of learning, writers and artists. All totalitarian governments make a determined effort, particularly in the early stages of their revolution, to do away with such potential centres of resistance to their power. But few have tried so furiously or for so long to obliterate these "islands" altogether as Hoxha's régime had done. It is not, however, clear how far this remorseless onslaught has in fact succeeded. Its persistence seems to suggest that the régime is not very happy with the results that have been achieved. Although the traditional Albanian family has undergone great changes, the maintenance of the family unit is still a major concern of the government's population and labour policies. Yet despite the great strains and stresses to which they have been subjected over many years, the ancient network of family and tribal loyalties may still prove strong enough to provide many Albanians with the only remaining refuge and personal escape hatch from the incessant pressures and rigours of the régime. As the persecution of ecclesiastical organizations has surpassed even that of the nazi régime in Germany, churches and mosques are no longer physically present to serve as "islands of separateness". People's religious beliefs have consequently entered into a dark, mysterious zone where no one can say with any degree of certainty what secret forms they might take or whether they will survive or not. The régime itself looks upon religion as a kind of submerged "island". The same thing could be said about the university of Tirana and some of the writers and artists who were in the forefront of the movement for more intellectual and political freedom during the cultural revolution. They had set a precedent of dissent which, in a time of crisis, might give birth to an intellectual ferment similar to the one that preceded the Hungarian uprising of 1956 and the reform movement in Czechoslovakia in 1968. Hoxha's régime may also have unwittingly laid the foundations of another possible "island of separateness" when it decided to copy the techniques of Mao's cultural revolution by pressing young people, workers and various other groups into innumerable campaigns under its direct supervision. The workers' rights to exercise control over government departments are enshrined in the 1976 constitution. After Chou En-lai's death in January 1976 and the failure of Teng Hsiao-ping to succeed him as prime minister there were riots in Peking between radical and moderate groups reminiscent of the upheavals which accompanied the cultural revolution of the 1960s. Albanians trained to employ similar methods at the behest of the communist party might be tempted to make use of them for quite different ends in a similar crisis. However, in terms of the criteria set out by Friedrich and Brzezinski the Albanian régime is ideologically, politically and economically much closer to North Korea, Vietnam, Cambodia (after April 1975) and to China itself than to any of the communist states of eastern Europe.

Under Hoxha's leadership the country has become an enclosed camp where Mao's totalitarian doctrines, interlaced with local Stalinist practices, have been tried out under perfect laboratory, almost test-tube, conditions. This may be one of the reasons that the Chinese leaders have lavished such extragavant praise on his revolutionary prowess and political skill. Perhaps their great admiration for Hoxha is tinged with envy for the opportunity he was given of working on such a small and amenable scale. As a result of this experiment, the communist régime which had replaced the wooden plough with modern agricultural machinery and made important advances in industry, education, public health, social welfare and in several other fields was also responsible for squeezing the Albanians into a totalitarian straitjacket of an all-enveloping character and vicious strength. Their release from it could well turn out to be almost as difficult, painful and lonely an undertaking as their release from foreign domination of one sort or another had been. The great tragedy of the Albanians is that their full awareness of the steel hoops of this modern totalitarian bondage coincided with the discovery that their recurring nightmare about the icy indifference of the rest of the world may not be a figment of the imagination after all.

Postscript

OCTOBER 1976

W HEN M AO T SE - T UNG died on 9 September 1976 the Albanian authorities proclaimed three days of national mourning. This was not merely a symbolic gesture but also an outward sign of deep anxiety about the future of Chinese-Albanian relations in the post-Mao era. In their message of condolence to the central committee of the Chinese communist party, the Albanian leaders quoted Mao as having stated some years earlier that

> the strength which emanated from the friendship between China and Albania is truly inexhaustible. May our two parties and peoples unite yet more closely with true Marxists throughout the world and the revolutionary peoples of various countries; may they fight side by side to bury the common enemies of the world: US imperialism and Soviet revisionism.

The Albanian message expressed the conviction that Mao's words would continue to serve as a permanent source of inspiration in furthering the cause of Chinese-Albanian friendship. But these brave sentiments concealed certain real fears and anxieties. There was, in the first place, the fear that sooner or later an individual, or group of individuals, who favoured a break with Mao's unyielding hostility to the Soviet Union might gain power in Peking. If this were to happen, the Albanian régime was likely to be the principal sufferer. Secondly, there was the question whether Mao's successors would remain loyal to his revolutionary domestic policies or would attempt to modify them in some way. Any modification would almost unavoidably involve the Albanians in the painful process of re-adjusting their own Maoist domestic policies to such changes as may have taken place in China, accompanied by the customary dismissals and purges. Thirdly, the anxieties and fears caused by Mao's death were compounded by the prospect that the situation in Yugoslavia might have become so unstable in the event of Tito's death as to effect the security of the Albanian régime, possibly the very independence of the country itself.

SELECTED READING LIST

BIBLIOGRAPHY
P. L. Horecky (edit.) *Southeastern Europe. A Guide to Basic Publications.* (Albania : pp. 73–115) Chicago & London. 1969.

NEWSPAPERS, PERIODICALS, ETC.
Zëri i Popullit (Voice of the People), official newspaper of the Albanian workers' (communist) party.
Bashkimi (Union), official newspaper of the democratic front.
Rruga e Partisë (The Party Path), theoretical monthly of the Albanian workers' (communist) party.
Nëndori (November), monthly magazine of the Albanian writers' and artists' union.
New Albania, political and social bi-monthly magazine. Tirana.
BBC Summaries of World Broadcasts.
Radio Free Europe (Munich) Research Papers.

GENERAL WORKS
F. Fejtö. *A History of the People's Democracies. Eastern Europe since Stalin.* London. 1974.
M. Hasluck. *The Unwritten Law of Albania.* Cambridge. 1954.
History of the Party of Labour of Albania. Tirana. 1971.
H. Hodgkinson. *The Adriatic Sea.* London. 1955.
E. Hösch. *The Balkans. A Short History from Greek times to the present day.* London. 1972.
E. Hoxha. *Vepra* (Works). Tirana. 1968 onwards.
S. Islami and others. *Historia e Shqipërisë* (History of Albania). 2 vols. Tirana. 1959–1965.
E. K. Keefe and others. *Area Handbook for Albania.* Washington. 1971.
P. Lendvai. *Eagles in Cobwebs. Nationalism and Communism in the Balkans.* London. 1970.
N. C. Pano. *The People's Republic of Albania.* Baltimore. 1968.
H. Seton-Watson. *The Pattern of Communist Revolution. A Historical Analysis.* London. 1960.

H. Seton-Watson. *The East European Revolution.* London. 1961.
S. Skendi (edit.) *Albania.* New York & London. 1957.

INTRODUCTION (From ancient Illyrians to modern Albanians)
and CHAPTER 1 (Long night of Ottoman rule)
A. Gegaj. *L'Albanie et l'Invasion Turque au XVe siècle.* Paris.
1937.
F. W. Hasluck. *Christianity and Islam under the Sultans.* 2 vols.
Oxford. 1929.
H. Inalcik. *Arnawutluk* (Albania) in *Encyclopedia of Islam.*
Vol. 1. London. 1960.
H. Inalcik. *The Ottoman Empire. The Classical Age:
1300–1600.* London. 1973.
F. S. Noli. *George Castrioti Scanderbeg.* New York. 1947.
D. Obolensky. *Byzantine Commonwealth. Eastern Europe,
500–1453.* London. 1971.
S. Skendi. *Religion in Albania during the Ottoman rule* in
Südost Forschungen. v. 15. Munich. 1956.
S. Skendi. *Crypto-Christianity in the Balkan Area under the
Ottomans* in *Slavic Review,* American Quarterly of Soviet and
East European Studies, Vol. XXVI, No. 2, June 1967.

CHAPTER 2 (Delayed Independence)
J. W. Baggally. *Ali Pasha and Great Britain.* Oxford. 1938.
Lord Byron. *Childe Harold's Pilgrimage.*
Lord Byron. *Selected Prose.* ed. P. Gunn. London. 1972.
N. Douglas. *Old Calabria.* London. 1962.
M. E. Durham. *The Burden of the Balkans.* London. 1905.
M. E. Durham. *High Albania.* London. 1909.
M. E. Durham. *The Struggle for Scutari.* London. 1914.
M. E. Durham. *Twenty Years of Balkan Tangle.* London. 1920.
E. P. Hamp. *The Position of Albanian* in *Proceedings of Con-
ference on Indo-European Linguistics.* Los Angeles. 1963.
J. C. Hobhouse (Lord Broughton). *Travels in Albania and other
provinces of Turkey* in 1808 and 1810. 2 vols. London. 1858.
T. S. Hughes. *Travels in Greece and Albania.* 2 vols. London.
1830.
E. Lear. *Journals of a Landscape Painter in Albania etc.* London.
1851.
S. E. Mann. *Albanian language and literature* in *Arnawutluk*
(Albania) in *Encyclopedia of Islam.* Vol. 1. London. 1960.

W. Plomer. *Ali the Lion.* London. 1936.

G. Remérand. *Ali de Tebélen, Pacha de Janina: 1744–1822.* Paris. 1928.

D. Shuteriqi (edit.) *Historia e Letërsisë Shqipe* (History of Albanian Literature). 2 vols. Tirana. 1959–1960.

S. Skendi. *The Albanian National Awakening 1878–1912.* New Jersey. 1967.

E. P. Stickney. *Southern Albania or Northern Epirus in European International Affairs: 1912–1923.* Stanford, Calif. 1926.

S. Story (edit.) *The Memoirs of Ismail Kemal Bey.* London. 1920.

CHAPTER 3 (Ahmet Zogu's authoritarian régime)

G. Ciano. *Diaries 1939–1943.* London. 1946.

G. Ciano. *L'Europa verso la catastrofe.* Milan. 1948.

Lord Kinross. *Atatürk. The Rebirth of a Nation.* London. 1964.

C. A. Macartney. *National States and National Minorities.* London. 1934.

S. E. Mann. *Albanian Literature: An Outline of prose, poetry and drama.* London. 1955.

H. Nicolson. *Peacemaking 1919.* London. 1933.

G. Petrotta. *Svolgimento storico della cultura e della letteratura Albanese.* Palermo. 1950.

P. Quaroni. *Diplomatic Bags. An Ambassador's Memoirs.* London. 1966.

V. Robinson. *Albania's Road to Freedom.* London. 1941.

J. Swire. *Albania: The Rise of a Kingdom.* London. 1929.

J. Swire. *King Zog's Albania.* London. 1937.

CHAPTER 4 (Foreign occupation and civil war)

J. Amery *Sons of the Eagle. A study in guerilla war.* London. 1948.

J. Amery. *Approach March.* London. 1973.

E. F. Davies. *Illyrian Venture. The story of the British Military Mission to Enemy-occupied Albania 1943–44.* London. 1952.

A. Ermenji. *Tridhjetë-vjetori i fillimit të luftës civile* (Thirtieth anniversary of the beginning of the Albanian civil war) in *Flamuri*, 28 Nov. 1973. Rome.

H. Neubacher. *Sonderauftrag Südost 1940–45. Bericht eines fliegenden Diplomaten.* Göttingen. 1957.

A. Puto. *Nëpër analet e diplomacisë Angleze* (A survey of British diplomatic documents of the Second World War) in *Nëndori*, Tirana, No. 12 1972; Nos. 1, 2 and 3, 1973.

CHAPTER 5 (Communists in power)
H. F. Armstrong. *Tito and Goliath*. London. 1951.
E. Barker. *Macedonia*. London. 1950.
V. Dedijer (edit.) *Il sangue tradito: relazioni jugoslavo-albanesi, 1938–1949. Documenti ufficiali, lettere, fotografie, memoriali co-ordinati ed elaborati*. Varese. 1949.
V. Dedijer. *Tito Speaks. His self-portrait and struggle with Stalin*. London. 1953.
M. Djilas. *Conversations with Stalin*. London. 1962.
L. Gardner. *The Eagle Spreads his Claws. A history of the Corfu channel dispute and of Albania's relations with the West, 1945–1965*. London. 1966.
E. Leggett. *The Corfu Incident*. London. 1974.

CHAPTER 6 (From Tito to Stalin)
A Chronology of Events in Albania 1944–1952. (Mimeographed). New York. 1955.
B. Page and others. *Philby: The Spy who Betrayed a Generation*. London. 1969.
K. Philby. *My Silent War*. London. 1968.

CHAPTER 7 (From Khrushchev to Mao Tse-tung)
J. F. Brown. *The New Eastern Europe. The Khrushchev Era and After*. London. 1966.
E. Crankshaw. *The New Cold War: Moscow v. Pekin*. London. 1963.
M. Frankland. *Khrushchev*. London. 1966.
W. E. Griffith. *Albania and the Sino-Soviet Rift*. Cambridge, Mass. 1963.
H. Hamm. *Albania: China's Beachhead in Europe*. London. 1963.
G. F. Hudson and others. *The Sino-Soviet Dispute*. London. 1961.
N. S. Khrushchev. *The Crimes of the Stalin Era. Special Report to the 20th Congress of the Communist Party of the Soviet Union*. New York. 1956.

A. Logoreci. *Albania: A Chinese Satellite in the Making?* in *The World Today*, May 1961. London.

A. Logoreci. *Albania: The Anabaptists of European Communism* in *Problems of Communism*, May-June 1967. Washington.

S. Skendi. *Albania* in S. D. Kertesz (edit.) *East Central Europe and the World: Developments in the Post-Stalin Era*. Indiana. 1962.

S. Skendi. *Albania and the Sino-Soviet Conflict* in *Foreign Affairs*. April 1962. New York.

CHAPTER 8 (Agrarian and Industrial Revolutions), CHAPTER 9 (Ideological and Political Turmoil) and CHAPTER 10 (Cultural and Social Changes)

T. Beeson. *Discretion and Valour. Religious conditions in Russia and Eastern Europe*. London. 1974.

Disa Probleme të Studimeve Shoqërore (Some Problems of Social Studies). Marxist-Leninist Institute. Tirana. 1969.

H. Hodgkinson. *Albanian Oil* in *Albania,* National Committee "Free Albania" Rome. 1962.

Konferenca Kombëtare e Studimeve Shoqërore (Proceedings of the national conference of social studies). 5 vols. Marxist-Leninist Institute. Tirana. 1970.

G. Murry. *Albanie: terre de l'homme nouveau. Paris.* 1972.

N. C. Pano. *The Albanian Cultural Revolution* in *Problems of Communism*, July-August 1974. Washington.

F. Pipa. *Nji Shekull Shkollë Shqipe: 1861–1961* (A century of Albanian education). Rome. 1961.

P. R. Prifti. *Albania and the Sino-Soviet Conflict* in *Studies in Comparative Communism*, Vol. VI, No. 3, 1973. Los Angeles.

P. R. Prifti. *The Albanian Party of Labor and the Intelligentsia* in *East European Quarterly*, Vol. VIII, No. 3, 1974. New York.

S. Schram. *Mao Tse-tung*. London. 1966.

S. Schram. *The Political Thought of Mao Tse-tung*. London. 1969.

S. Schram (edit.) *Authority, Participation and Cultural Change in China*. Cambridge. 1973.

S. Schram (edit.) *Mao Tse-tung Unrehearsed. Talks and Letters: 1956–71.* London. 1974.

J. I. Thomas. *Education for Communism: School and State in the People's Republic of Albania*. Stanford, Calif. 1969.

CHAPTER 11 (Totalitarian Isolation)

Amnesty International report: interviews with former political prisoners from Albania, 10 January 1976, at Centro emigrazione per profughi stranieri, Latina, Italy.

C. J. Friedrich and Z. K. Brzezinski. *Totalitarian Dictatorship and Autocracy*. New York. 1965.

M. Latey. *Tyranny. A Study in the Abuse of Power*. London. 1972.

A. Pipa. *Libri i Burgut* (Prison Notebook). New York. 1959.

P. R. Prifti. *Albania's Expanding Horizons* in *Problems of Communism*, Jan.-Feb. 1972. Washington.

L. Schapiro (edit.) *Political Opposition in One-Party States*. London. 1972. (includes J. Birch, *The Albanian Political Experience*; H. Seton-Watson, *On Totalitarianism*; C. J. Friedrich, *In Defence of a Concept*).

INDEX

Compiled by Harold E. Crowe